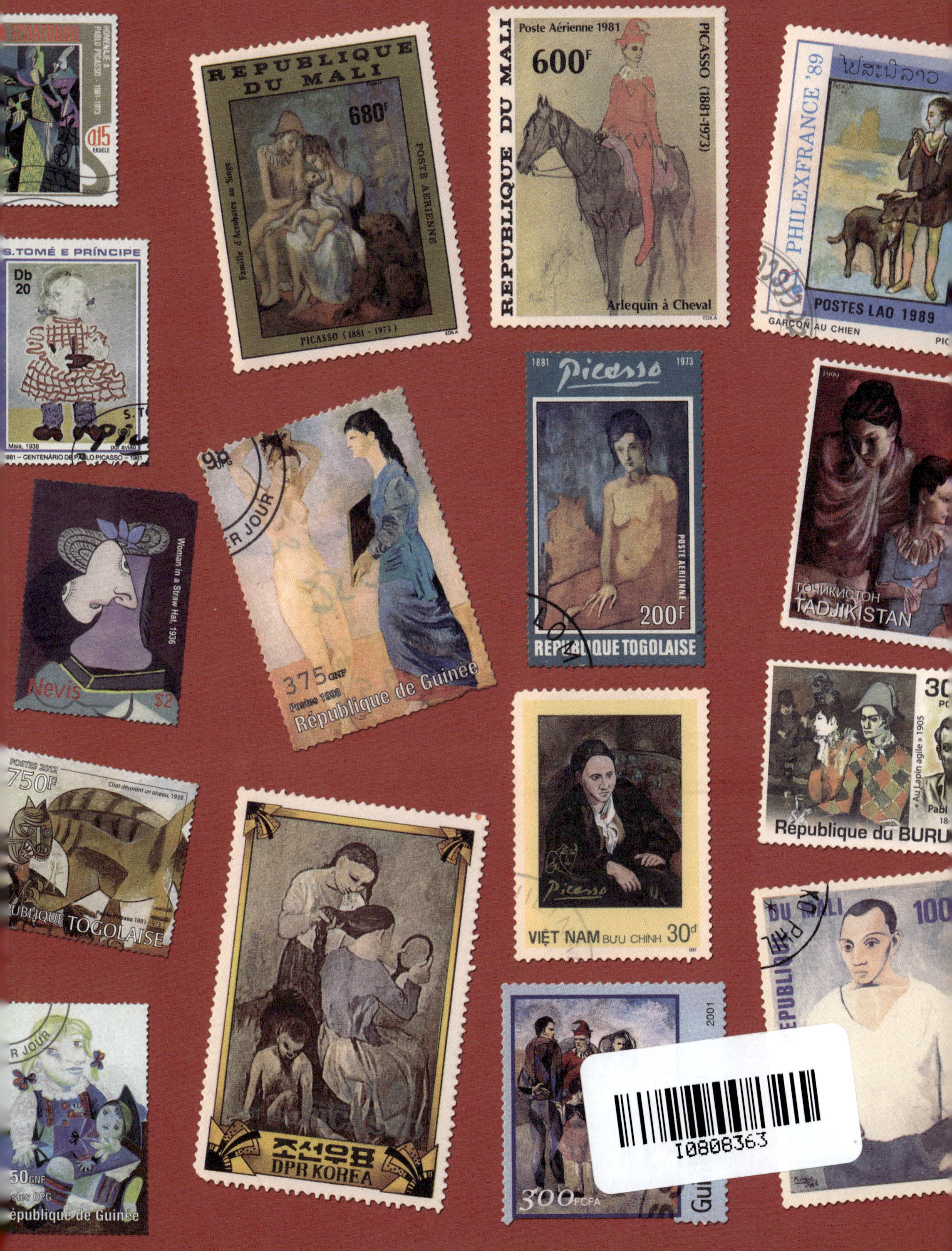
REPUBLIQUE DU MALI
680F
POSTE AERIENNE
Famille d'Acrobates au Singe
PICASSO (1881 - 1973)
REPUBLIQUE DU MALI
Poste Aérienne 1981
600F
PICASSO (1881-1973)
Arlequin à Cheval
PHILEXFRANCE '89
POSTES LAO 1989
GARÇON AU CHIEN
S.TOMÉ E PRÍNCIPE
Db 20
Maia, 1938
1881 – CENTENÁRIO DE PABLO PICASSO – 1981
1881 Picasso 1973
POSTE AERIENNE
200F
REPUBLIQUE TOGOLAISE
Woman in a Straw Hat, 1936
Nevis
$2
375 GNF
République de Guinée
ТОҶИКИСТОН
TADJIKISTAN
République du BURU
« Au Lapin agile » 1905
POSTES 2012
750F
Chat dévorant un oiseau, 1939
TOGOLAISE
VIỆT NAM BƯU CHÍNH 30d
조선우표
DPR KOREA
REPUBLIQUE DU MALI
2001
300 FCFA
épublique de Guinée

I0808363

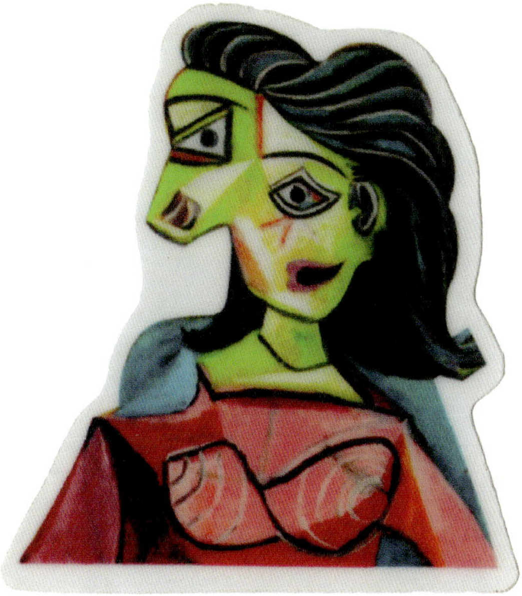

POSTMARKED PICASSO

HIS PAINTINGS ON STAMPS

Library of Congress Control Number: 2022944456

Stamp images are from the author's stamp collection.
Edited by Ian Robertson
Designed by Christopher Bower
Cover design by Christopher Bower
Type set in Promixa Nova

ISBN: 978-0-7643-6584-3
Printed in China

Published by Schiffer Publishing, Ltd.
4880 Lower Valley Road
Atglen, PA 19310
Phone: (610) 593-1777; Fax: (610) 593-2002
Email: Info@schifferbooks.com
Web: www.schifferbooks.com

FSC
www.fsc.org
MIX
Paper | Supporting responsible forestry
FSC® C104723

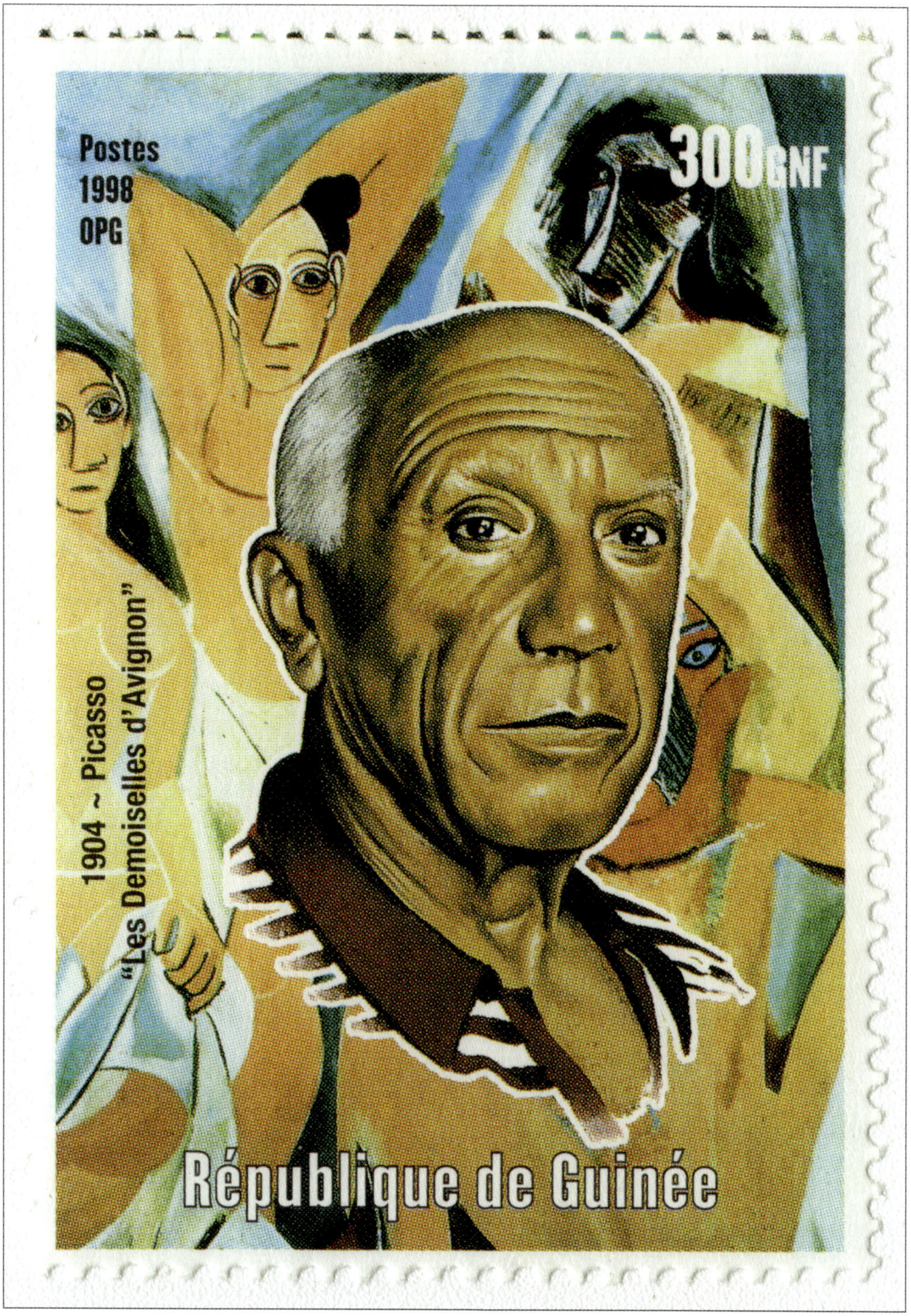

Les Demoiselles d'Avignon This stamp contains a portrait of Pablo Picasso with a background of Picasso's 1907 *Les Demoiselles d'Avignon*. The 300-franc stamp was issued possibly in 1998 in the name of the Republic of Guinea, a country on the western coast of Africa formerly known as French Guinea. The stamp is part of a nine-stamp sheet titled *Events of the 20th Century: 1900–1909*.

POSTMARKED PICASSO

HIS PAINTINGS ON STAMPS

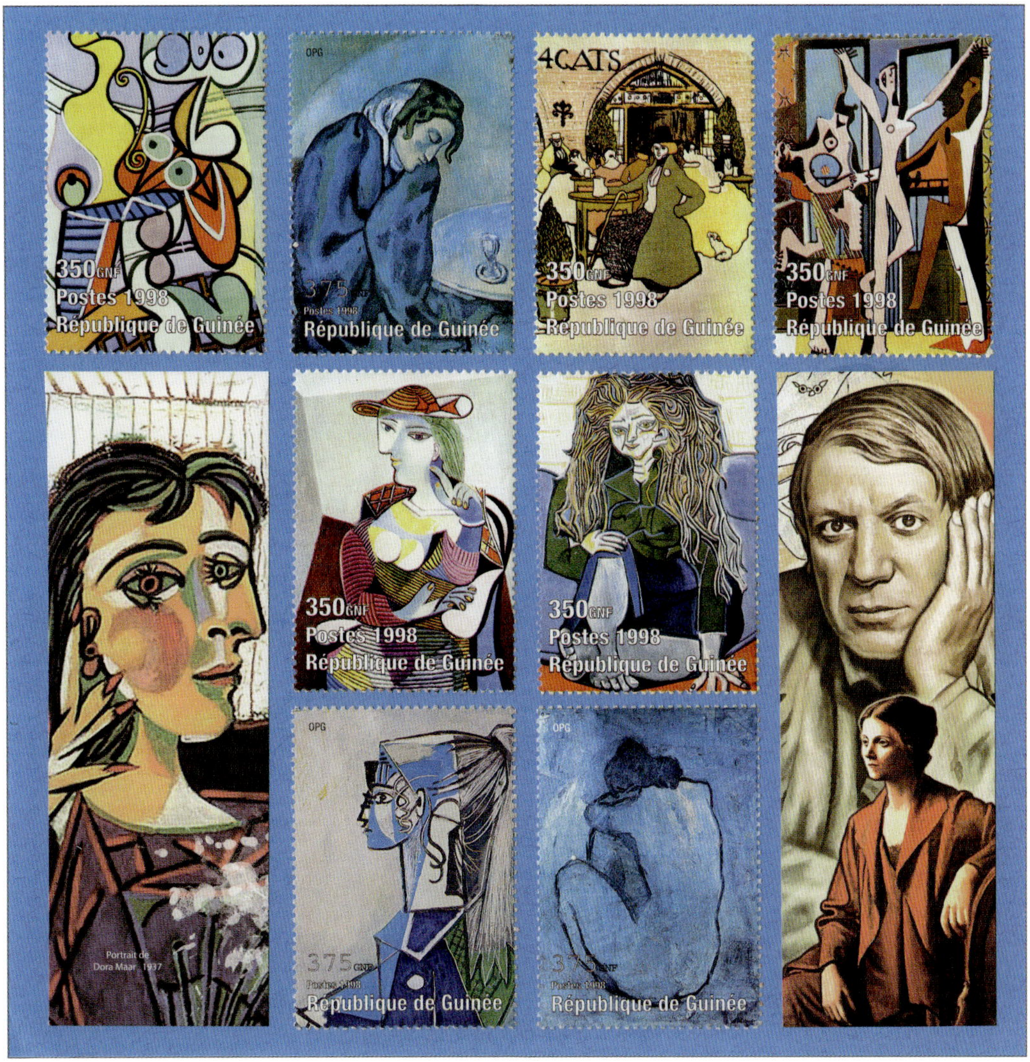

Donald D. Spencer

SCHIFFER PUBLISHING

4880 Lower Valley Road • Atglen, PA 19310

DEDICATION

to Steven and Anne Spencer

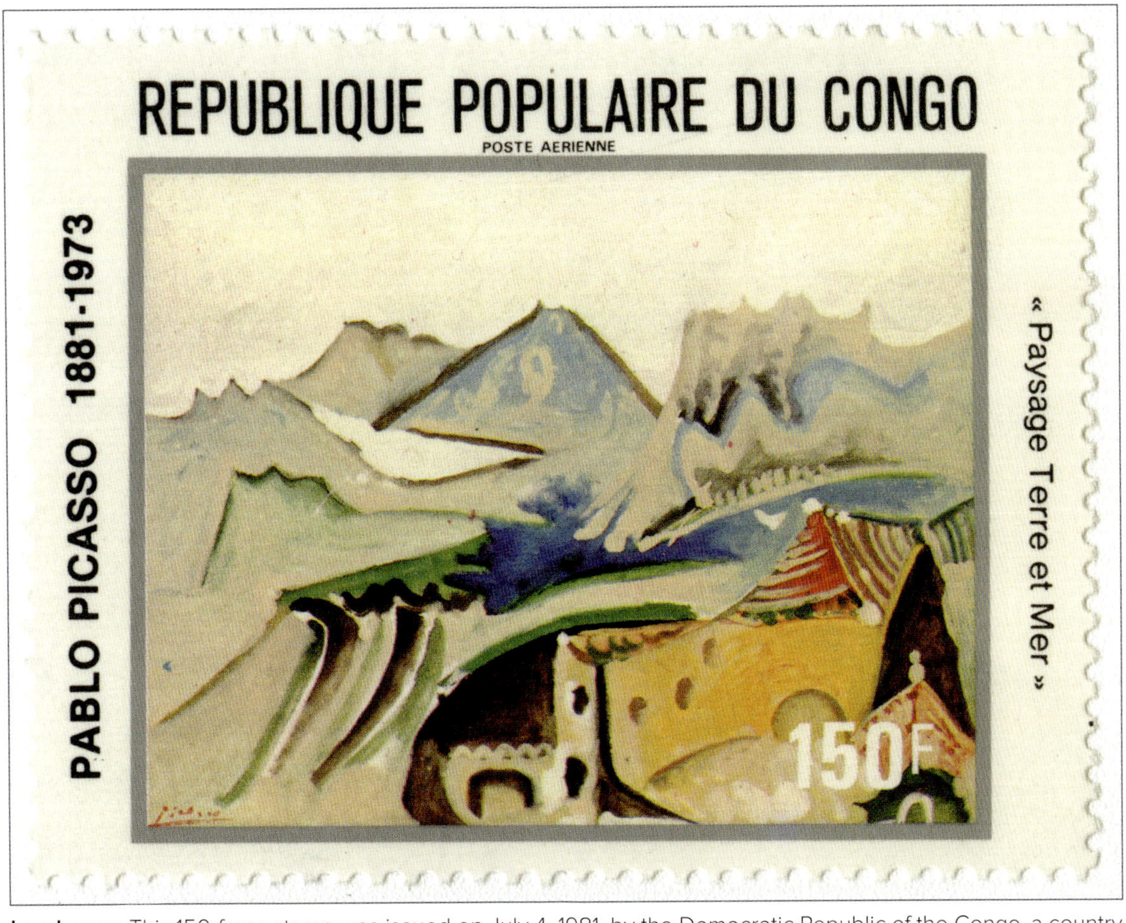

Landscape This 150-franc stamp was issued on July 4, 1981, by the Democratic Republic of the Congo, a country located in central Africa.

CONTENTS

Preface . . . 11
Introduction . . . 13

Chapter 1: Early Years (1881–1900) . . . 16
Chapter 2: The Blue Period (1901–1904) . . . 18
Chapter 3: The Rose Period (1905–1906) . . . 22
Chapter 4: Cubism (1907–1914) . . . 24
Chapter 5: Neoclassicism and Surrealism (1917–1935) . . . 26
Chapter 6: The Violent Years (1936–1945) . . . 30
Chapter 7: Postwar Years (1946–1954) . . . 32
Chapter 8: Late Works (1955–1973) . . . 34
Chapter 9: Picasso Painting Stamps . . . 38
- 1895–1900 . . . 40
- 1901–1903 . . . 42
- 1904–1906 . . . 58
- 1907–1916 . . . 74
- 1917–1935 . . . 78
- 1936–1945 . . . 92
- 1946–1954 . . . 100
- 1955–1972 . . . 104

Glossary . . . 110
Bibliography . . . 113
Index . . . 114

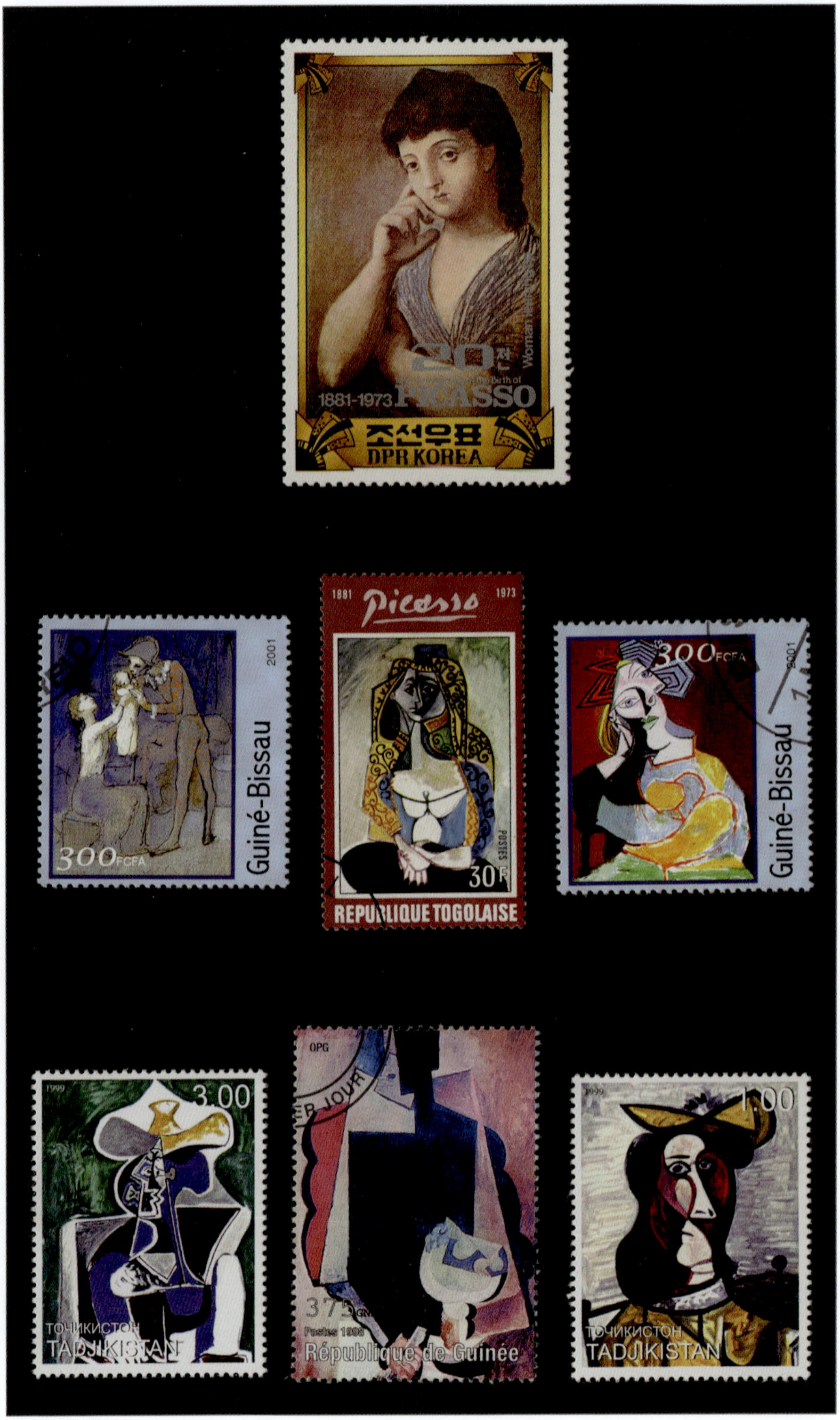

Picasso art on postage stamps Pablo Picasso's art appears on stamps issued by countries throughout the world.

PREFACE

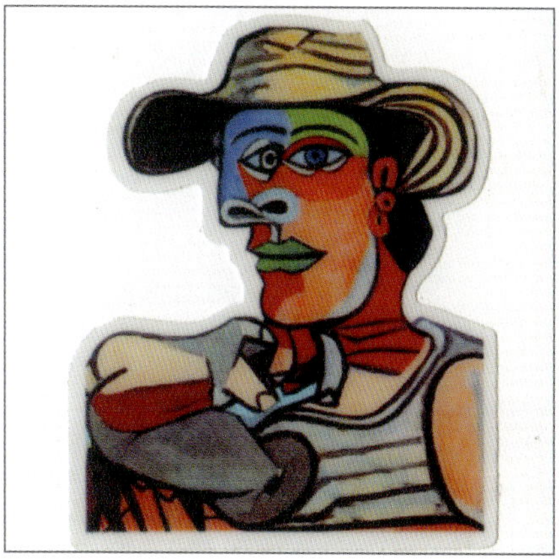

Pablo Picasso died the wealthiest and most famous artist of the twentieth century. He originated or contributed to many of the major artistic movements of modern times. Born in Spain, Picasso made his first visit to Paris, France, at nineteen. He soon became known for his thin, sad figures in the paintings of the "Blue Period," and later for the romantic harlequins and acrobats of his "Rose Period." In 1906 he began studying new forms, eventually leading to the development of "cubism." *Les Demoiselles d'Avignon*, which he completed in 1907, marked an important turning point in Picasso's career. It was not the subject matter of *Les Demoiselles d'Avignon* that shocked critics; rather, the geometric style of the figures and the distortion and fragmentation of pictorial space.

In the early 1920s he painted the full and powerful figures of his "neoclassical" work. In the 1930s Picasso reached new and vital stature as a painter with his famous *Guernica* painting of 1937, Picasso's bitter and impassioned comment on the events of the Spanish Civil War. In this work Picasso depicts fear and horror following the destruction of the Basque town Guernica during bombing raids by the German Condor Legion. In Picasso's later output he devoted himself primarily to graphic work. He also took works by other famous painters as models, re-creating them in his own style.

Picasso paintings spawned an industry of Picasso books, Picasso stamps, Picasso postcards, and Picasso maximum cards that celebrate his genius. This book portrays the artist's most famous paintings on postage stamps issued by countries throughout the world. In addition to Picasso paintings on stamps, the book also contains a brief history of his most famous paintings and a few maximum cards.

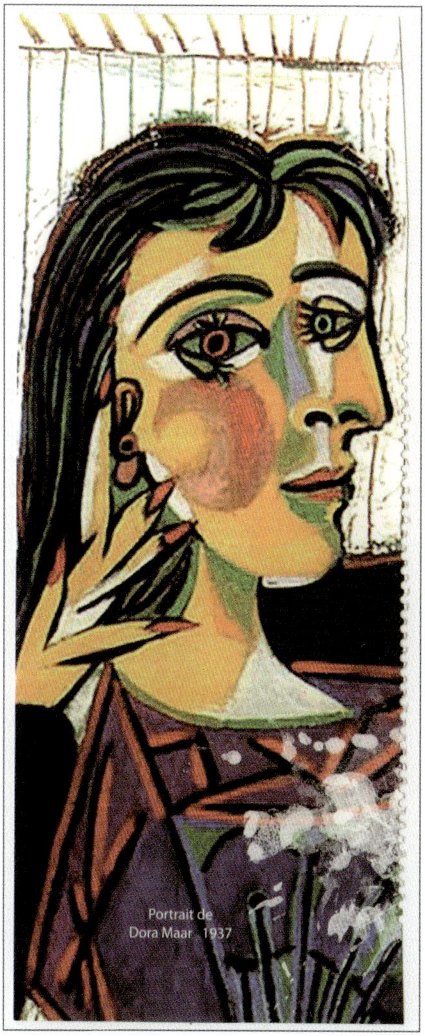

Portrait of Dora Maar This 1937 Picasso artwork was used by Burundi in 2011 on a stamp souvenir sheet that celebrated the 130th anniversary of the birth of Pablo Picasso.

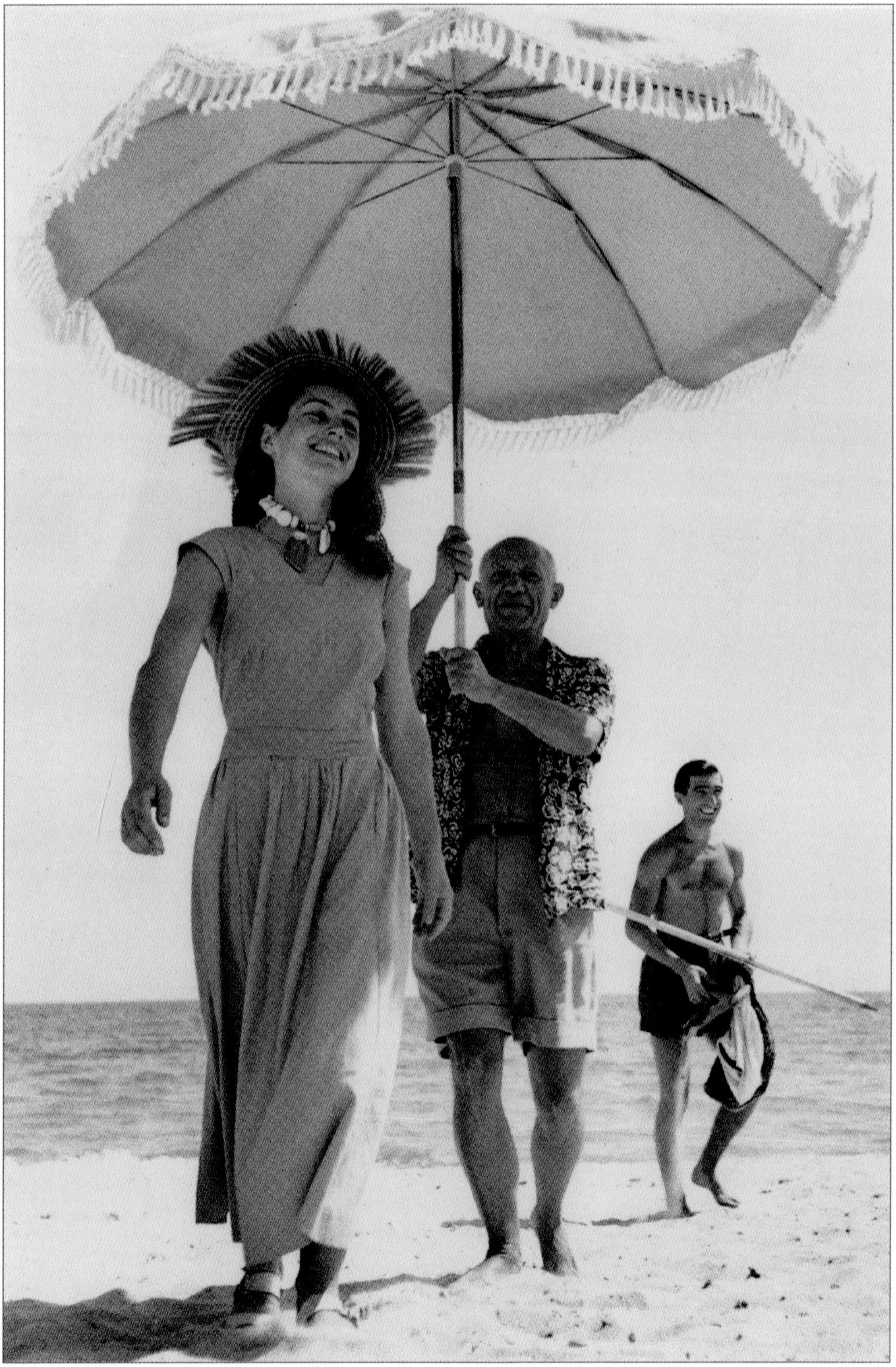

Françoise Gilot and Picasso at the beach This postcard scene shows Picasso in one of his more pixie moods on a Riviera beach, shielding Françoise Gilot from the sun.

INTRODUCTION

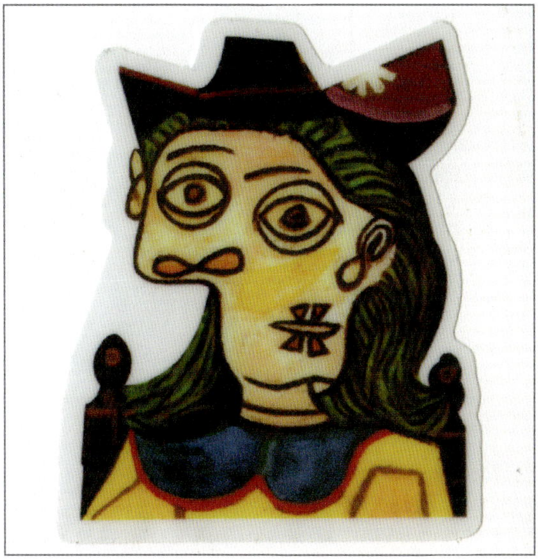

Many of Picasso's paintings have been honored on stamps worldwide. Contained herein are postage stamps that illustrate or describe pictures that were painted by Picasso. Paintings on stamps present a whole new way of looking at art.

Pablo Picasso showed great talent from an early age. When he was nineteen he left his native Spain and moved to Paris, where he met many famous artists. At twenty-one he had a one-man show in Paris and joined the city's artistic life. When Picasso first lived in Paris, he and his friend were so poor that they had only one bed between them and had to take turns to sleep! While one painted, the other slept in the bed.

Picasso's style developed from the "Blue Period" (1901–1904) to the "Rose Period" (1904–1906) to the pivotal work *Les Demoiselles d'Avignon* (1907), and the subsequent evolution of "cubism." Soon thereafter his work was characterized by "neoclassicism" and a renewed interest in drawing and figural representation.

Picasso was inspired by many things, including his surroundings, his girlfriends and wives, other famous artists, and Spanish and African art. Picasso was always original. His art explored humans and their situations. In the 1920s, Picasso and his wife, Olga (whom he married in 1918), continued to live in Paris, traveled frequently, and spent their summers at the beach. From 1925 to the 1930s Picasso was involved to a certain degree with the "surrealists." In 1932, with large exhibitions at Paris and Zurich galleries, Picasso's fame increased markedly. By 1936 the Spanish Civil War had affected Picasso, the expression of which culminated in his painting *Guernica* (1937). From the late 1940s onward he lived in the South of France.

In 1943 Picasso met Françoise Gilot, with whom he lived for the next ten years. In 1954 Picasso met Jacqueline Rogue, whom he married in 1961. They moved to Mougins, a commune in southeastern France that was a fifteen-minute drive from Cannes. There, Picasso continued his prolific work in painting, drawing, sculpture, and ceramics until his death on April 8, 1973.

The legendary life and career of Pablo Picasso (1881–1973) spanned most of the twentieth century and ushered in some of its most significant artistic revolutions. In every stage of his life and career, whether inspired by personal tragedies, wartime traumas, or private elations, Picasso's genius was fueled by a passion and authenticity that saw him push boundaries ever further, flouting all outward conventions and criticisms as he invented and reinvented the rules of the game, time after time. Picasso achieved universal renown and immense fortune for his revolutionary artistic accomplishments and became one of the best-known figures in twentieth-century art.

There is a lot of money in art; paintings by famous artists regularly fetch millions at auction. It is hardly surprising that some unscrupulous painters paint fakes. Many fake Picasso paintings have been recorded. Also many fake or illegal stamps with Picasso paintings have been found. Several paintings by Picasso rank among the most expensive paintings in the world. Many of these paintings sold for several million dollars. On May 11, 2015, the painting *Woman of Algiers* set a record for the highest price ever paid for a painting when it sold for $179.3 million at Christie's in New York.

Picasso was also a well-known womanizer. He was married twice but had many lovers throughout his life and left behind four children by three different women. His first wife, Olga, stayed married to him until she died in 1955, though they had been separated since 1935, when Olga discovered his affair with seventeen-year-old Marie-Thérèse Walter. Many of Picasso's girlfriends were much younger, including Françoise Gilot; she was just twenty-one years old when she met Picasso, who was forty years her senior. Picasso painted many pictures of his wives (Olga Koklova and Jacqueline Roque), mistresses (Fernande Oliver, Eva Gouel, Marie-Thérèse Walter, Dora Maar, Françoise Gilot), and children (Paulo [Paul], Maya, Claude, Paloma).

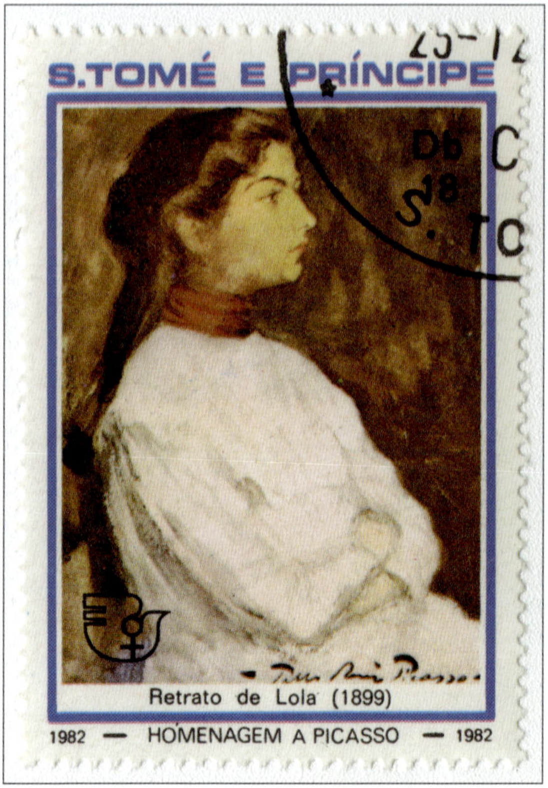

Picasso painted this portrait of his sister Lola. On December 24, 1982, the Democratic Republic of Sao Tome and Principe Islands issued an 18-dobra stamp with this image.

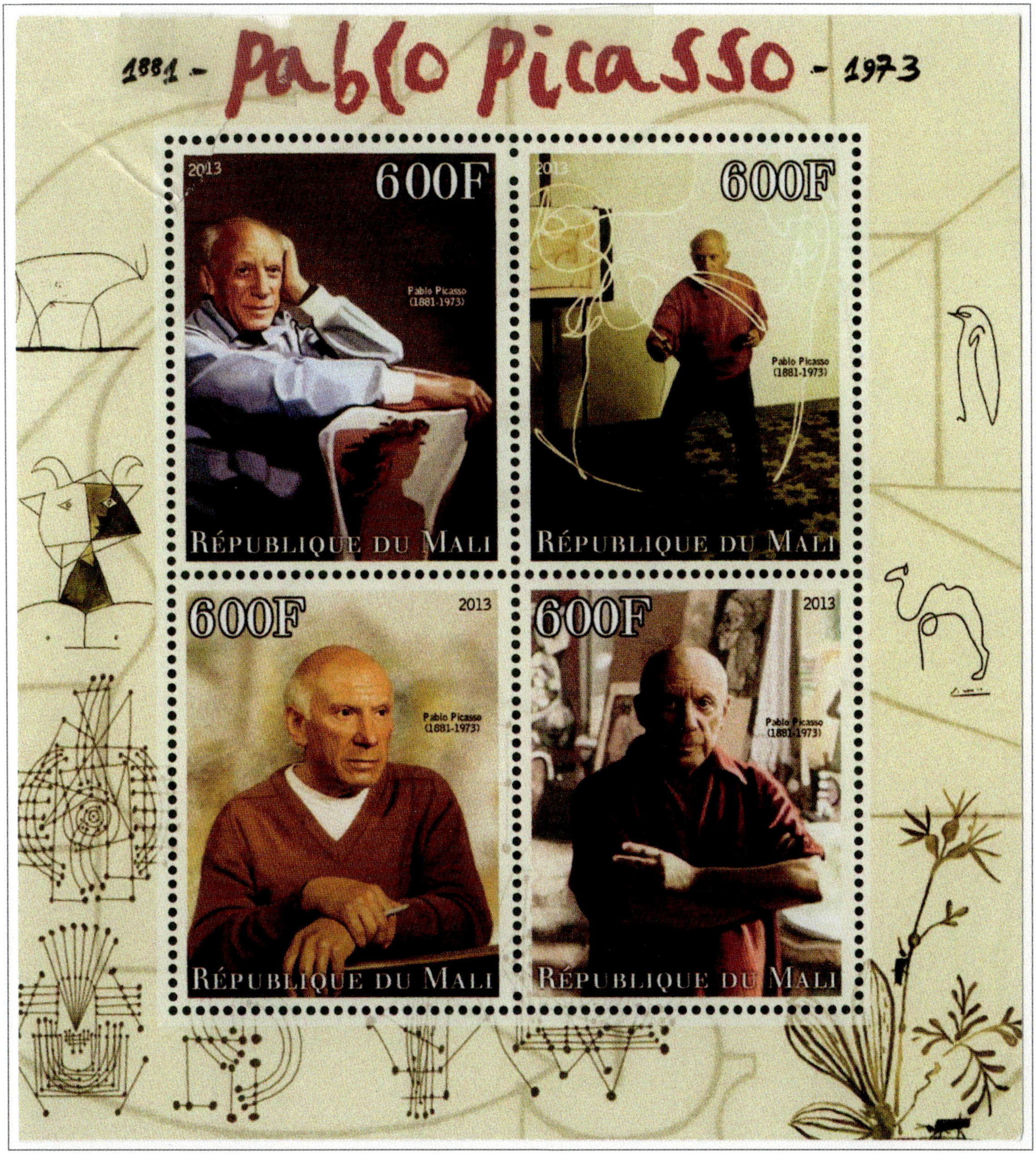

Pablo Picasso In 2013 the Republic of Mali issued this four-stamp sheet containing images of Picasso. During the first decade of the twentieth century, his style changed as he experimented with different theories, techniques, and ideas. After 1906, the fauvist work of the slightly older artist Henri Matisse motivated Picasso to explore more-radical styles, beginning a fruitful rivalry between the two artists, who were subsequently often paired by critics as the leaders of modern art.

CHAPTER 1:
EARLY YEARS (1881–1900)

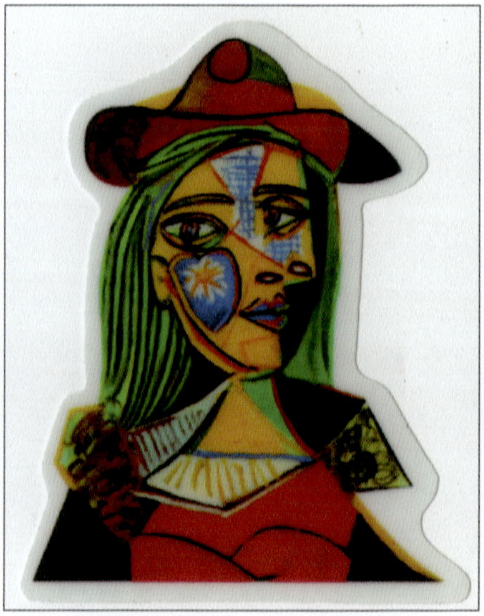

Pablo Ruiz Picasso was born on October 25, 1881, in Málaga, a provincial town in southern Spain, the son of Doña María Picasso y López and Don José Ruiz y Blasco. He first used the surnames of both parents, and in 1901 he decided to use only his mother's middle name.

As a child, Picasso showed incredible artistic talent and was considered a prodigy. Picasso's father, who was also an artist, gave all of his art supplies to thirteen-year-old Pablo because he showed such amazing talent. In 1894 Picasso showed his paintings for the first time in a Corunna junk shop. In 1885 the family moved to Barcelona, where his father worked at the art school and Picasso entered the School of Fine Arts. In 1895 Picasso painted *Girl with Bare Feet*.

No doubt about it, Picasso was brilliant. Artistically he was years ahead of his classmates, who were all five to six years older than he was. But Picasso disliked being told what to do, and he was often thrown into detention. For being a bad student he was placed in a bare cell with whitewashed walls and a bench to sit on. However, Picasso liked it there, since he took along a sketch pad and passed the time drawing.

In 1896 Picasso presented his work to the public for the first time. At sixteen years old Picasso had already learned everything that the art schools could teach him. It was in 1896 that Picasso painted *Portrait of the Artist's Mother*, *Portrait of the Artist's Father*, and *First Communion*.

In 1897 Picasso, with the financial support of his family, moved to Madrid to continue his studies. In this year Picasso painted *Science and Charity*, showing a doctor and a nun caring attentively for a patient. Picasso's father submitted this painting to an art exhibit in Madrid.

By 1899, Paris was the most important art center in the world. Here, artists and writers met in cafés and studios, and owners encouraged the latest trends in art. Picasso was now a fully trained professional painter. In 1899 Picasso was a regular guest at the cabaret/café Els Quatre Gats in Barcelona, Spain, the meeting place for the literary and artistic avant-garde of Barcelona. He worked in the studio of his friend Carles Casagemas, also a painter. In October 1900 Picasso traveled to Paris with Casagemas. He returned to Barcelona at the end of the year. In 1901 Casagemas committed suicide in Paris. His friend's death deeply affected Picasso. In autumn 1901 Picasso's first pictures of the "Blue Period" were painted.

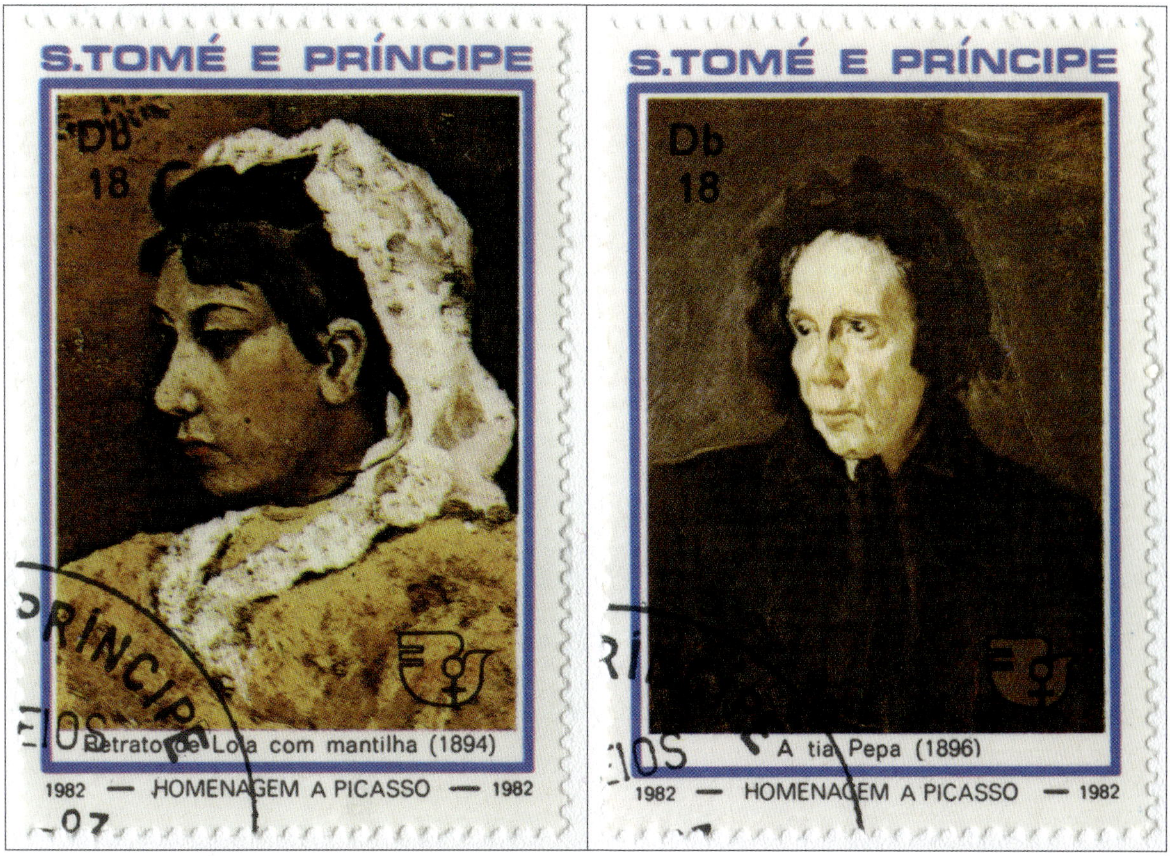

Early-years stamps Stamps that contain Picasso pictures painted by Pablo Picasso during his early years (1894–1899): Sister *Lola with Mantilla* and *Aunt Pepa*.

CHAPTER 2:
THE BLUE PERIOD (1901–1904)

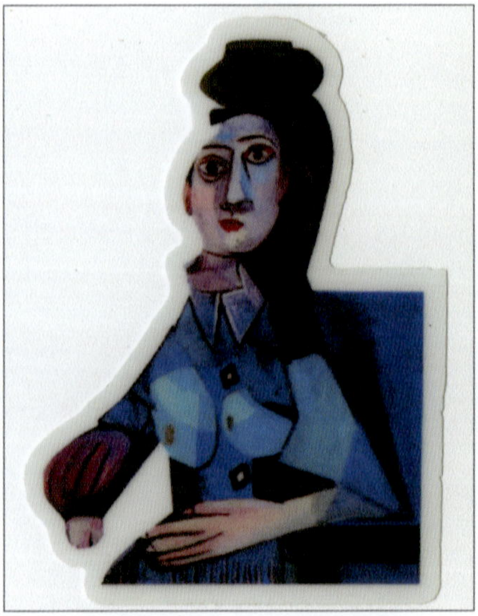

The "Blue Period" of Picasso (1901–1904) was when he painted essentially monochromatic paintings in shades of blue and blue green, only occasionally warmed by other colors. These works, inspired by Spain but painted in Paris, are now some of his most popular works. Many of Picasso's "Blue Period" works seem to reflect his experience of relative poverty and instability, depicting street urchins, beggars, the old and frail, the blind, social outsiders, circus people, prisoners, poor or despairing people in general, and drunks and prostitutes. In 1901 Picasso was influenced by the suicide of his friend Carlos Casagemas, who took his own life at the L'Hippodrome Café in Paris by shooting himself in the right temple on February 17, 1901. Picasso started painting in blue when he learned of Casagemas's death. Picasso–normally an outgoing socializer–withdrew from his friends. Picasso's bout of depression lasted several years. From 1901 to 1903 he painted several posthumous portraits of Casagemas, culminating in the gloomy painting *Life*, which was painted in 1903 and is now in the Cleveland Museum of Art.

In May 1902 Picasso traveled to Paris again and stayed there for the rest of the year, working in Casagemas's former studio.

Picasso's third stay in Paris (October 1902 onward) resulted in his financial situation becoming progressively worse. In January 1903 he returned to Barcelona to Casagemas's former studio. In the following fourteen months, nearly fifty paintings were completed, including *Life*, *Celestine*, *The Old Guitarist*, and *The Blind Man's Meal*. In April 1904 Picasso made his final move to Paris. In autumn 1904 Picasso met Fernande Oliver, with whom he lived until 1911.

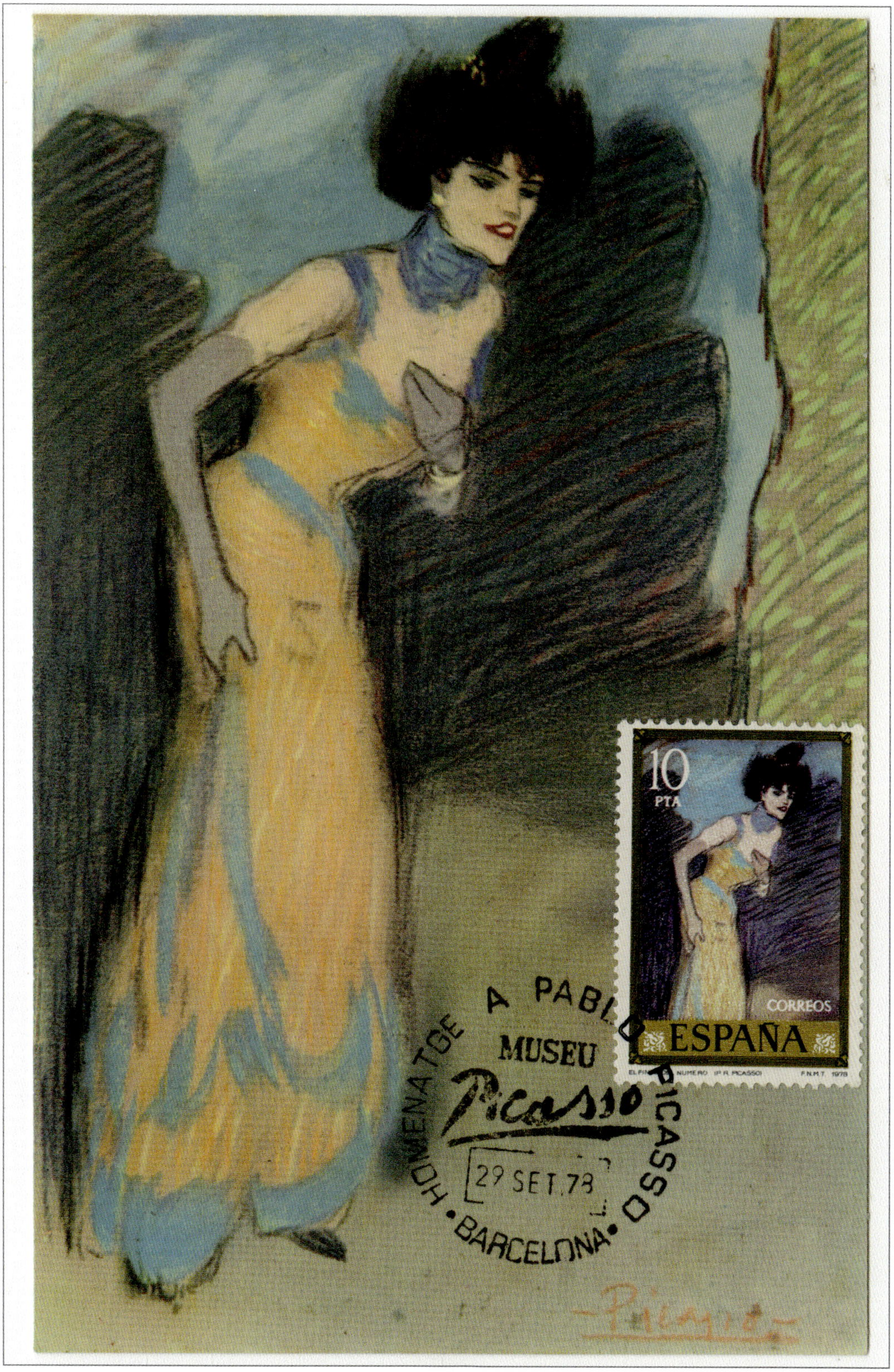
10
PTA
CORREOS
ESPAÑA
F.N.M.T. 1978
HOMENATGE A PABLO PICASSO
MUSEU
Picasso
29 SET.78
BARCELONA

Picasso's paintings during the "Blue Period" showed his sadness over what he saw and felt about the poor lives of those around him. Some of the paintings that Picasso painted in Paris and in Barcelona, Spain, included the following:

The Burial of Casagemas (1901)
The Death of Casagemas (1901)
Lady in Blue (1901)
Waiting (1901)
The Kept Woman (1901)
Portrait of Cabarets (1901)
Harlequin and His Companion (1901)
The Absinthe Drinker (1901)
Child Holding a Dove (1901)
Harlequin Leaning on a Table (1901)
The Girl with the Chignon (1901)
The Aperitif (1901)
Woman Ironing (1901)
Evocation—the Burial of Casagemas (1901)
The Blue Room (1901)
Self-Portrait (1901)
Drunk Woman Drowsing (1902)
The Two Sisters (1902)
Mother and Child on the Seashore (1902)
Prostitutes in a Bar (1902)
Woman Huddled on the Ground with the Sea in the Background (1902)
The Soup (1902)
The Tragedy (1903)
Life (1903)
The Sick Child (1903)
Couple in a Café (1903)
Sebastian Junyer-Vidal with a Woman in a Café (1903)
The Blue Glass (1903)
Portrait of Señora Soler (1903)
The Soler Family (1903)
Bust of a Woman (1903)
The Blind Man's Meal (1903)
The Old Guitarist (1903)
The Old Jew (1903)

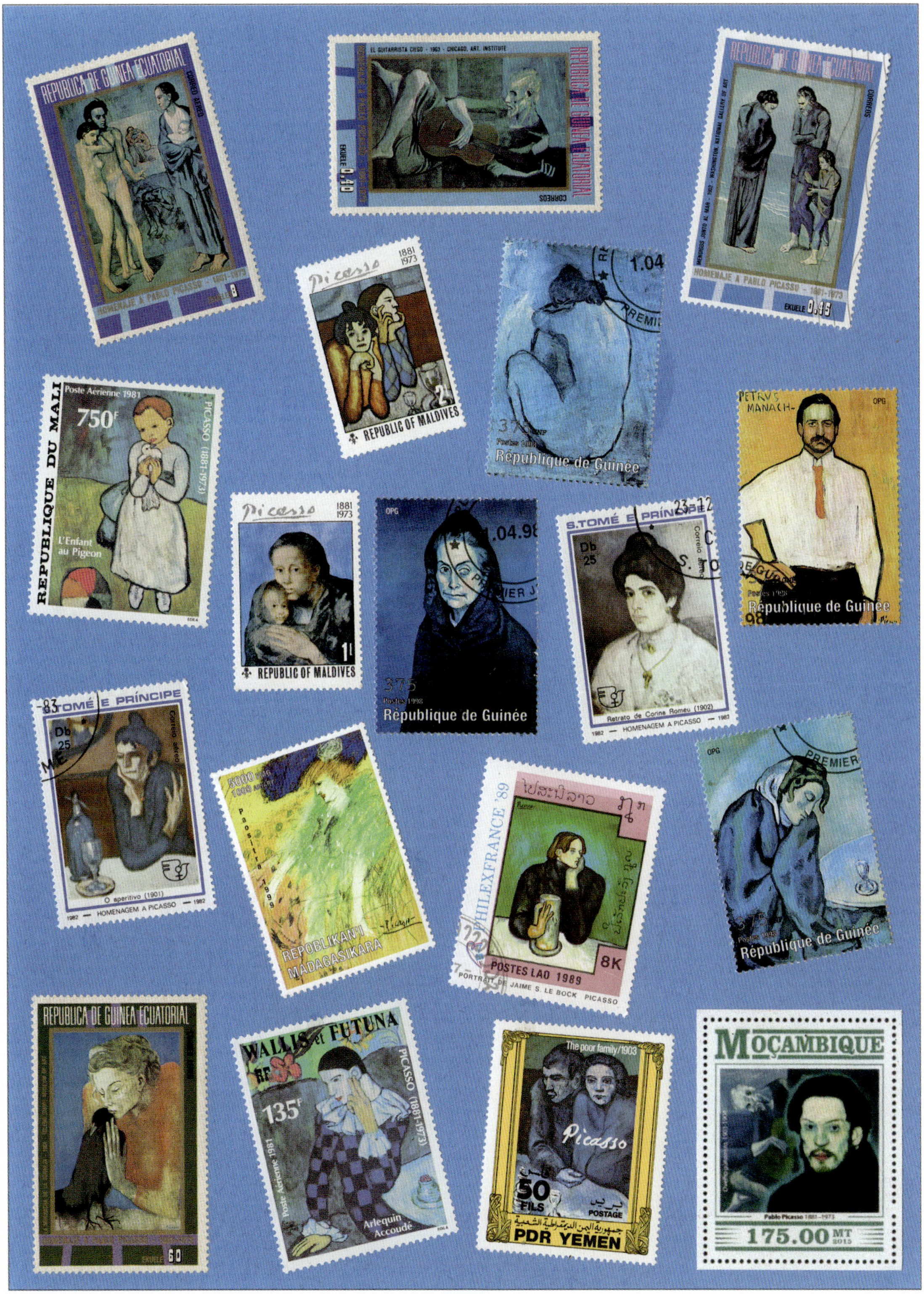

Blue-Period stamps Stamps that contain Picasso pictures painted during the "Blue Period" (1901–1904)

CHAPTER 3:
THE ROSE PERIOD (1905–1906)

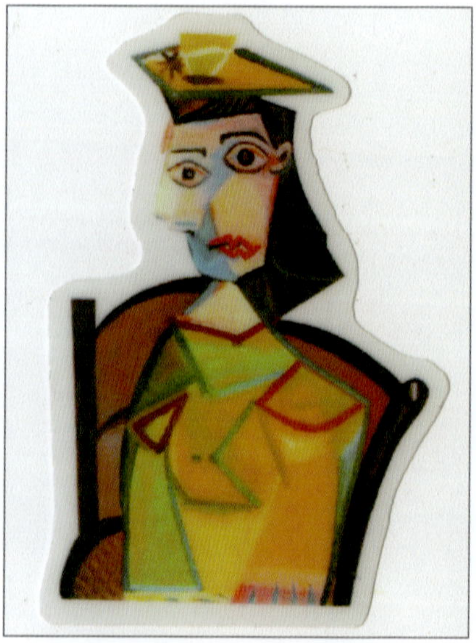

Picasso's "Blue Period" was followed by his "Rose Period." Picasso's bout with depression gradually ended, and as his psychological state improved, he moved toward more-joyful, more-vibrant works and emphasized the use of pinks ("rose" in French) and other warm hues to express his shift in mood and subject manner. Picasso's "Rose Period" paintings were a happier type of painting, showing clowns and performers at the circus. Picasso's pictures of his "Rose Period" sold well, and consequently his financial situation improved.

Some of the paintings Picasso painted during the "Rose Period" include the following:

The Toilette (1905)
Acrobat and Young Harlequin (1905)
Family of Acrobats with Ape (1905)
Acrobat on a Ball (1905)
Boy with a Dog (1905)
Harlequin with Glass (1905)
Sitting Nude (1905)
Mother and Child (1905)
Family of Traveling Entertainers (1905)
Two Brothers (1906)
Portrait of Gertrude Stein (1906)
La Coiffure (1906)
Pablo Picasso Self-Portrait (1906)

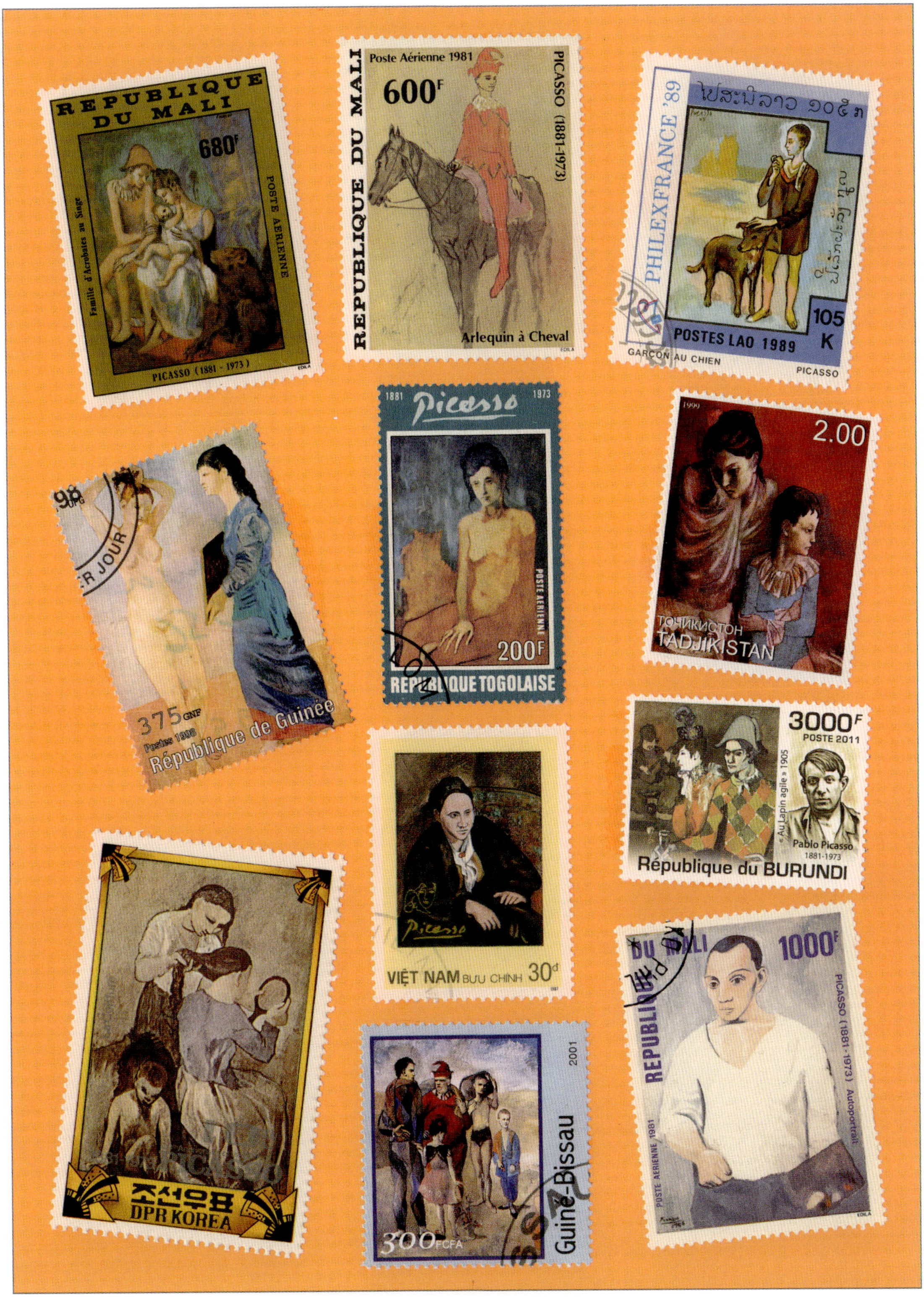

Rose-Period stamps Stamps that contain Picasso pictures painted during the "Rose Period" (1905–1906)

CHAPTER 4:
CUBISM (1907–1914)

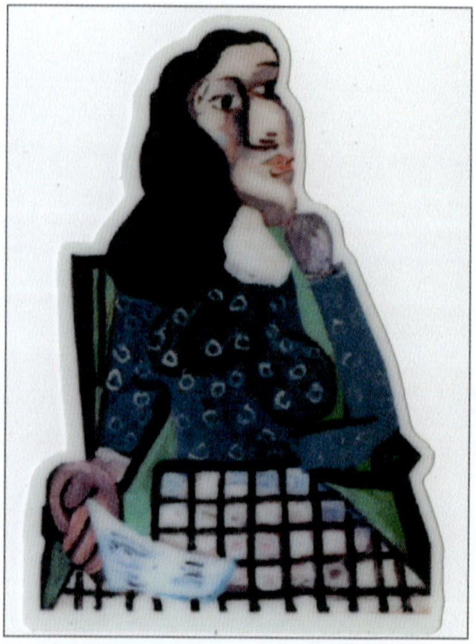

In 1907 Picasso began to paint pictures that looked more like puzzles with the pieces out of order. Picasso reduced everything—landscapes, figures, and houses—to geometric patterns, or cubes. It was a new way of seeing things in art. This new art was called "cubism." Cubism changed the concept of art and led the way to "surrealism" and "modern art."

"Cubism" was the first movement into the abstract art of the twentieth century. It began in Paris with the work of Picasso and his good friend Georges Braque, who tried to paint three-dimensional reality into two-dimensional space. They painted things as they were "known to be" rather than as they appeared. Picasso's "cubist" paintings often showed all sides of an object or figure at once: table legs rose in the air, and two eyes appeared on the same side of a nose.

Picasso shocked the art world with his painting *Les Demoiselles d'Avignon* (*The Ladies of Avignon*) because it is not a realistic picture and because the women do not look beautiful. Picasso worked on this picture on and off for about a year. He wanted to paint a traditional subject in a new way. Many people say this picture marks the beginning of modern art.

Some of the paintings Picasso painted during the 1907–1914 period include the following:

Self-Portrait (1907)
Woman with a Fan (1907)
Les Demoiselles d'Avignon (1907)
Houses on a Hill (1909)
Woman with Pears (1909)
Portrait of Ambroise Vollard (1910)
Woman with Mandolin (1910)
Violin "Jolie Eva" (1912)
Still Life with Woven Cane (1912)
Guitare (1912)
Card Player (1914)

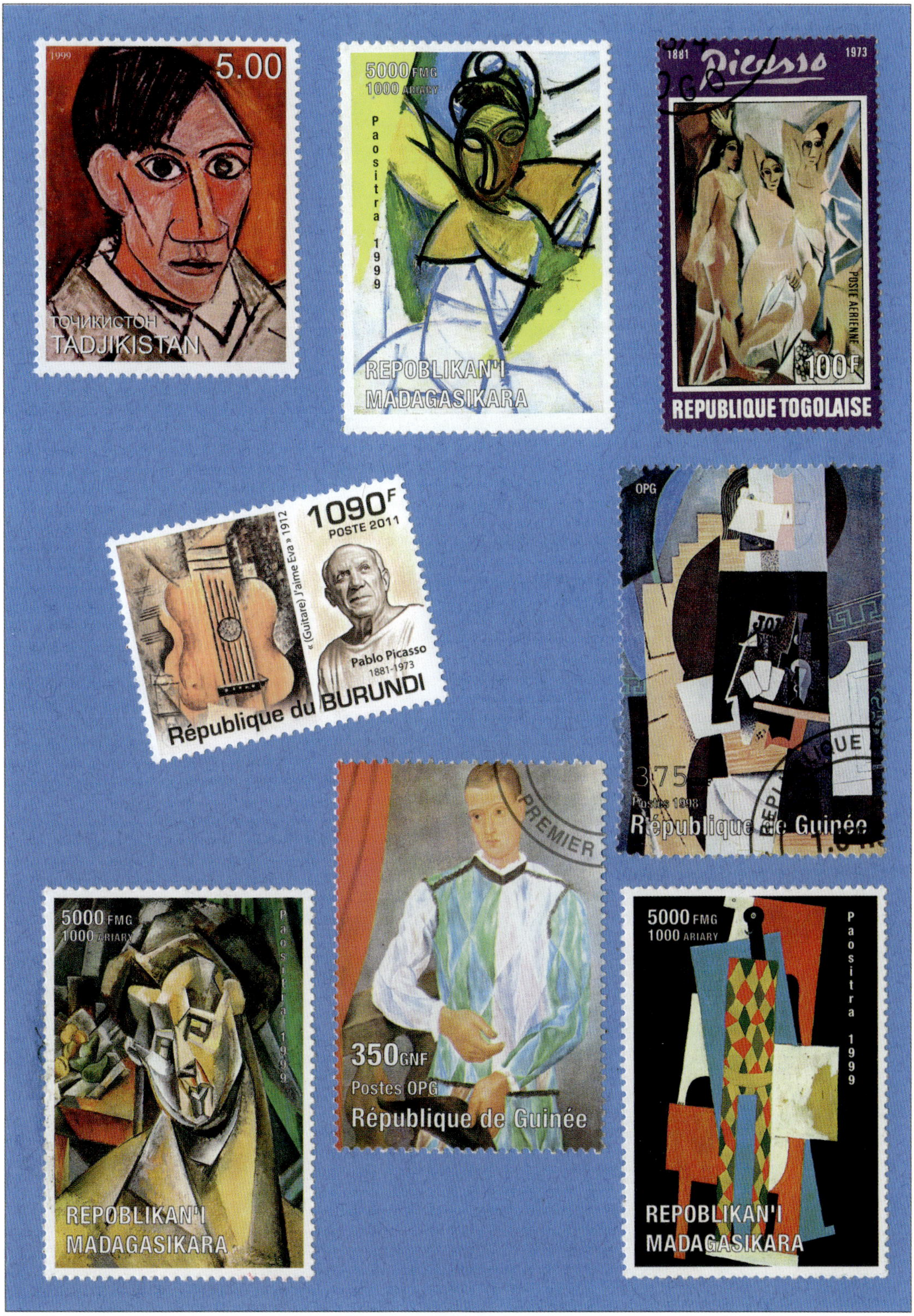

Cubism stamps Stamps that contain Picasso pictures painted during his cubism period (1907–1916)

CHAPTER 5:
NEOCLASSICISM AND SURREALISM (1917–1935)

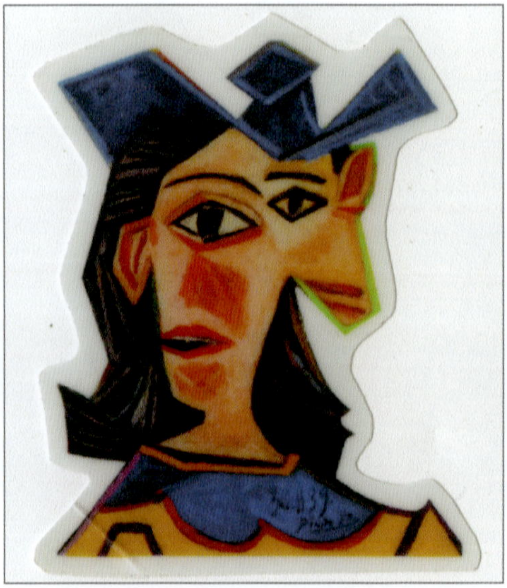

Picasso gradually shifted from "cubism"; in 1917 he started producing work in a neoclassical style. This change occurred shortly after his first visit to Italy, where he was inspired by the naturalism found in Italian Renaissance paintings. Aiming to emulate these Renaissance artists, he returned to figurative painting.

In 1918 Picasso went on a honeymoon to Biarritz, France, with his first wife, Olga. This is where he painted *The Bathers*, which illustrated bathing beauties in their old-fashioned swimsuits. The women in this picture seem to have rather strange bodies. They appear a little elongated, their limbs curling with playful energy. Picasso was having fun with this painting. It was a picture he kept for himself and never sold.

Examples of Picasso's paintings in the "neoclassicism" style include the following:

Harlequin (1917)
Olga in an Armchair (1918)
The Bathers (1918)
Pierrot Seated (1918)
Sleeping Peasants (1919)
Large Bather (1921)
Three Musicians (1921)
Seated Nude Drying Her Foot (1921)
Woman Running on the Beach (1922)
Paul on a Donkey (1923)
Family on the Beach (1923)
Mandolin and Guitar (1924)

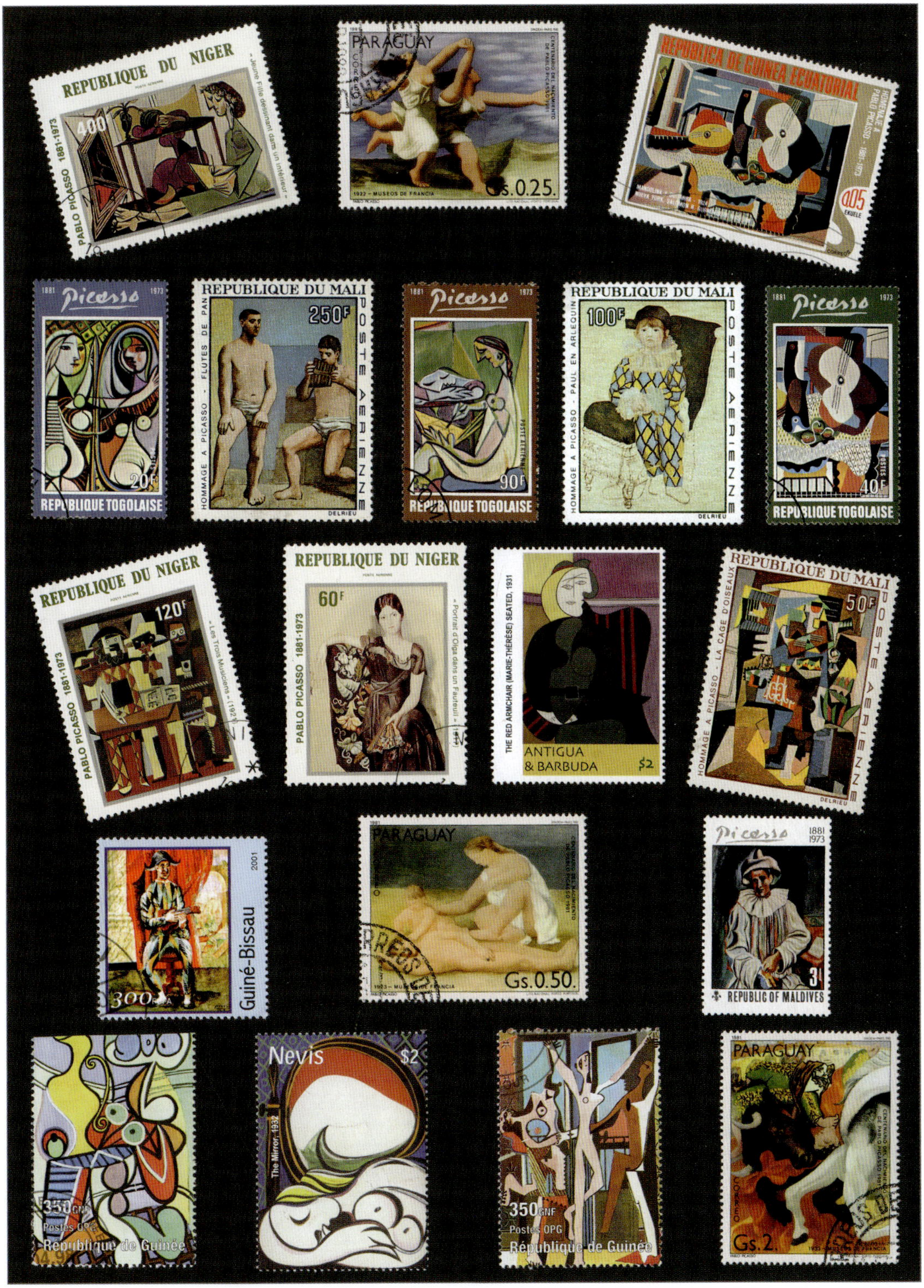

Neoclassicism and surrealism stamps Stamps that contain Picasso pictures painted during the neoclassicism and surrealism periods (1917–1935)

Following "neoclassicism," Picasso again moved away from naturalism. In 1925 he began working in a style called "surrealist," characterized by dreamy depictions of figures with disorganized facial features and twisted bodies. This "surreal" quality is emphasized by an unnatural palette of clashing colors and bright tones, as well as a contrast between geometric and organic forms.

Some of Picasso's paintings of the "surrealism" period include the following:

Baigneuse (1925)
The Three Dancers (1925)
Studio with Plaster Head (1925)
Paul as Harlequin (1925)
Paul as a Clown (1925)
Paul as Pierrot with Flowers (1929)
Large Female Nude in Red Chair (1929)
Figures at the Seashore (1931)
The Red Chair (1931)
Still Life on a Pedestal Table (1931)
Woman in Red Chair (1932)
Woman with a Flower (1932)
The Rescue (1932)
Nude, Green Leaves and Bust (1932)
Girl in Front of a Mirror (1932)
The Dream (1932)
Bullfight: Death of the Toreador (1933)
Bullfight (1934)
Minotaur (1934)
Minotauromachia (1935)
The Muse (1935)

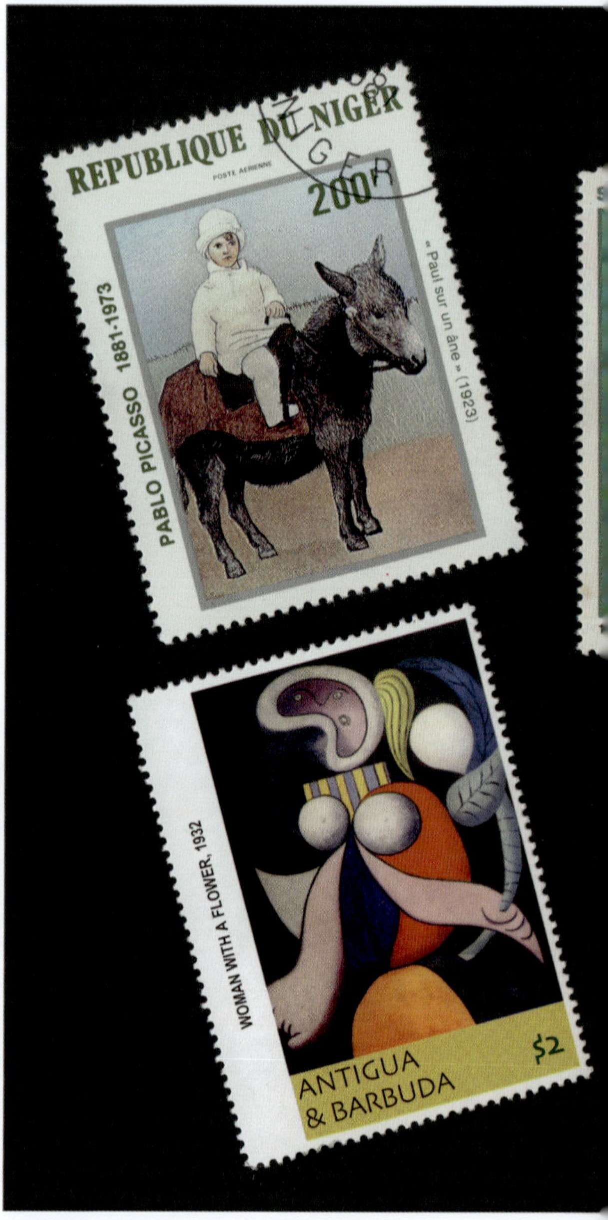

Neoclassicism and surrealism stamps

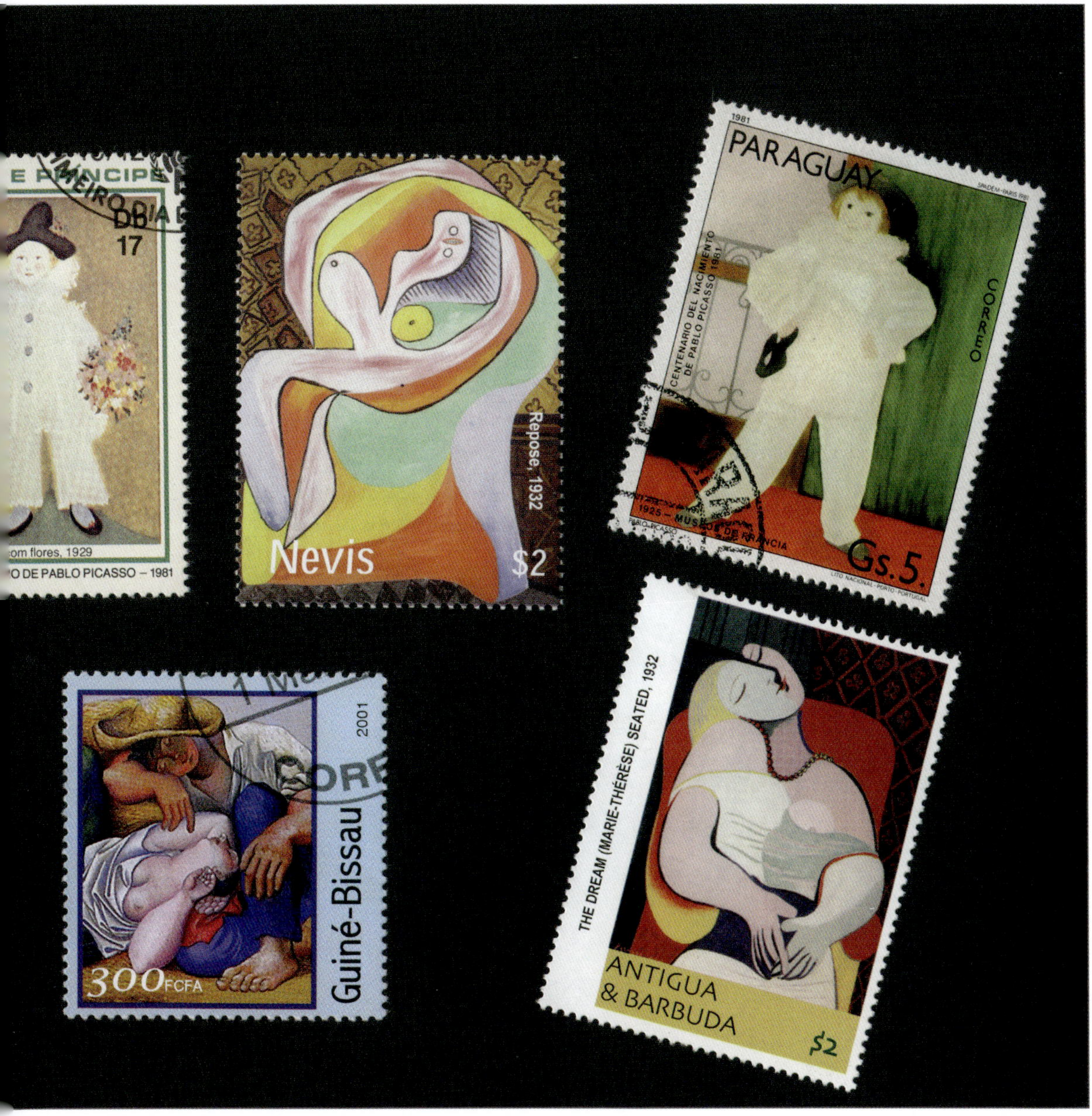
DE PABLO PICASSO – 1981
Repose, 1932
Nevis
$2
1981
PARAGUAY
CENTENARIO DEL NACIMIENTO DE PABLO PICASSO 1981
CORREO
Gs.5.
2001
Guiné-Bissau
300 FCFA
THE DREAM (MARIE-THÉRÈSE) SEATED, 1932
ANTIGUA & BARBUDA
$2

CHAPTER 6:
THE VIOLENT YEARS (1936–1945)

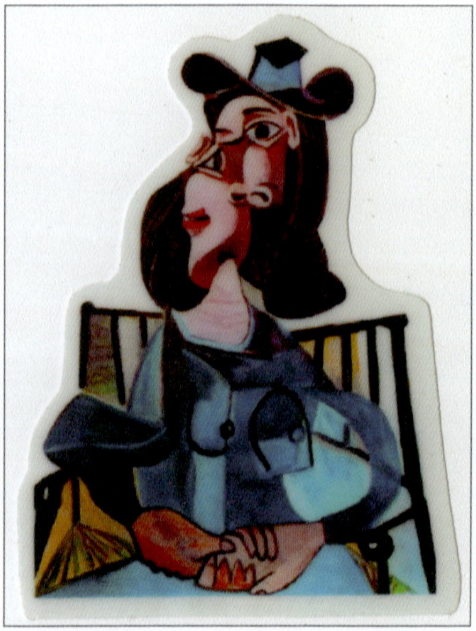

During the 1930s the world was going through a period of violence, fear, and death. Picasso's works during this dark period of war and social turmoil—the "Violent Years"—are deeply marked by political and personal catastrophes. The Spanish Civil War came to a cruel climax in the bombing of the Spanish town Guernica, and Picasso's response was probably his most famous painting, which he painted within a few weeks of the event.

The painting *Guernica* was commissioned in 1937 for the Spanish Pavilion at the Exposition Universelle in Paris. In this work, Picasso depicts fear and horror following the destruction of the town Guernica during bombing raids by the German Condor Legion. Picasso adopted a political stance, saying that "painting was not invented to decorate homes. It is a weapon of attack and defense against the enemy." Picasso's huge, shocking scene of death and destruction got a mixed reception in Paris and was criticized for being hard to understand. When a Nazi officer saw *Guernica*, he asked Picasso, "Was you who did it?" And Picasso is said to have responded, "No, you did!" Picasso wanted the painting to be displayed in Spain, and this finally happened in 1975. The painting now hangs in Madrid.

World War II saw ruthless fighting and bombing campaigns, and the systematic slaughter of millions in Nazi concentration camps. During the war, Picasso chose to stick it out in his studio in France. He was not allowed to exhibit, but he managed to have paintings sold, and he lived far more comfortably than most people did. After the war was over, many people found it difficult to come to terms with the horror of what had happened, and this was reflected in the art of the time.

Some of the paintings Picasso produced during the war years include the following:

Guernica (1937)
Seated Woman (1937)
Weeping Woman (1937)
Maya (1938)
Maya with a Doll (1938)
Cat Catching a Bird (1939)
The Yellow Pullover (Dora Maar) (1939)
Portrait of Sabartes (1939)
Woman Dressing Her Hair (1940)
Aubade (1942)
Studio Window (1943)

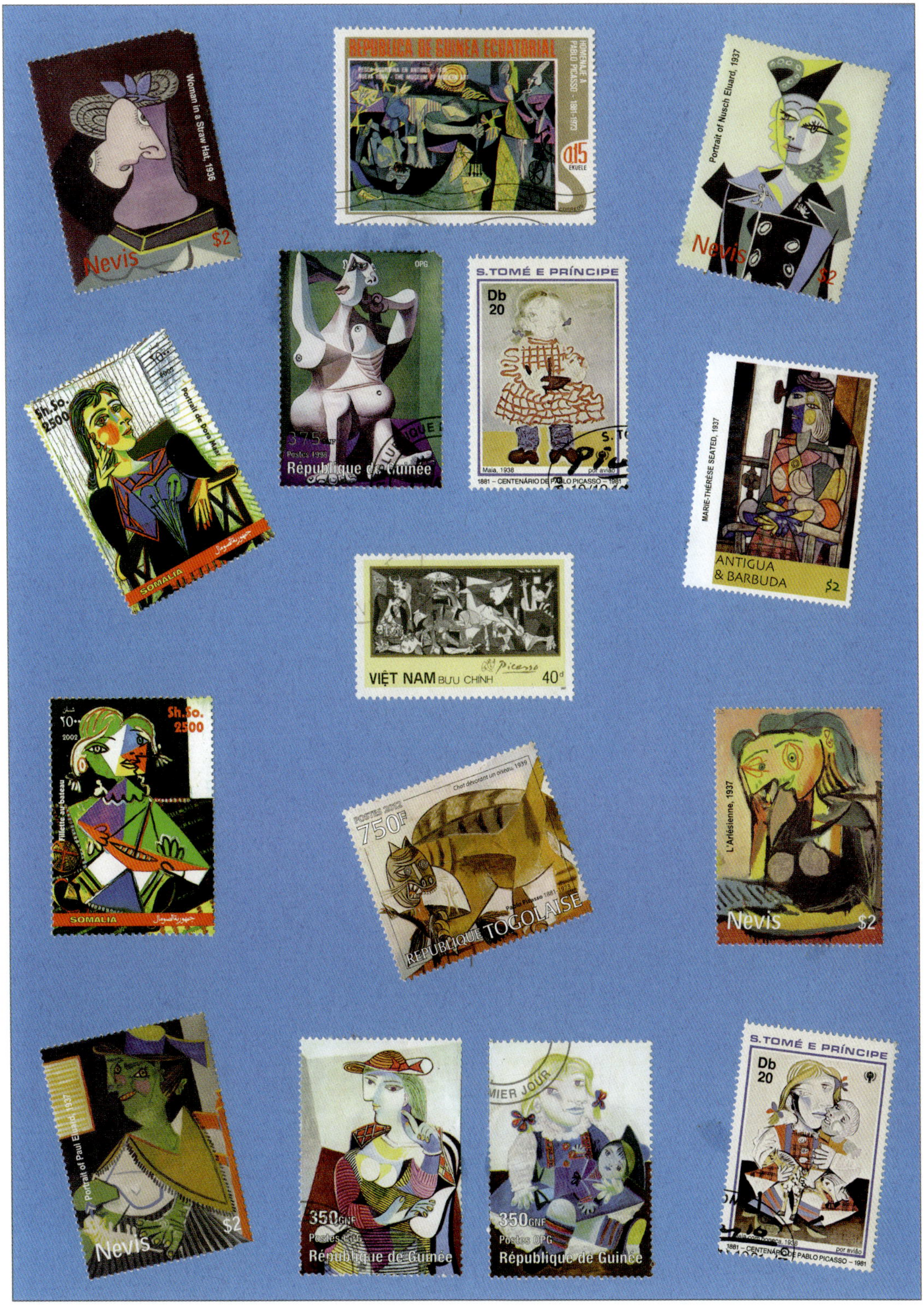

Violent-years stamps Stamps that contain Picasso works painted during the "violent years" (1936–1945)

CHAPTER 7:

POSTWAR YEARS (1946–1954)

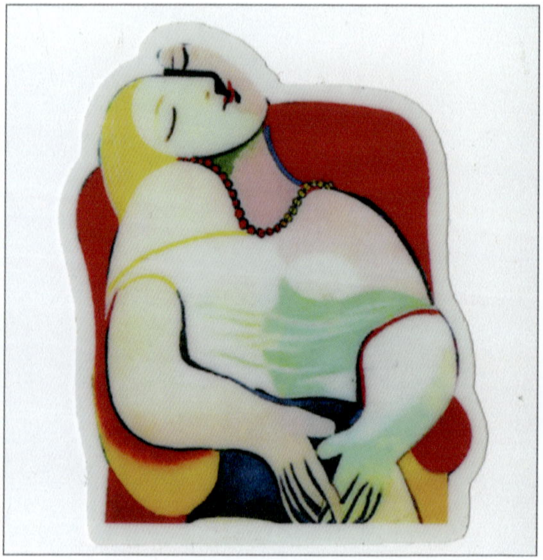

After World War II, Picasso's fame increased enormously. In America he was celebrated as the most significant artist of the twentieth century, and in France he became a public figure.

In 1951 Picasso responded to the war in Korea with a very specifically titled work. After American forces moved into Korea, he painted *Massacre in Korea*, which describes good and evil in opposition to each other in a vivid and unmistakable way. During the 1950s the world of children found its way into Picasso's paintings. In a number of pictures, Picasso shows his two youngest children, Claude and Paloma, absorbed in play.

Some of the paintings Picasso produced during the "Postwar Years" include the following:

Françoise as a Flower (1946)
Claude and Paloma at Play (1950)
Paloma with an Orange (1951)
Françoise, Claude and Paloma (1951)
Claude Drawing (1951)
Massacre in Korea (1951)
Paloma at Three Years Old (1952)
War (1952)
Peace (1952)
Paloma in Blue (1952)
Portrait of Madame (1952)
Woman with a Dog (1953)
Portrait of Sylvette (1954)
Children Drawing (1954)
Jacqueline with Flowers (1954)

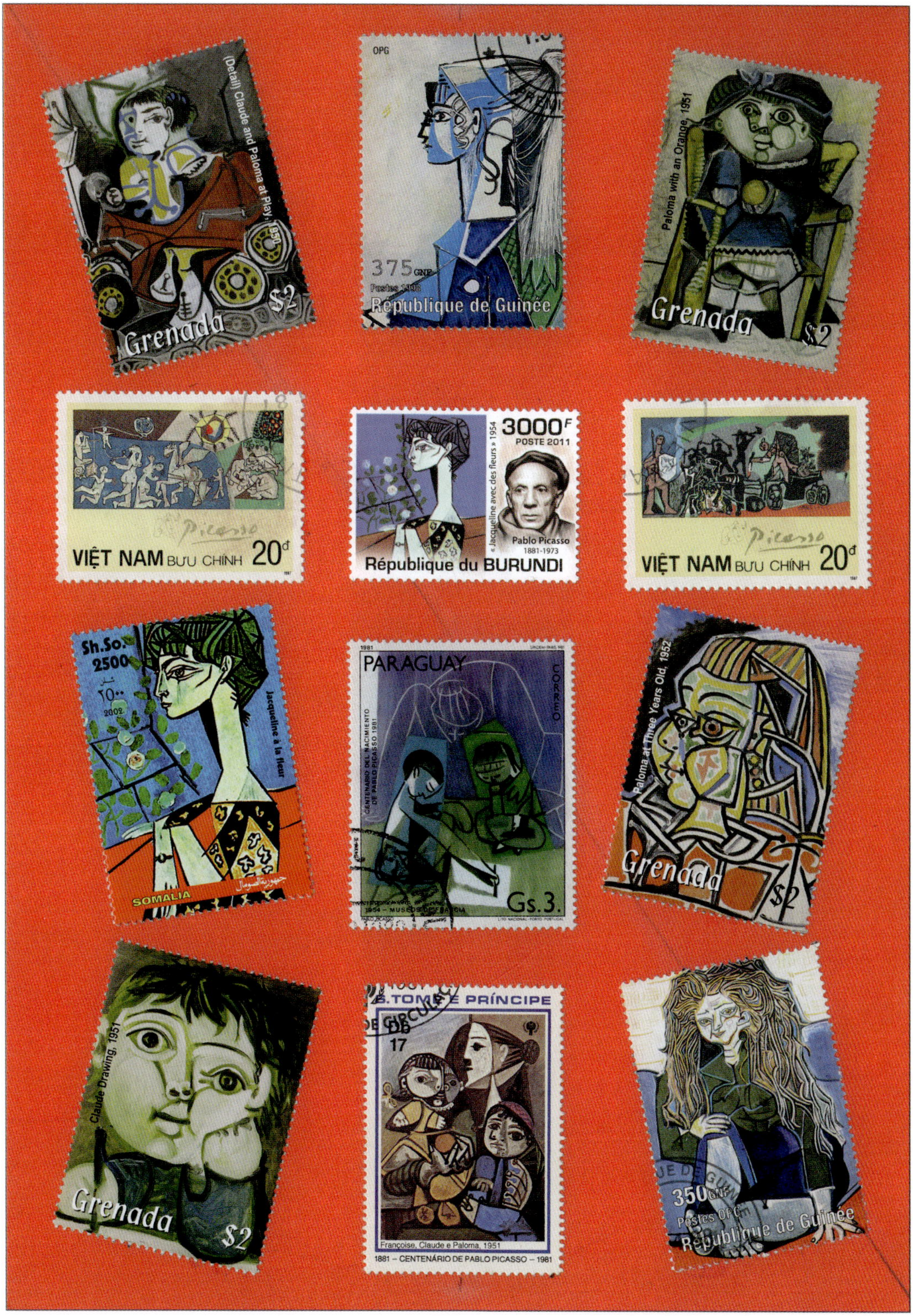

Postwar-years stamps Stamps that contain Picasso pictures painted during the postwar years (1946–1954)

CHAPTER 8:
LATE WORKS (1955–1973)

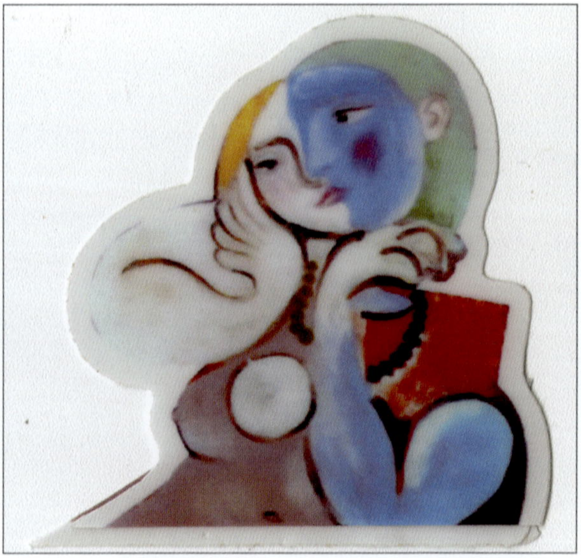

In the final part of Picasso's life, he gradually retreated from public life. He moved his home several times, usually in a vain attempt to escape from the many people clamoring to meet him. In 1961 Picasso married Jacqueline Roque, who had often modeled for him since their meeting in 1953. Toward the end of Picasso's life, he entered a phase of hectic productivity. He worked on several pieces simultaneously, painting up to five paintings a day. He often took works by other painters as models, re-creating them in his own style.

The paintings produced in Picasso's later years were not categorized into certain styles, since they each incorporated different elements of his past periods. This approach culminated in a mixed collection of paintings that illustrate the influence of his changing style and remind viewers of his endless talent.

Picasso died at ninety-one on April 8, 1973, in southern France. He left 13,500 paintings and designs, 100,000 prints and engravings, 34,000 book illustrations, and 300 sculptures and ceramics. No other artist has come close

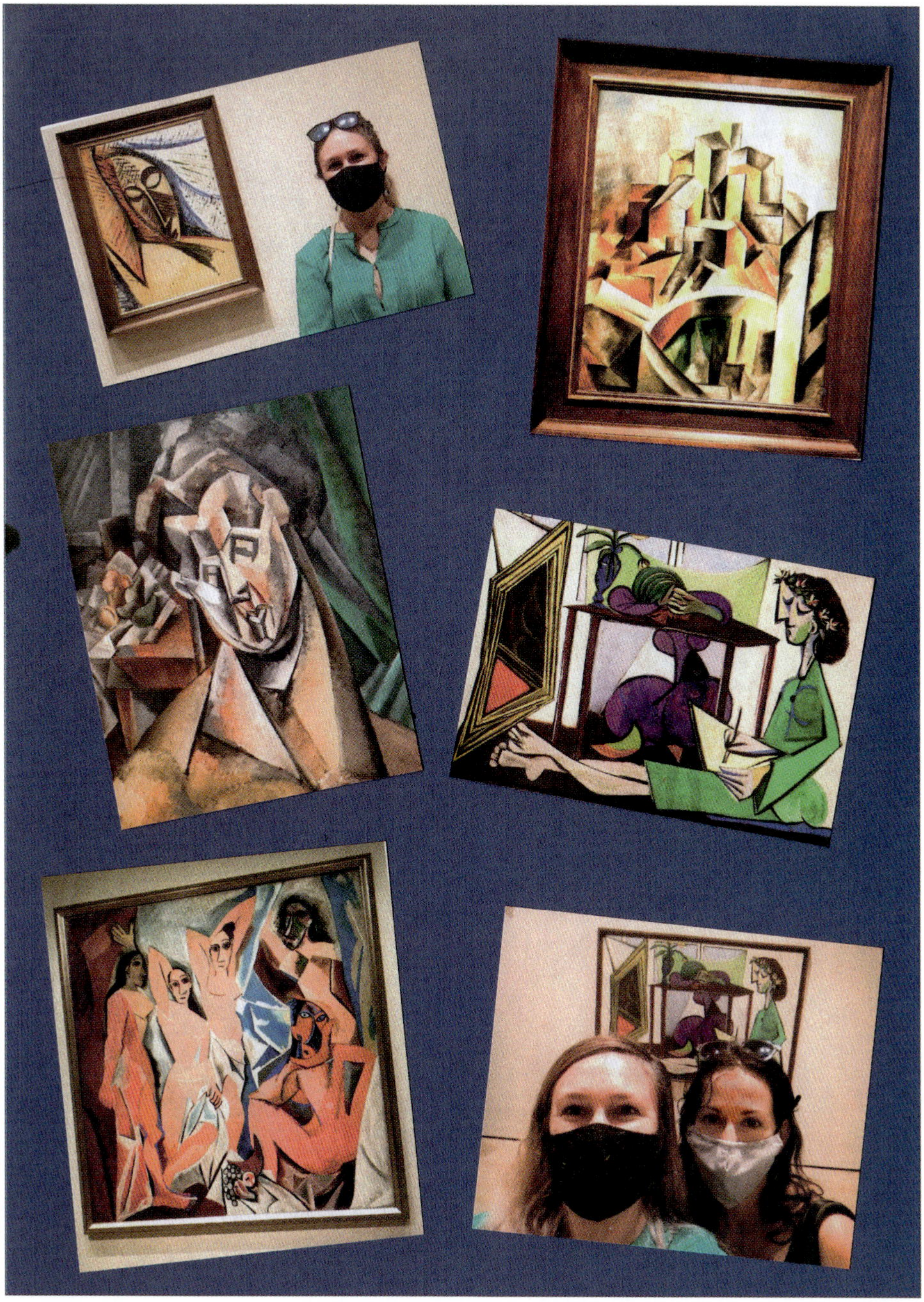

Picasso paintings at the Museum of Modern Art In July 2021 the author's granddaughter, Selena Alger-Schiffer, and her friend Mardi Sykes took these photographs of Picasso paintings at the Museum of Modern Art in New York City. They were required to wear masks because of the COVID-19 virus. The Museum of Modern Art is an art museum in midtown Manhattan, New York City. It plays a major role in developing and collecting modern art and is often identified as one of the largest and most influential museums of modern art in the world. The museum has a large collection of Picasso paintings, including *La Coiffure* (1905), *Les Demoiselles d' Avigon* (1907), *Woman with Pears* (1909), *Fruit Dish* (1909), *Card Player* (1914), *Green Still Life* (1914), *Harlequin* (1915), *Woman in White (1923), Still Life with a Cake* (1924), *Three Musicians* (1924), *Girl before a Mirror* (1932), *Two Figures on the Beach* (1933), and *Interior with Girl Drawing* (1935).

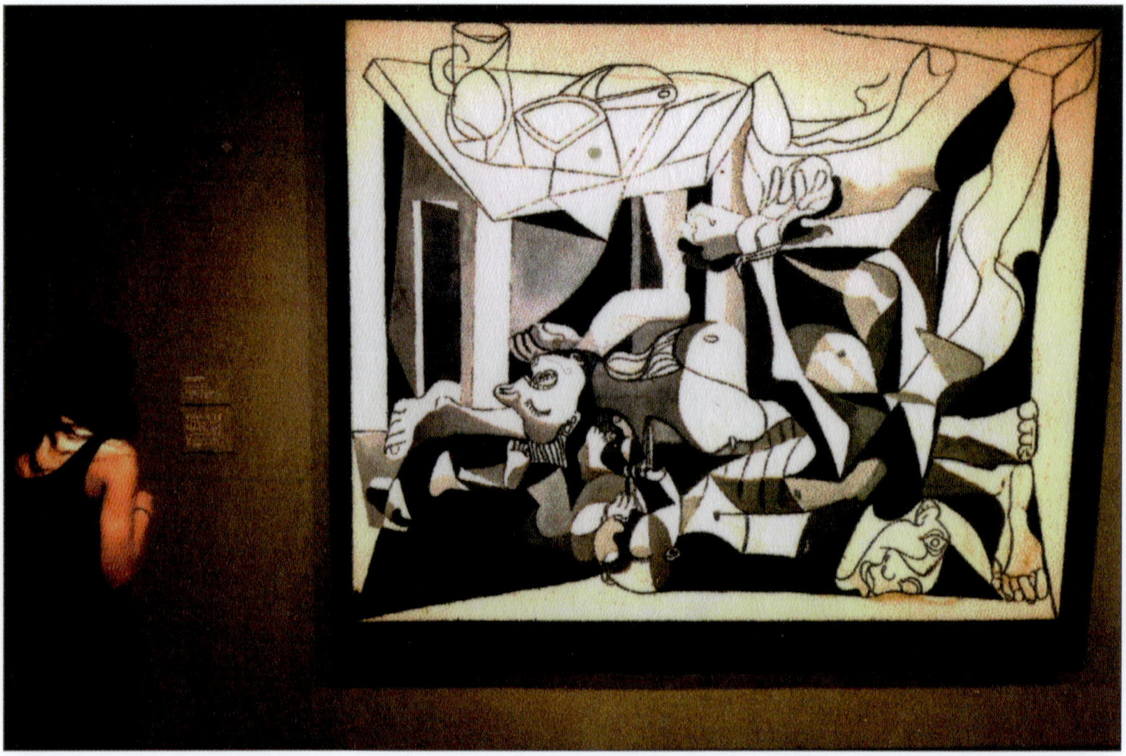

***The Charnel House* painting** Mardi Sykes looking at Picasso's *The Charnel House* (1945), an oil-and-charcoal-on-canvas painting at the Museum of Modern Art in New York City. *Photograph by Selena Alger-Schiffer*

to being so prolific during their lifetime. Before Picasso died, he left many paintings to places that meant a great deal to him during his life. In 1963, the Picasso Museum opened in Barcelona. Its initial collection was donated by Picasso's friend J'aime Sabartes, but after his friend died in 1968, Picasso continued to give works to the museum. In an agreement with the French government, Picasso left a personal selection of his work to France—enough to fill a museum. In 1985 the Picasso Museum opened in Paris. This museum contains 203 paintings, 85 ceramics, 191 sculptures, and more than 3,000 drawings, manuscripts, and engravings that span his life as an artist. No modern art museum is complete without some of Picasso's work.

Some of the pictures Picasso painted during his last years include the following:

Women of Algiers (1955)
Las Meninas (1957)
Infanta Margarita Maria (1957)
The Doves (1957)
Tête de Femme (1960)
The Artist and His Model (1963)
Cavalier with Pipe (1968)
Female Nude and Smoker (1968)
Rembrandt Figure and Eros (1969)
Large Heads (1969)
Girl in a Room (1969)
The Kiss (1969)
Cavalier with Pipe (1970)
Seated Woman (1970)
Seated Old Man (1971)
Musketeer with a Sword (1972)
Self-Portrait (1972)

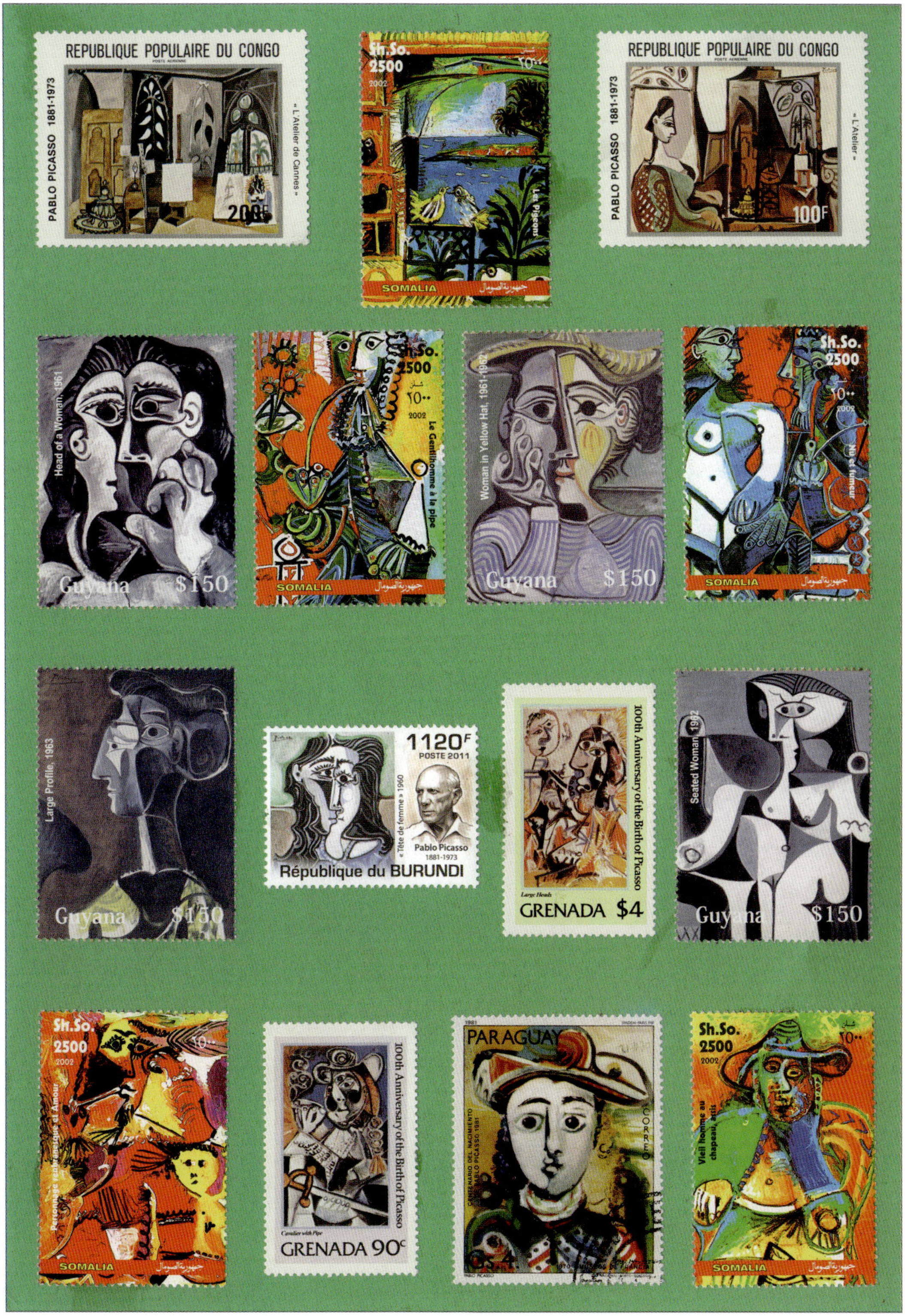

Late-works stamps Stamps that contain Picasso pictures painted during the "late works" years (1955–1973)

CHAPTER 9:

PICASSO PAINTING STAMPS

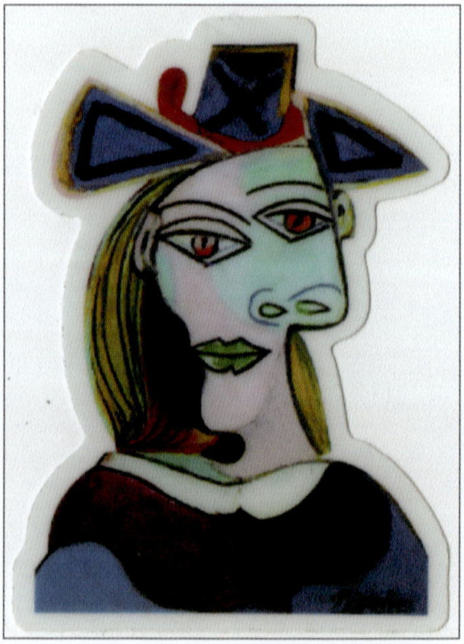

The following Picasso Painting Stamps are in this chapter:

Girl with Bare Feet (1895)
Science and Charity (1897)
Els Quatre Gats (1899)
Child Holding a Dove (1901)
Harlequin and His Companion (1901)
Harlequin Leaning on a Table (1901)
Self-Portrait (1901)
Portrait of Pedro Manach (1901)
Self-Portrait (1901)
Absinthe Drinker (1901)
Corina Pere Romeu (1902)
*The Old Guitarist (*1903)
*Life (*1903)
Beggars by the Edge of the Sea (1903)
Celestina (1903)
Woman with a Crow (1904)
The Toilette (1905)
Acrobat on a Ball (1905)
Boy with a Dog (1905)
Harlequin with Glass (1905)
Seated Nude (1905)
Family of Traveling Entertainers (1905)
Portrait of Gertrude Stein (1906)
LA Coiffure (1906)
Pablo Picasso Self-Portrait (1906)
Les Demoiselles d'Avignon (1907)
(Guitare) J'aime Eva (1912)
Card Player (1914)
Harlequin (1915)
Harlequin (1917)
Pierrot Seated (1918)
Three Musicians (1921)
Picasso and Olga (1923)

Family on the Beach (1923)
The Three Dancers (1925)
Studio with Plaster Head (1925)
Paul as Harlequin (1925)
Still Life on a Pedestal Table (1931)
Woman with a Flower (1932)
Girl in Front of a Mirror (1932)
Minotaur (1934)
The Muse (1935)
Woman with a Hat (1935)
Portrait of Dora Maar (1937)
Guernica (1937)
Seated Woman (1937)
Portrait of Maya with Her Doll (1938)
Portrait of Sabartes (1939)
Night Fishing at Antibes (1939)
Woman Dressing Her Hair (1940)
Françoise as a Flower (1946)
War (1952)
Peace (1952)
Jacqueline with Flowers (1954)
La Meninas (1957)
Tête de Femme (1960)
The Artist and His Model (1963)

1895–1900

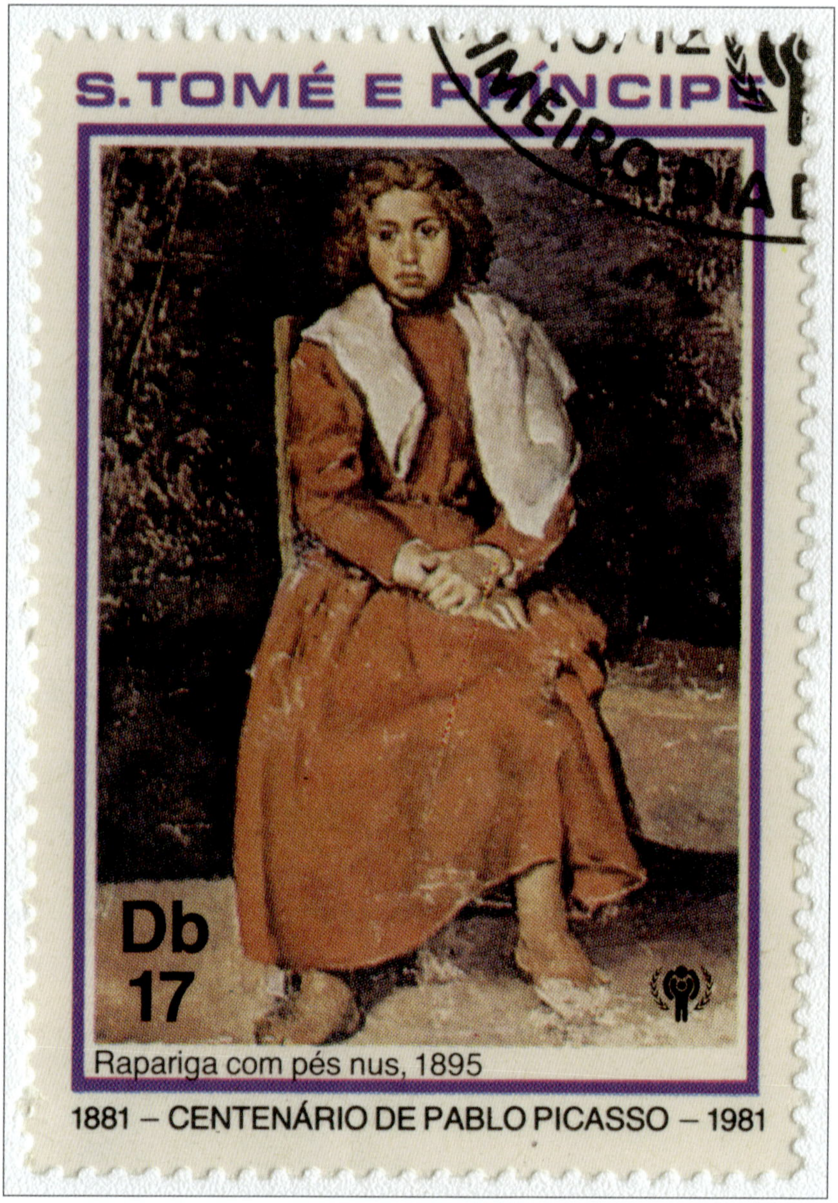

***Girl with Bare Feet* (1895)** Picasso's oil-on-canvas painting *Girl with Bare Feet* (*The Barefoot Girl*) was treasured by Picasso as a favorite early work. This portrait of a young, impoverished girl was painted from a live model before he entered art school. Already Picasso was so skillful that the girl's body and face are rendered with great confidence. The painting is in the Picasso Museum in Paris, France. This is a seventeen-dobra stamp issued on December 10, 1981, by the Democratic Republic of Sao Tome and Principe, an island nation in the Gulf of Guinea, off the coast of central Africa. The stamp illustrated Picasso's 1895 painting.

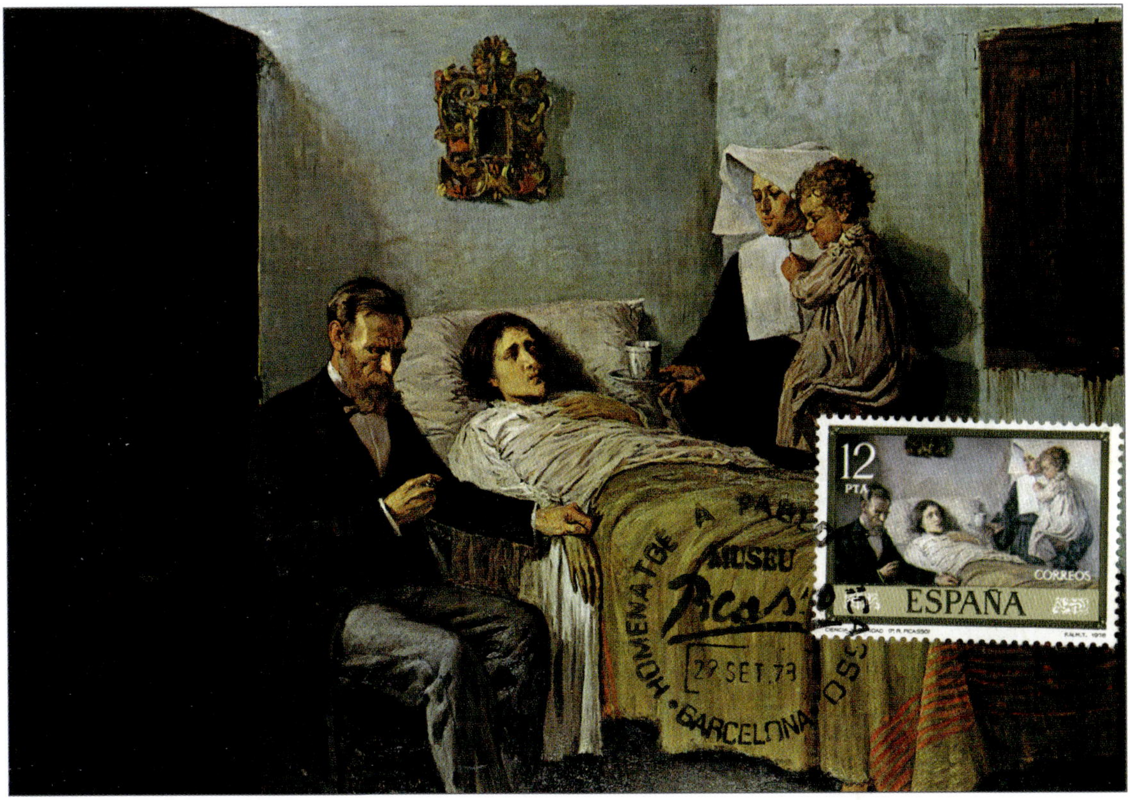

***Science and Charity* (1897)** For this painting–an allegory in which a doctor represents science and a nun stands for charity–Picasso's father helped him choose the subject and posed as the doctor. This oil-on-canvas painting of the woman patient, doctor, nun, and child is in the Picasso Museum in Barcelona, Spain. This maximum card (maxicard) and stamp were issued in Barcelona on September 29, 1978. The card and stamp use Picasso's 1897 image of *Science and Charity*.

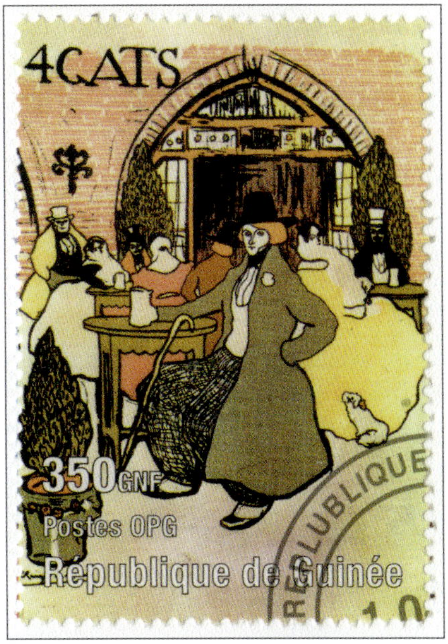

***Els Quatre Gats* (1899)** An advertisement for Picasso's favorite restaurant in Barcelona, Spain. Picasso produced this colored pencil and india ink poster for El Quatre Gats (the Four Cats) restaurant in 1899. Picasso shows the Frenchman's influence in his use of bright colors and heavily outlined images. The drawing is in the Picasso Museum in Barcelona, Spain. This stamp was issued on April 1, 1998, by the Republic of Guinea. The stamp used Picasso's 1899 drawing of the Four Cats restaurant.

1901–1903

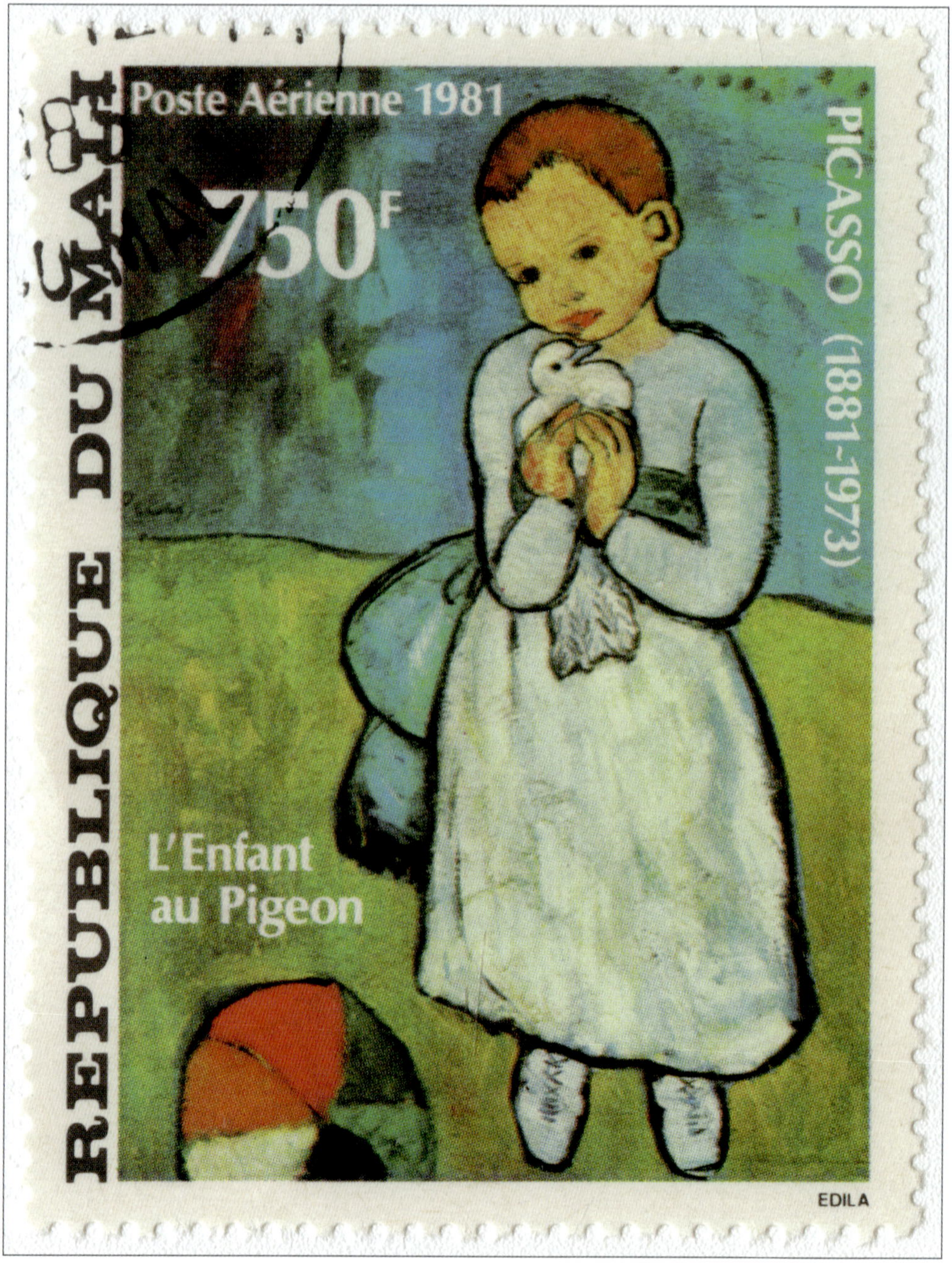

***Child Holding a Dove* (1901)** This oil-on-canvas painting is in the National Gallery in London, England. This 750-franc stamp was issued on July 15, 1981, by the Republic of Mali, a sovereign state in West Africa. Picasso's 1901 *Child Holding a Dove* was featured on the stamp.

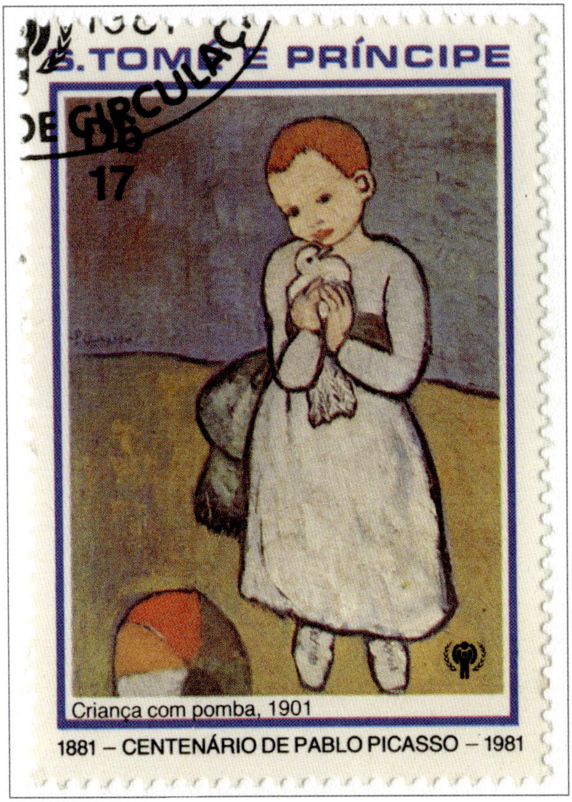

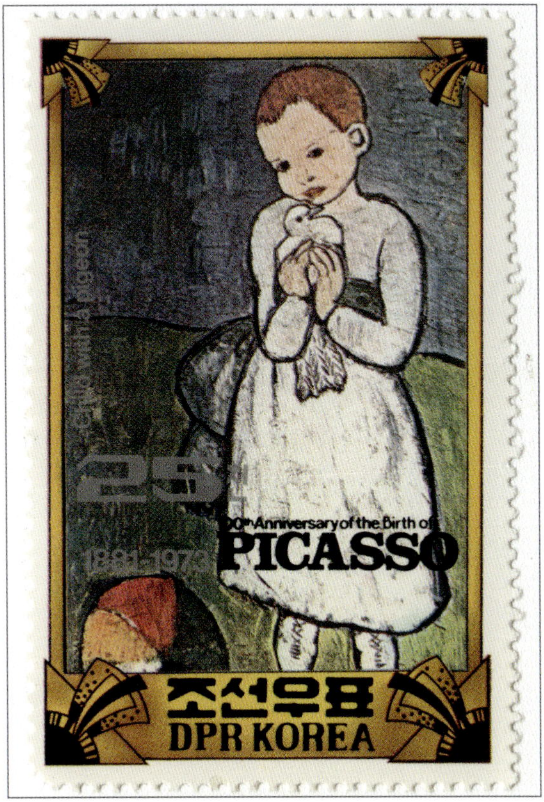

Child Holding a Dove (1901) These three stamps used Picasso's painting *Child Holding a Dove* (*top left*): St. Thomas and Prince Islands, December 10, 1981; (*top right*): North Korea (DPR Korea), March 30, 1982; and (*right*): North Vietnam, December 30, 1977.

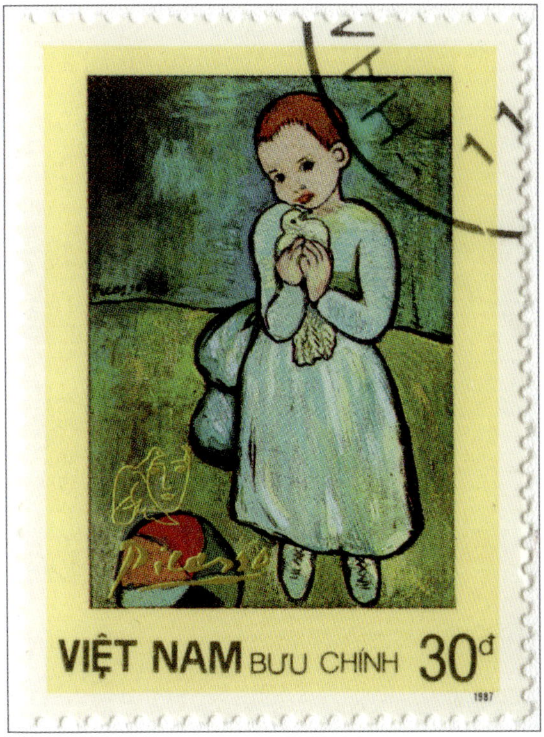

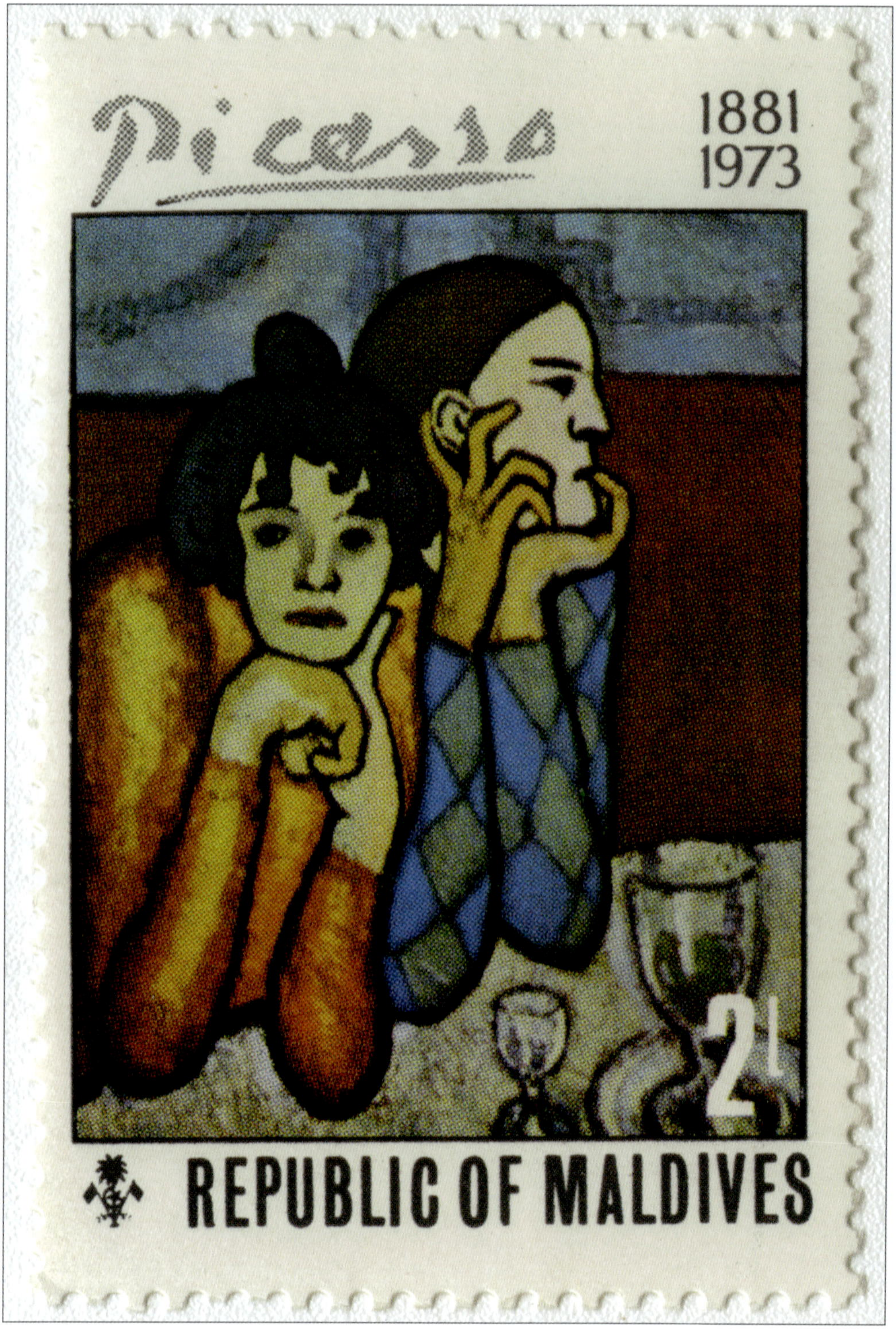

***Harlequin and His Companion* (1901)** This painting is in the Pushkin State Museum of Fine Arts, Moscow, Russia. This stamp was issued by the Republic of Maldives, a South Asian island country in the Indian Ocean. Shown on the stamp is Picasso's 1901 *Harlequin and His Companion*.

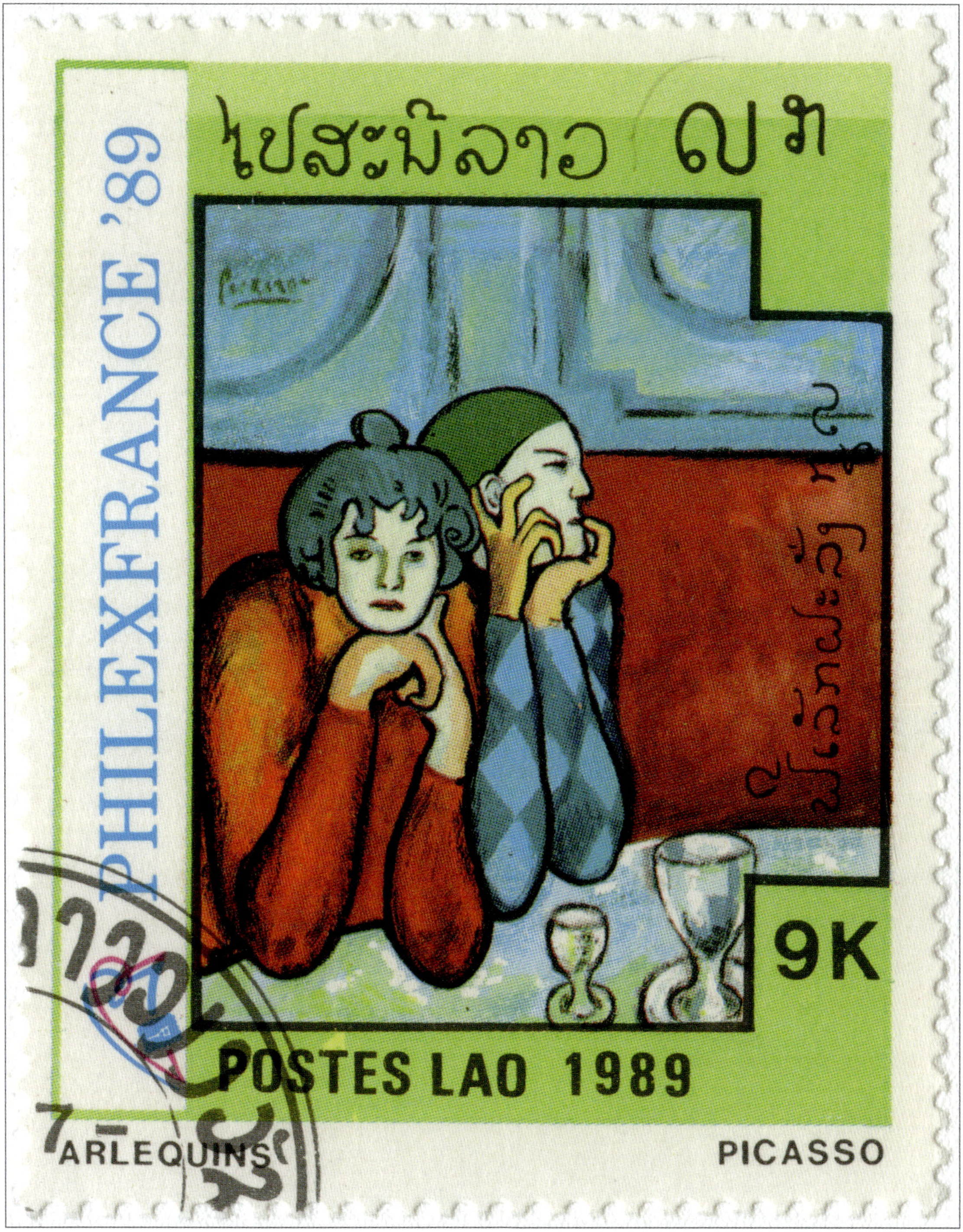

***Harlequin and His Companion* (1901)** In 1989, the Lao People's Democratic Republic issued this 9-kip stamp to honor the PHILEXFRANCE '89 event.

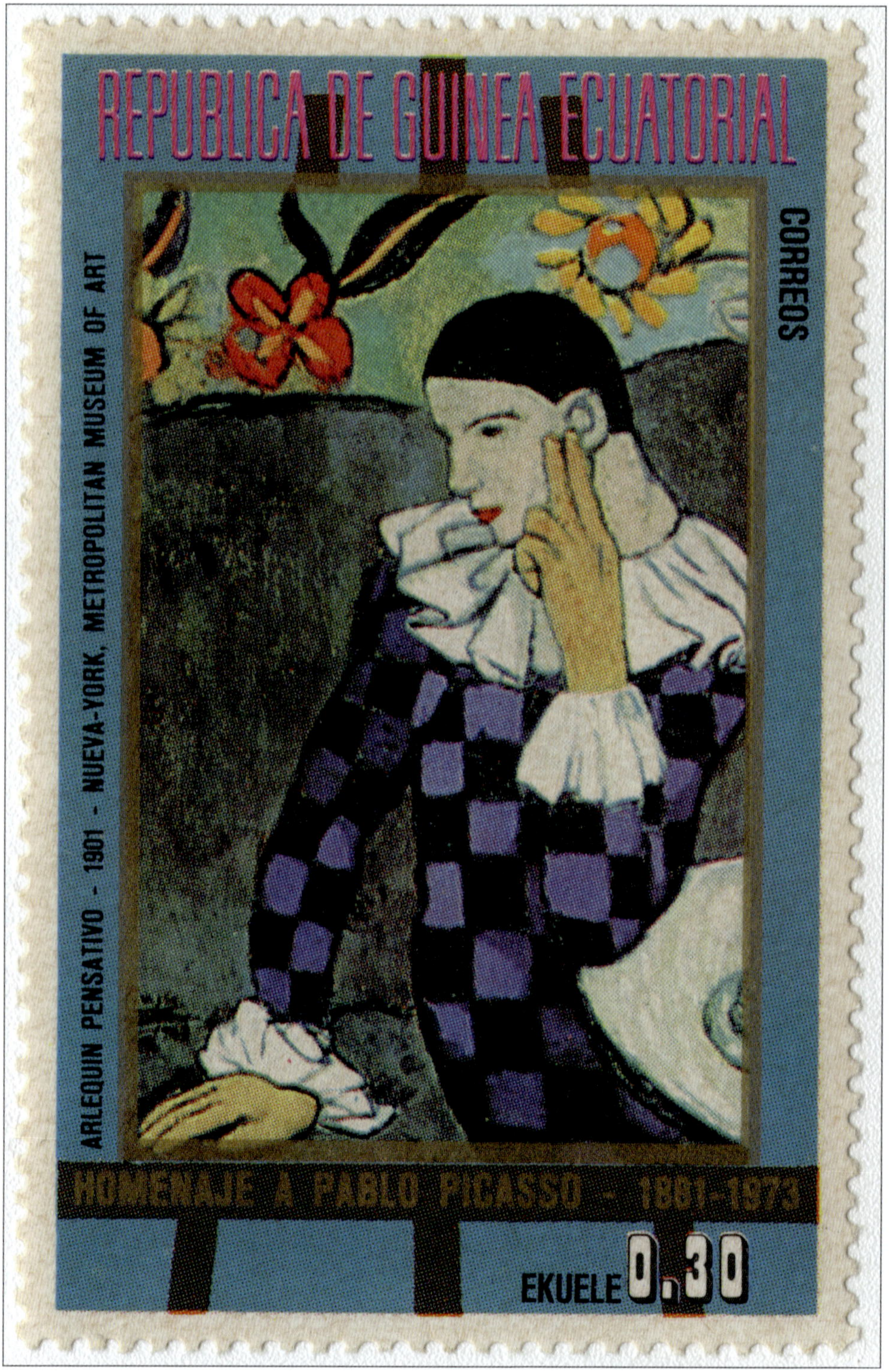

***Harlequin Leaning on a Table* (1901)** An oil-on-canvas painting (*Harlequin Leaning on a Table*, 1901) in the Metropolitan Museum of Art in New York. On December 20, 1973, the Republic of Guinea Ecuatorial issued a stamp with this image.

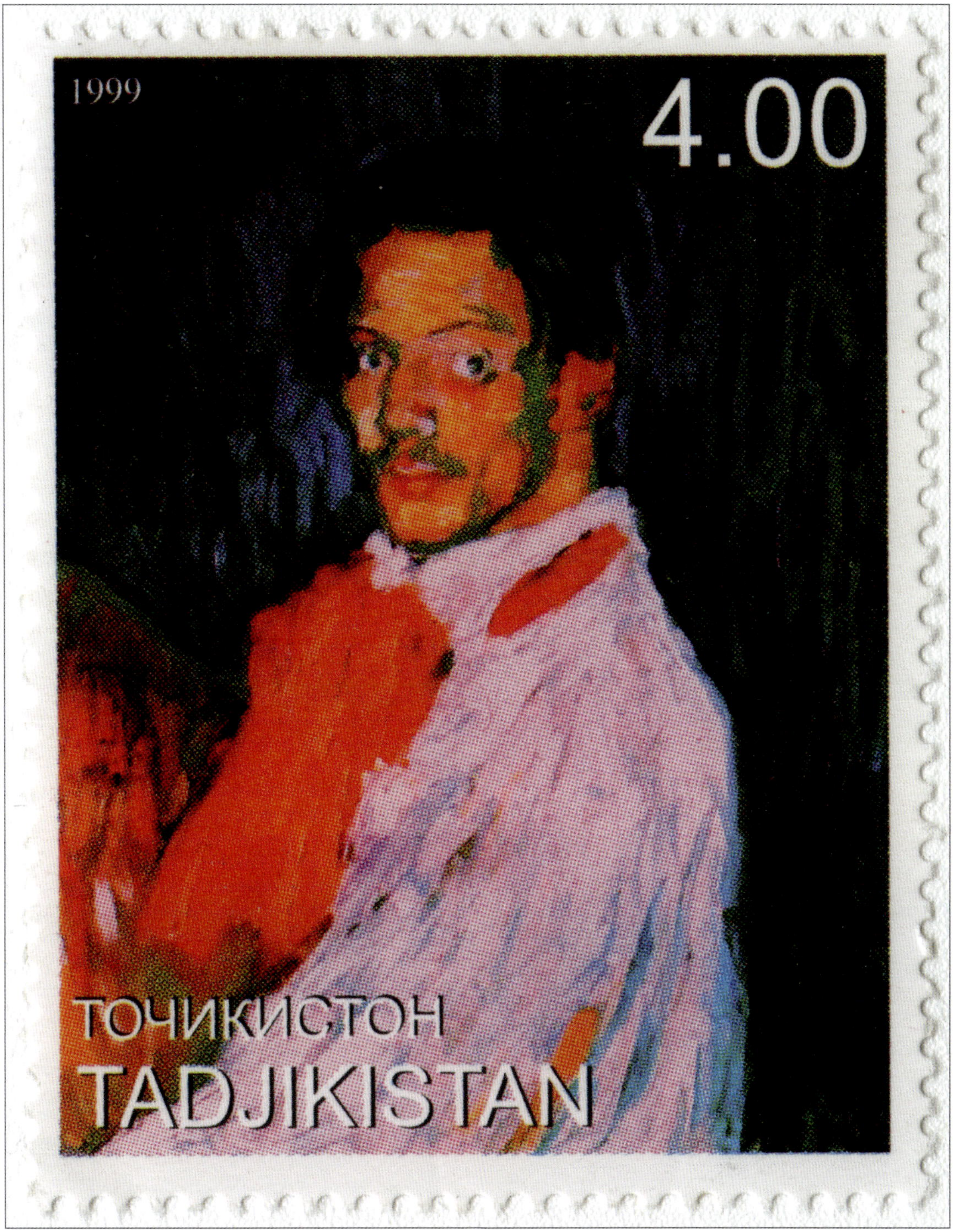

***Self-Portrait* (1901)** A four-ruble stamp featuring this painting (*Self-Portrait*, 1901) was issued, possibly in 1999, in the name of the Republic of Tajikistan, a sovereign state in central Asia.

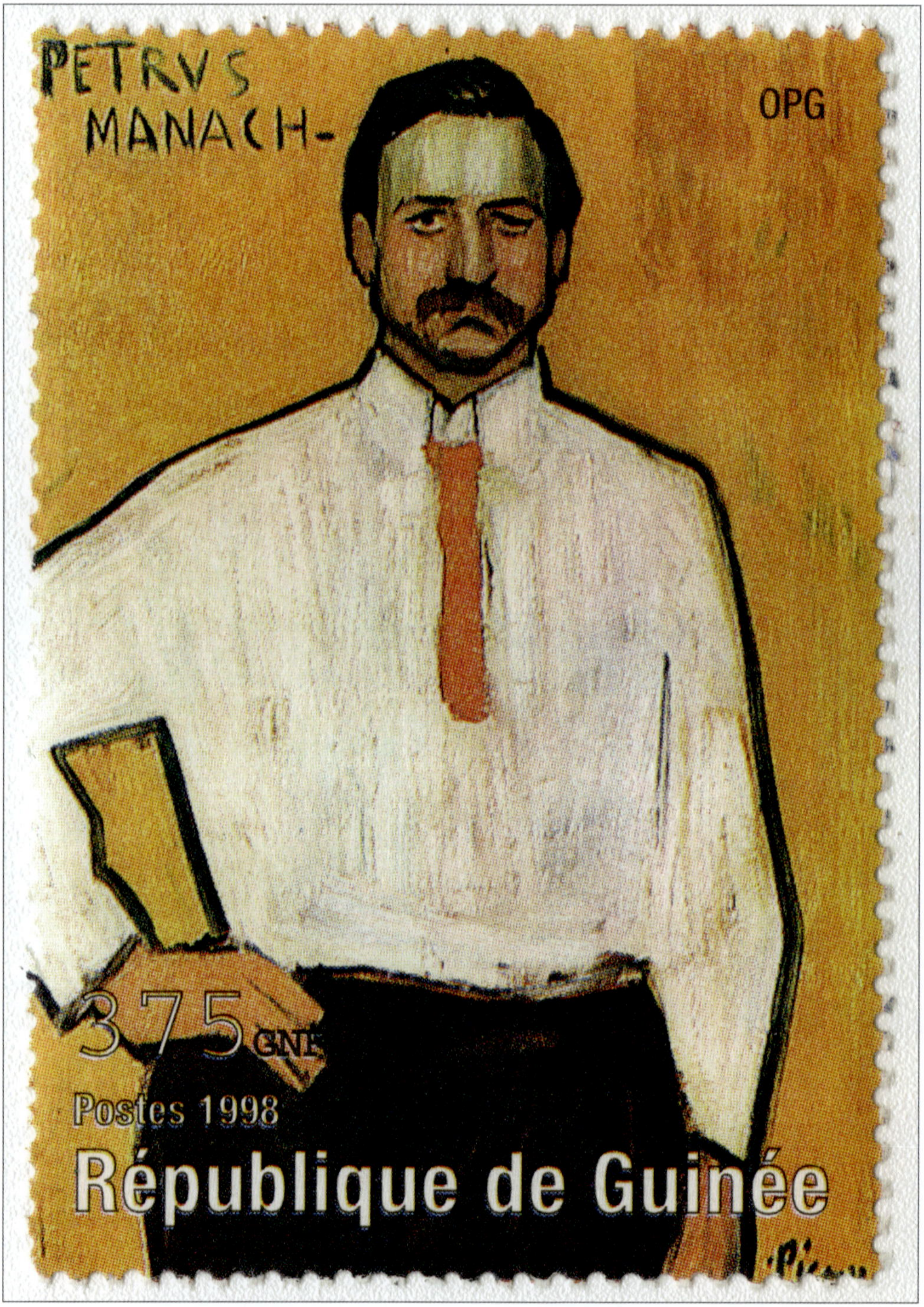

***Portrait of Pedro Manach* (1901)** Picasso painted a portrait of art dealer Pedro Manach in oil on canvas. This Spanish industrialist was Picasso's first patron and financial supporter in Paris. He offered the penniless Picasso a fixed sum of 150 francs a month for his paintings and set up contracts with artists and dealers. The painting is in the National Gallery of Art in Washington, DC. The stamp was issued in 1998 by the Republic of Guinea.

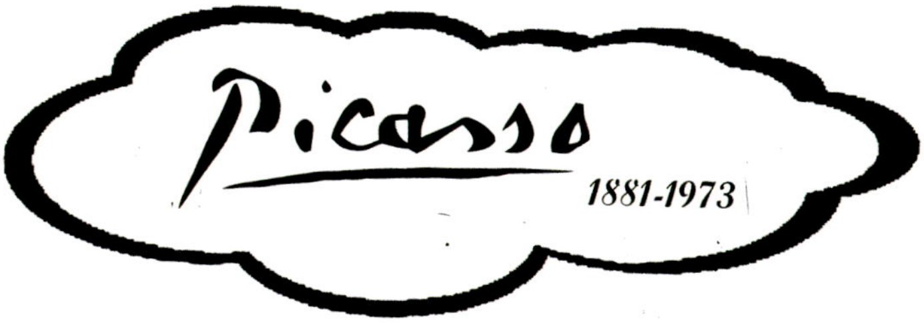

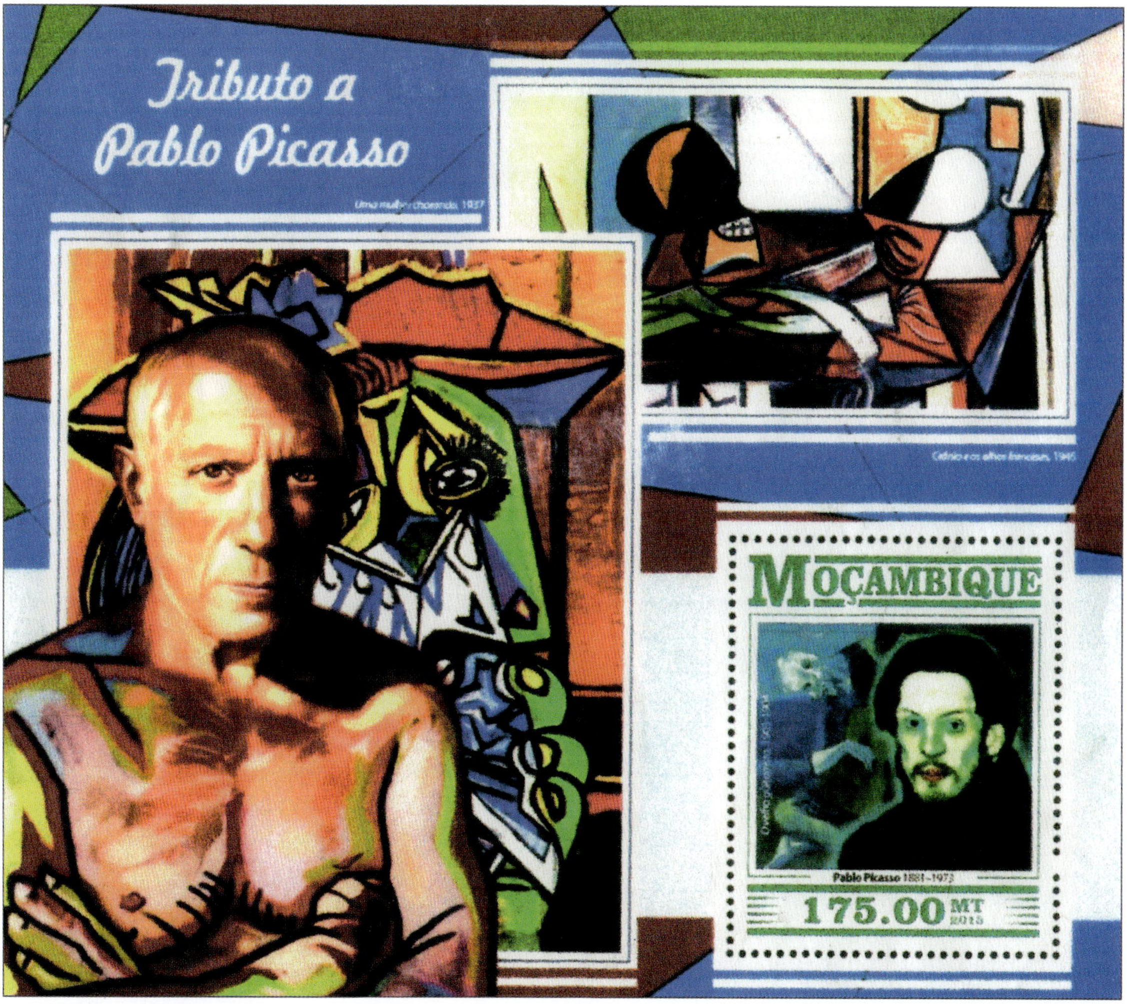

***Self-Portrait* (1901)** A 175-metical stamp souvenir sheet was issued, possibly in 2015, in the name of the Republic of Mozambique, a sovereign state in Southeast Asia. It contains a stamp that features Picasso's 1901 *Self-Portrait* and other Picasso paintings.

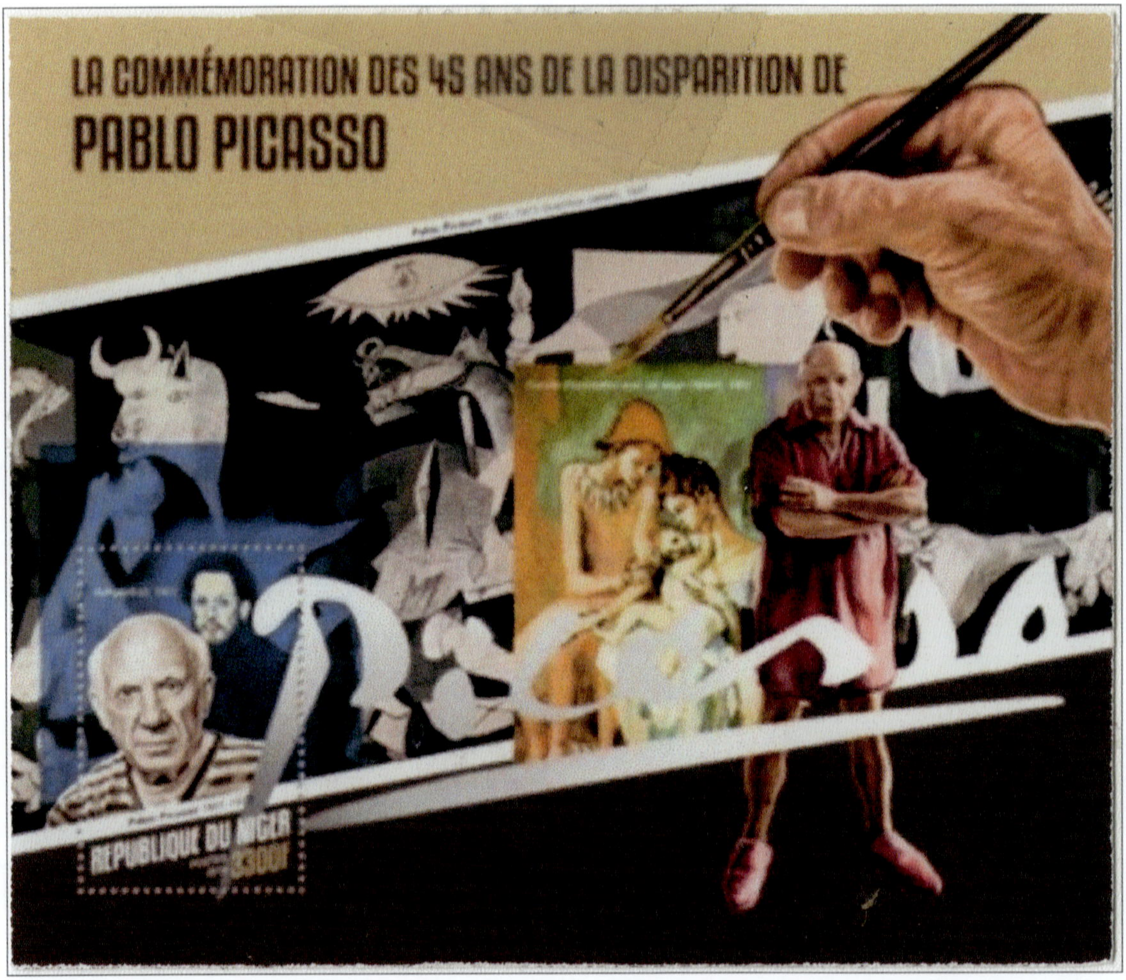

***Self-Portrait* (1901)** This stamp souvenir sheet was issued, possibly in 2018, in the name of the Republic of Niger, a sovereign state in West Africa. It shows several paintings by Picasso, including this 1901 *Self-Portrait*.

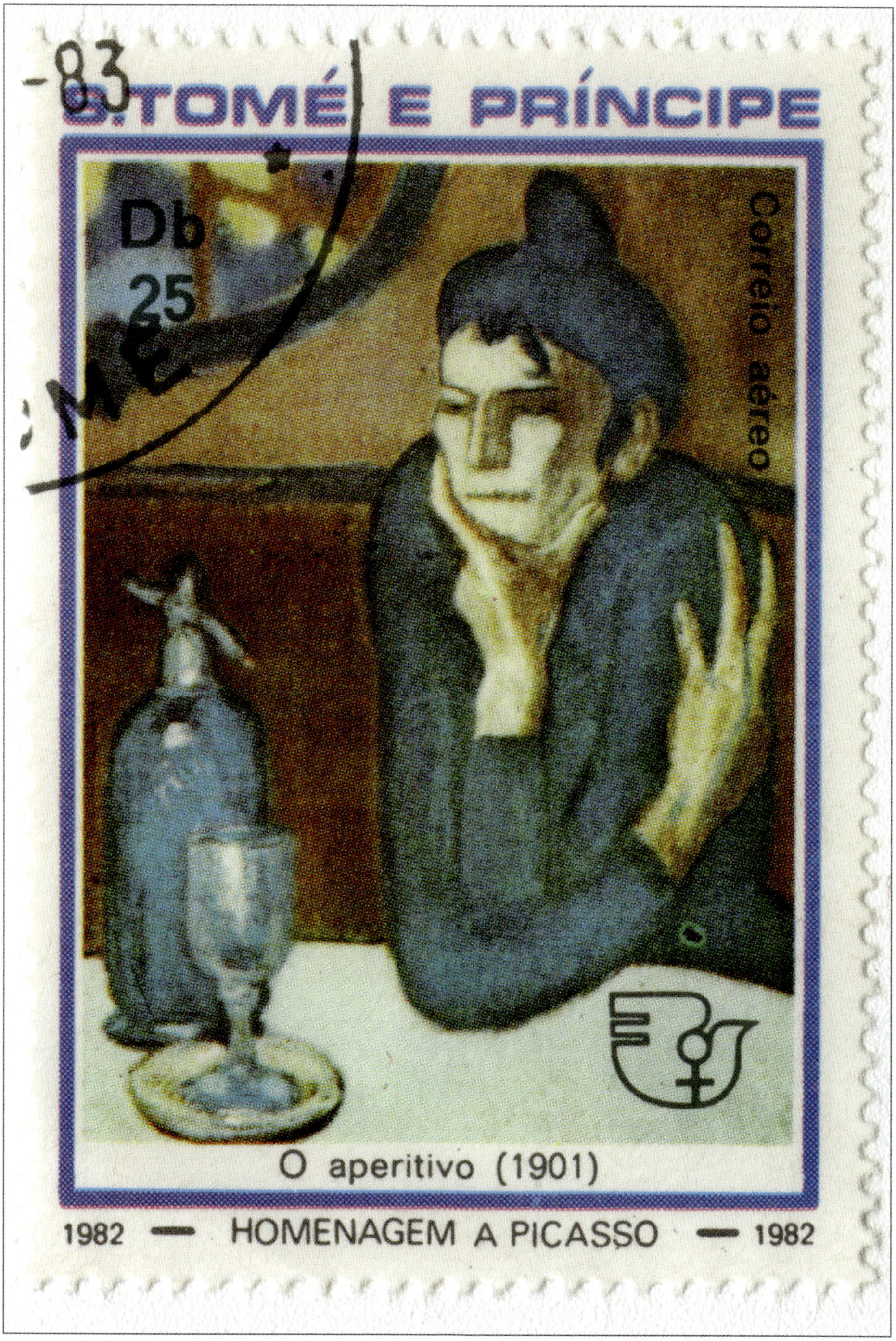

Absinthe Drinker **(1901)** The absinthe drinker staring numbly ahead is a symbol of the gloomy underside of city nightlife. Picasso set the alcoholic woman in the corner of a café, a glass of absinthe in front of her. Painted at the beginning of Picasso's "Blue Period," the color blue remains restricted to individual objects. A twenty-five-dobra stamp using this image was issued on December 24, 1982, by the Democratic Republic of Sao Tome and Principe, an island nation in the Gulf of Guinea, off the coast of central Africa.

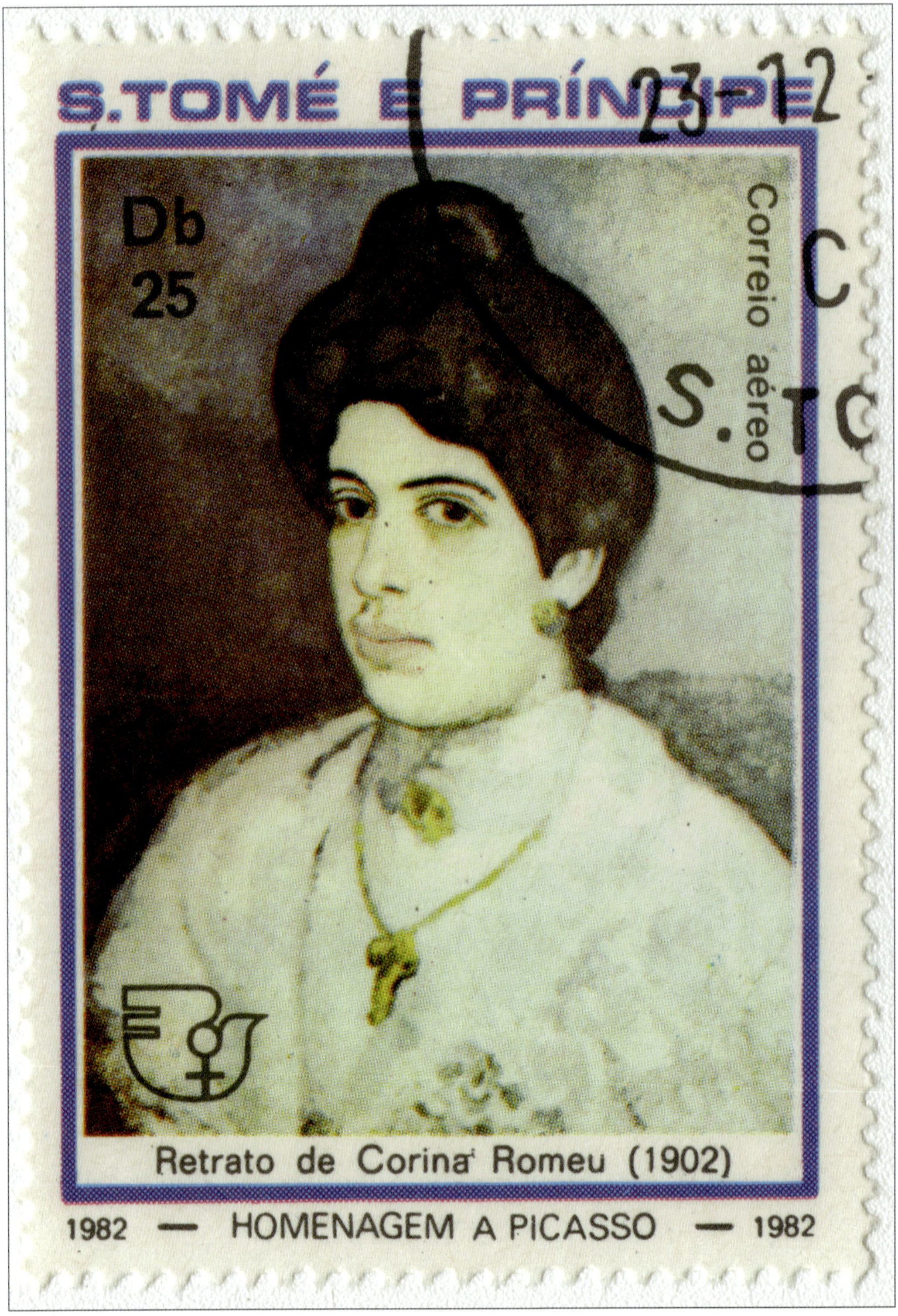

***Corina Pere Romeu* (1902)** This image (*Corina Pere Romeu*, 1902) on a twenty-five-dobra stamp was issued on December 24, 1982, by the Democratic Republic of Sao Tome and Principe Islands.

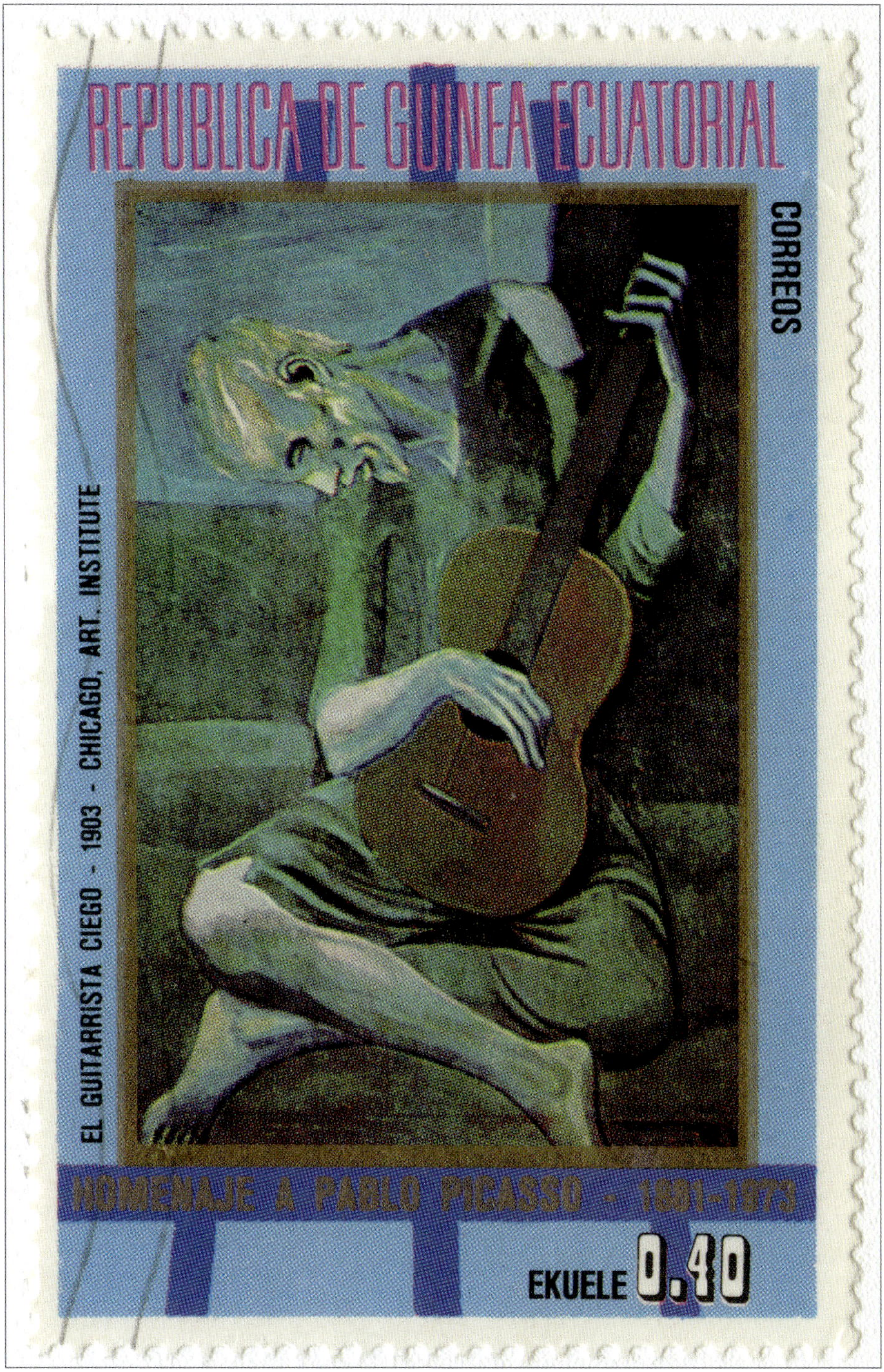

***The Old Guitarist* (1903)** An oil-on-panel, dark-themed painting portraying an old, weak man hunched over his guitar, playing the instrument on the streets of Barcelona, Spain. It was painted at a time when Picasso turned a sympathetic ear toward the downtrodden and those struck by poverty. The painting is in the Art Institute of Chicago. On December 20, 1973, the Republic of Guinea Ecuatorial issued this stamp showing Picasso's painting.

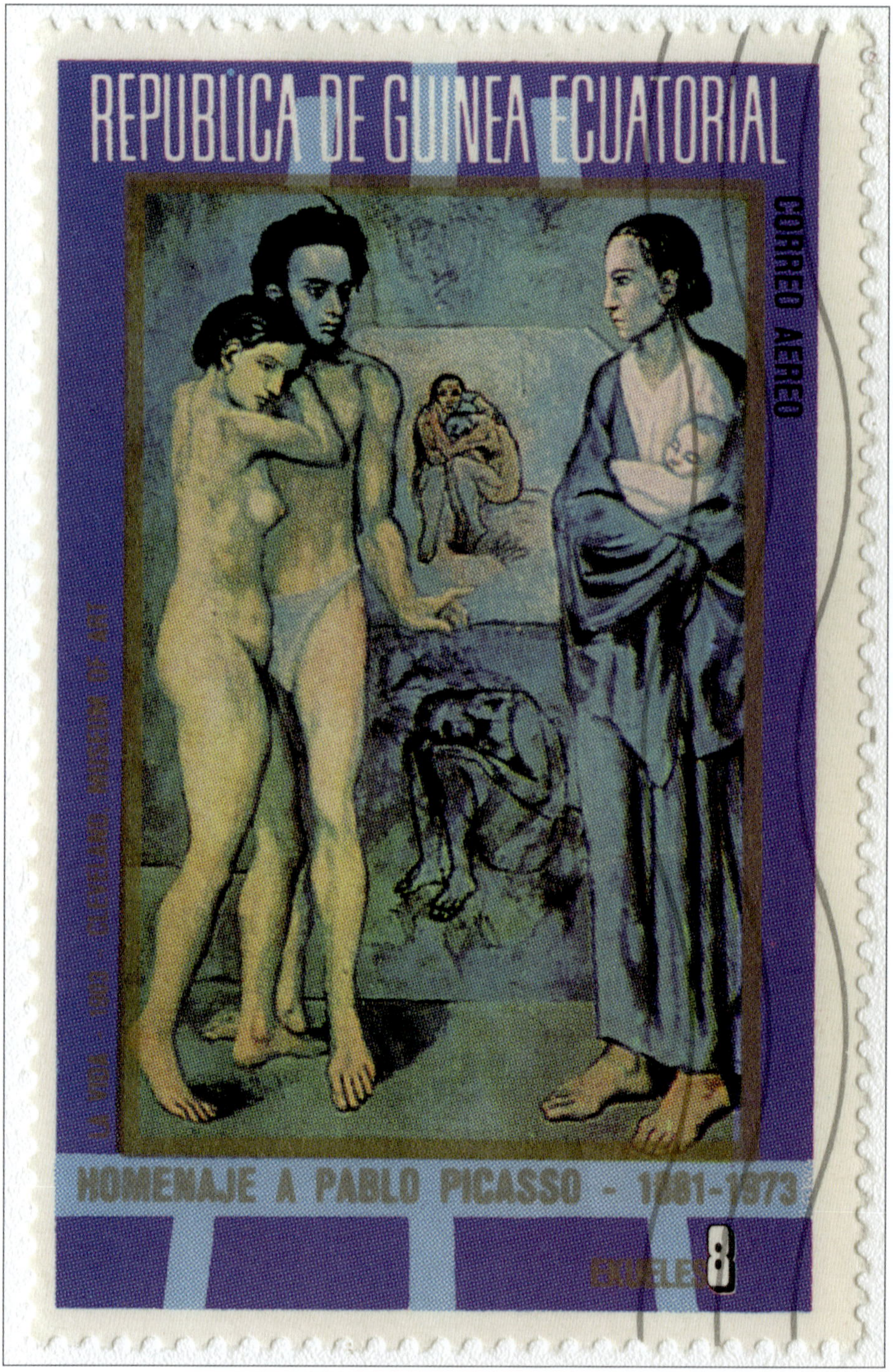

Life (1903) (*La Via*) An oil-on-canvas painting (*La Via*, 1903) of a naked couple clinging to each other on the left side of the picture. The man is pointing across to the mother in the blue cloak holding her sleeping child in her arms. It suggests Picasso's feelings about the hardships suffered by some families. The painting is in the Cleveland Museum of Art. On December 20, 1973, the Republic of Guinea Ecuatorial issued this stamp featuring the painting.

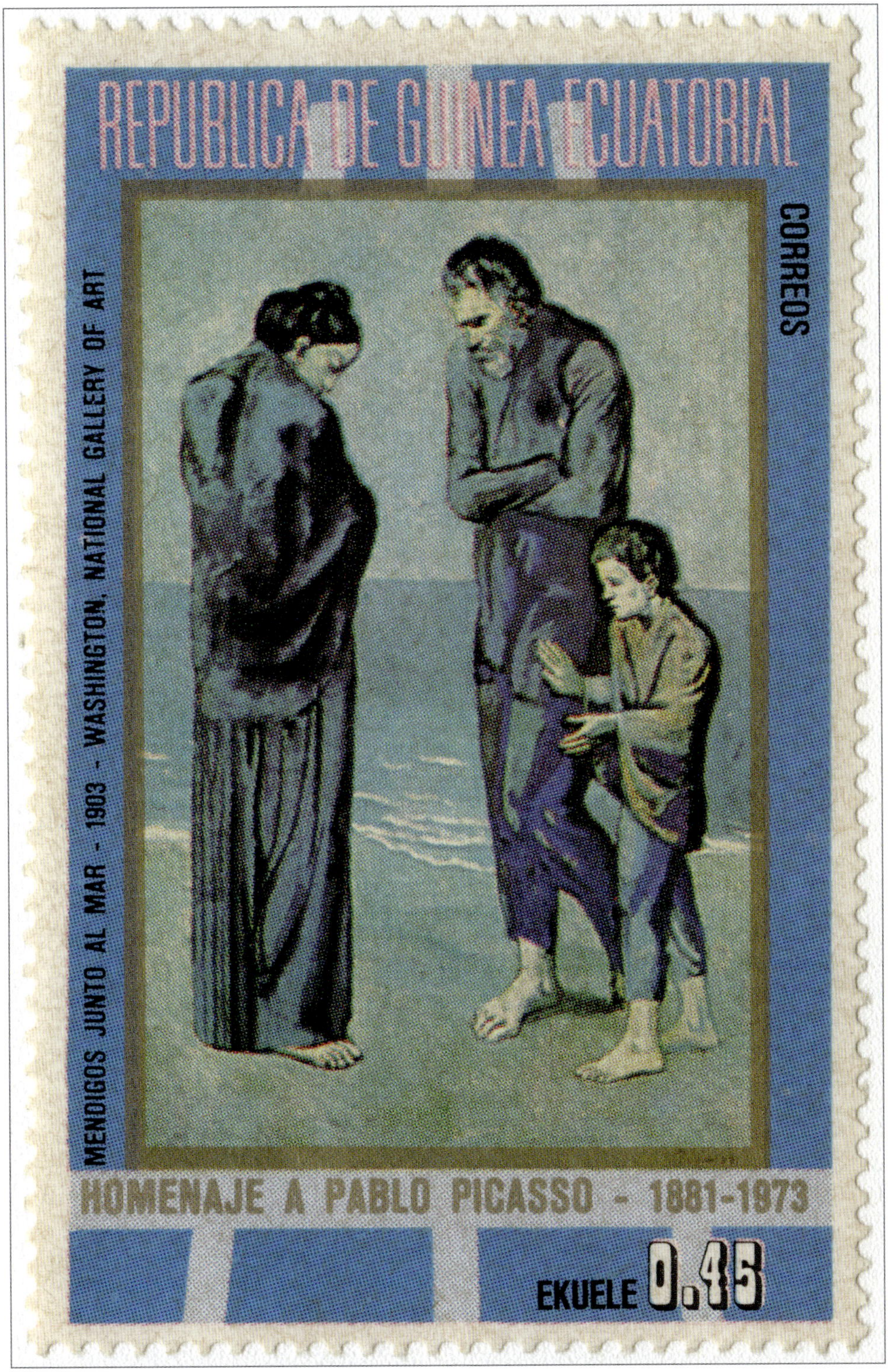

***Beggars by the Edge of the Sea* (1903)** An oil-on-wood painting originally titled *The Tragedy* (*Beggars by the Edge of the Sea*, 1903). It is in the National Gallery of Art in Washington, DC. On December 20, 1973, the Republic of Guinea Ecuatorial issued a stamp using the painting.

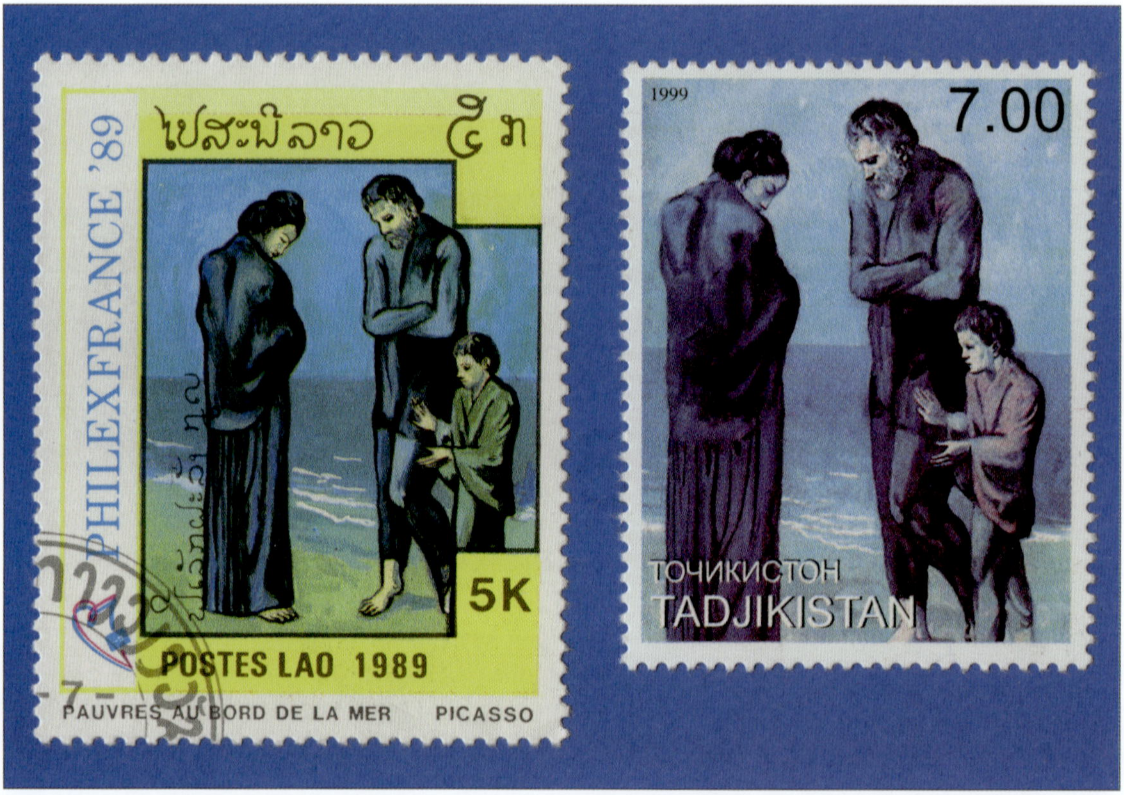

***Beggars by the Edge of the Sea* (1903)** Two stamps using the image (*Beggars by the Edge of the Sea*, 1903): the stamp on the left was issued in 1989 by the Lao People's Democratic Republic; the seven-ruble stamp on the right was issued possibly in 1999, in the name of the Republic of Tajikistan, a sovereign state in central Asia.

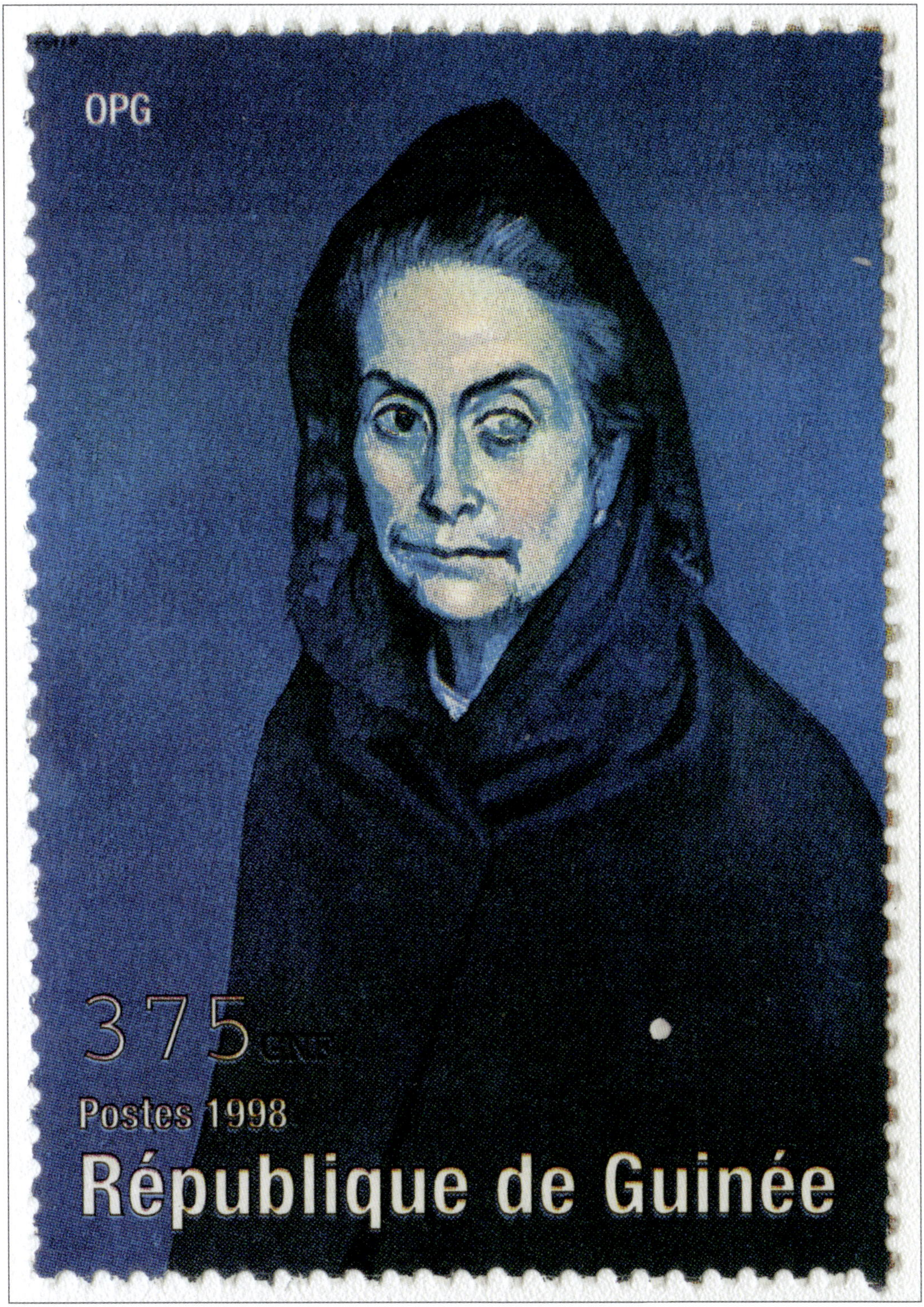

***Celestina* (1903)** An oil-on-canvas painting (*Celstina*, 1903) in the Picasso Museum in Paris. The Republic of Guinea, a country on the western coast of Africa, issued a stamp using this image to honor the twenty-fifth anniversary of the death of Picasso.

1904–1906

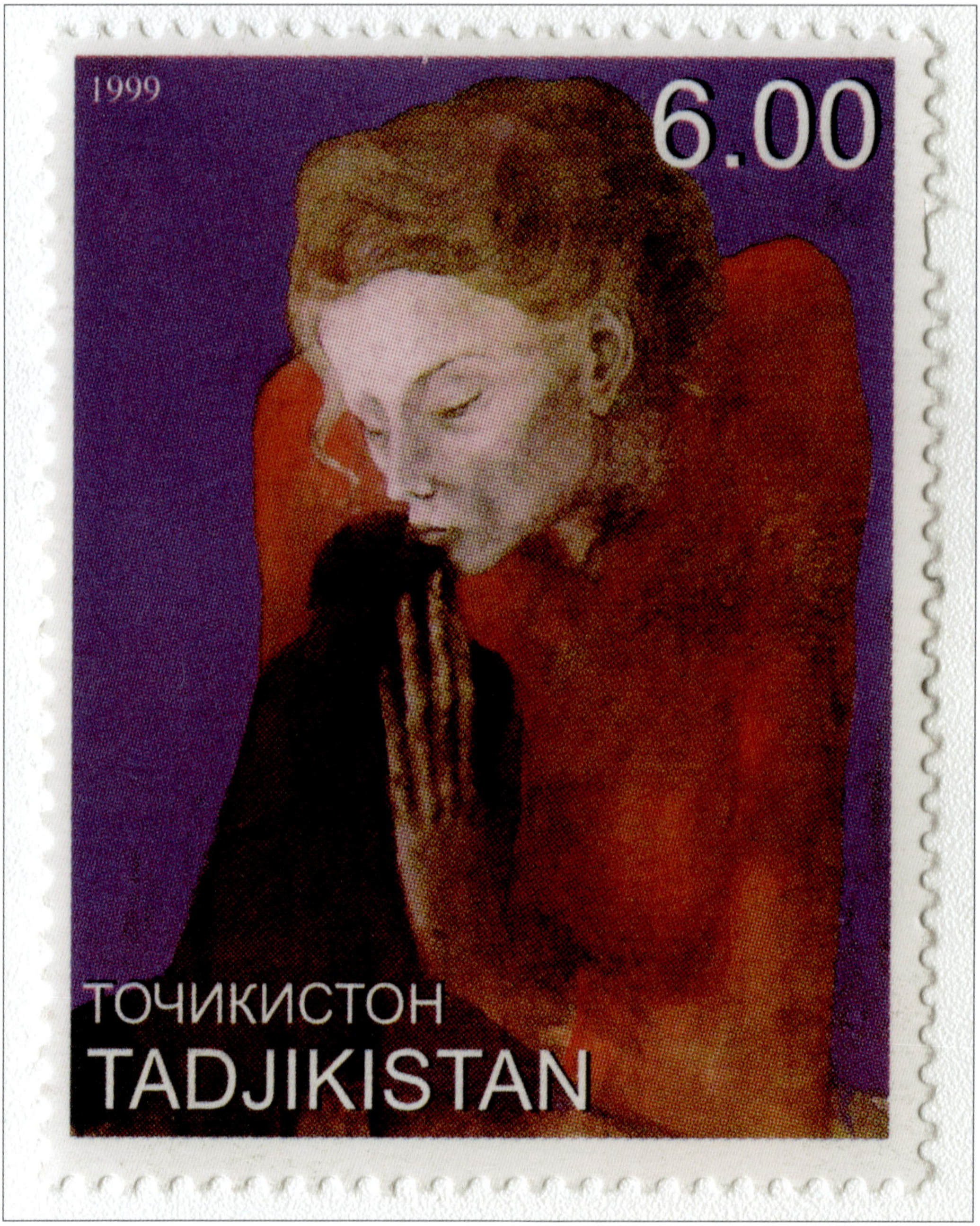

***Woman with a Crow* (1904)** The image (*Woman with a Crow*, 1904) was used to produce these two stamps. On the right is a PDR Yemen (1983) stamp; on the left is a six-ruble stamp that was issued, possibly in 1999, in the name of the Republic of Tajikistan.

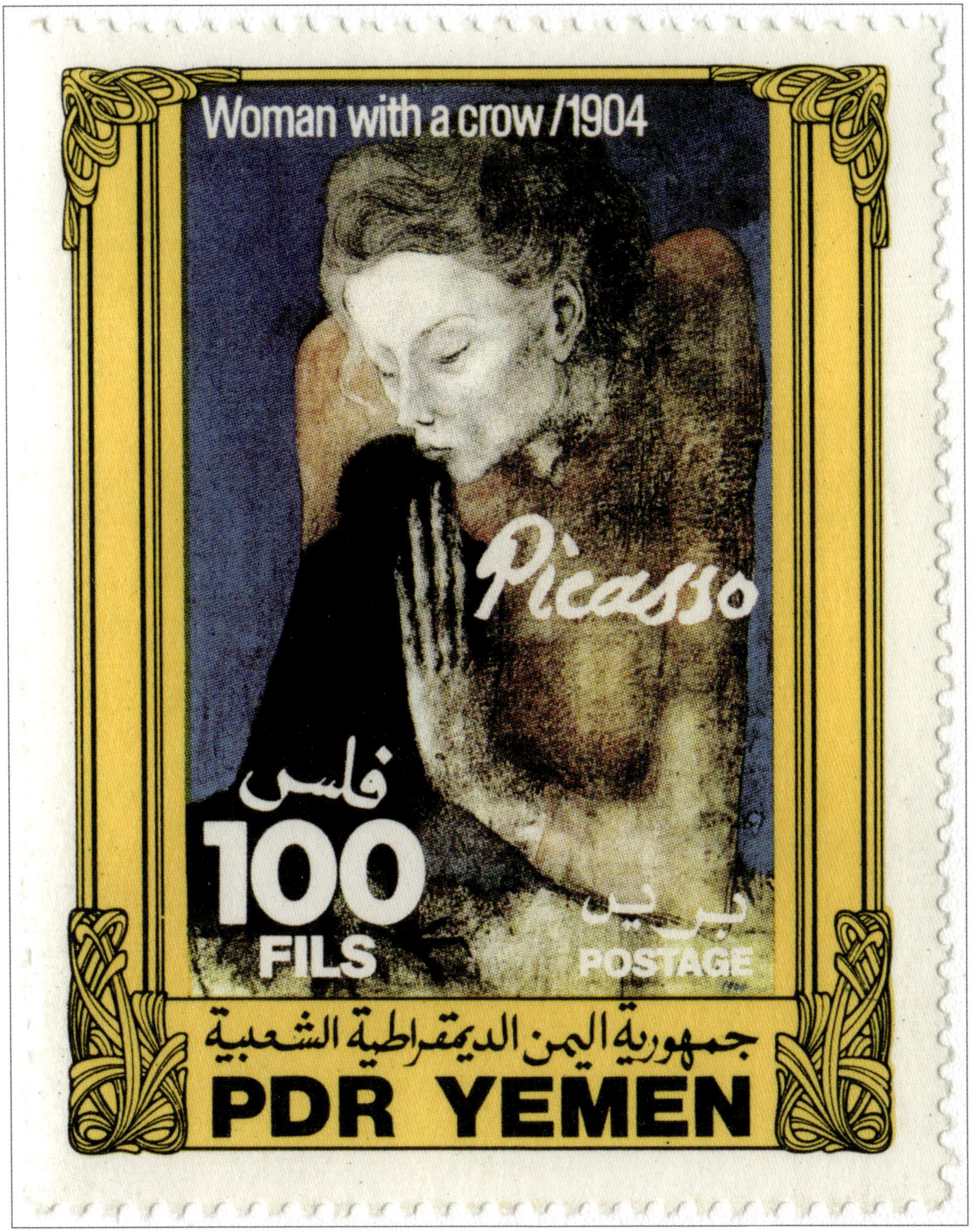
Woman with a crow / 1904
Picasso
فلس
100
FILS
بريد
POSTAGE
جمهورية اليمن الديمقراطية الشعبية
PDR YEMEN

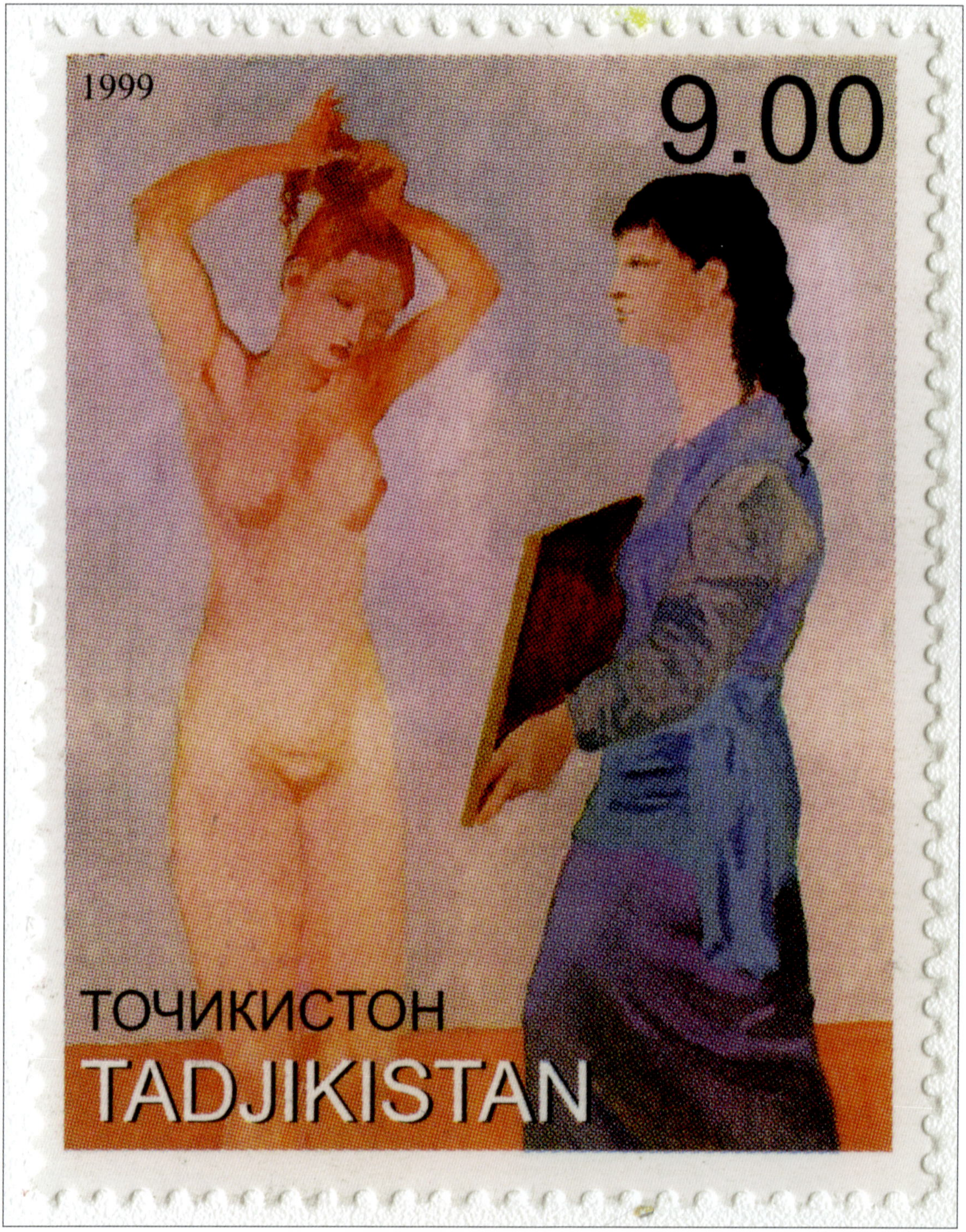

These two stamps used the painting *The Toilette*. The stamp on the right was issued in 1998 by the Republic of Guinea to honor the twenty-fifth anniversary of the death of Picasso. On the left is a stamp that was issued, possibly in 1999, in the name of the Republic of Tajikistan.

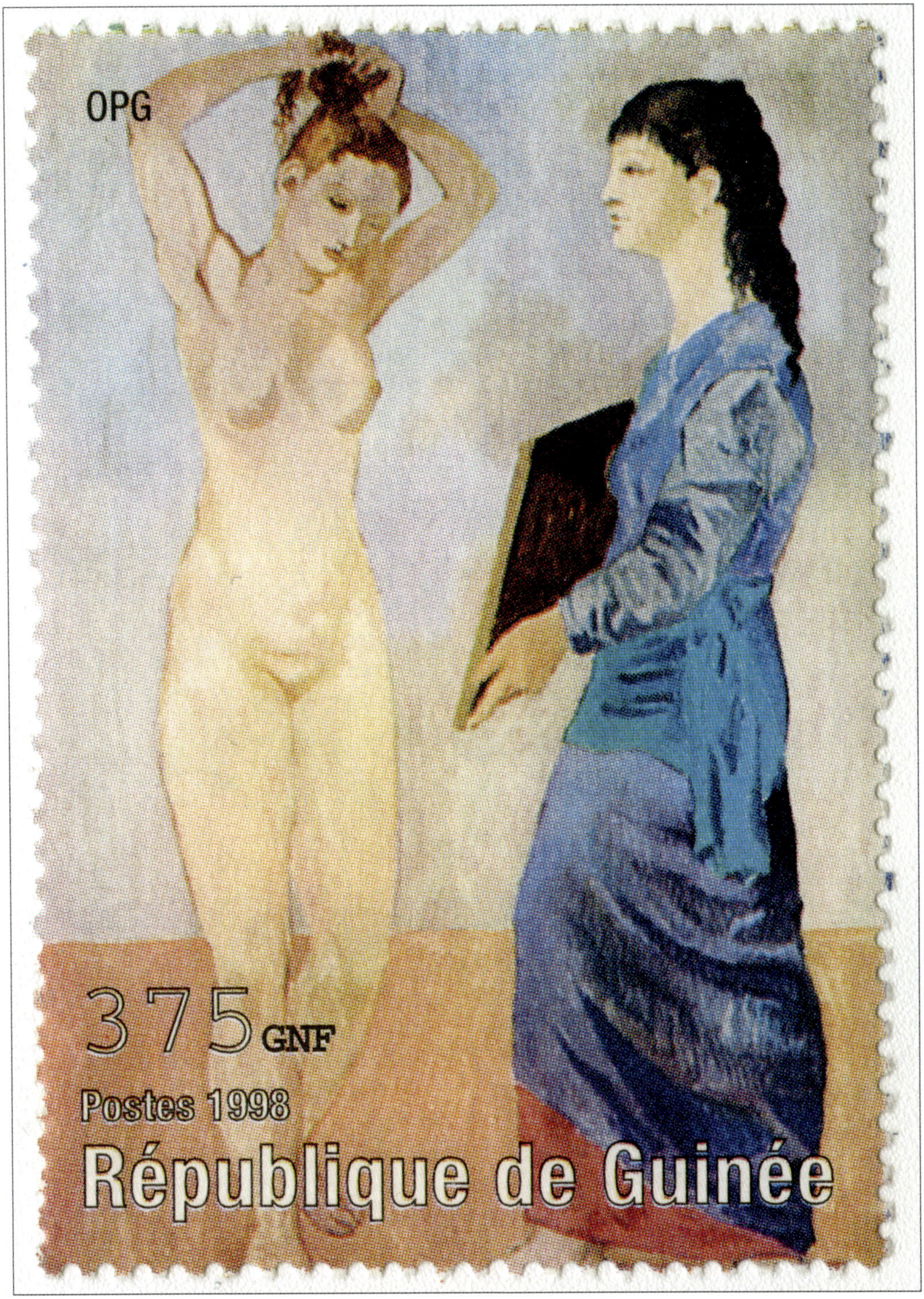
OPG
375 GNF
Postes 1998
République de Guinée

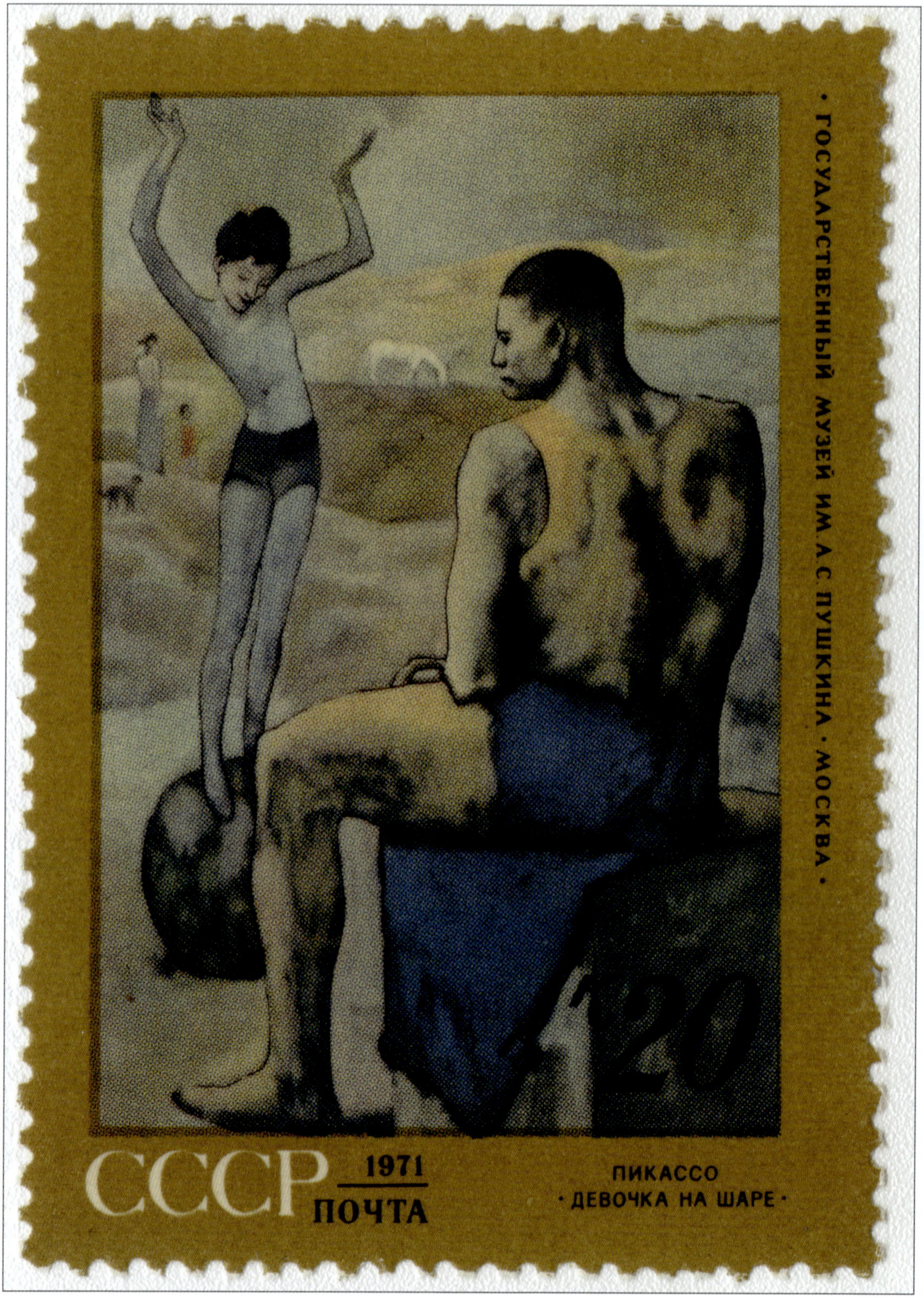

This Russian stamp was issued on July 7, 1971, using an image of *Acrobat on a Ball*.

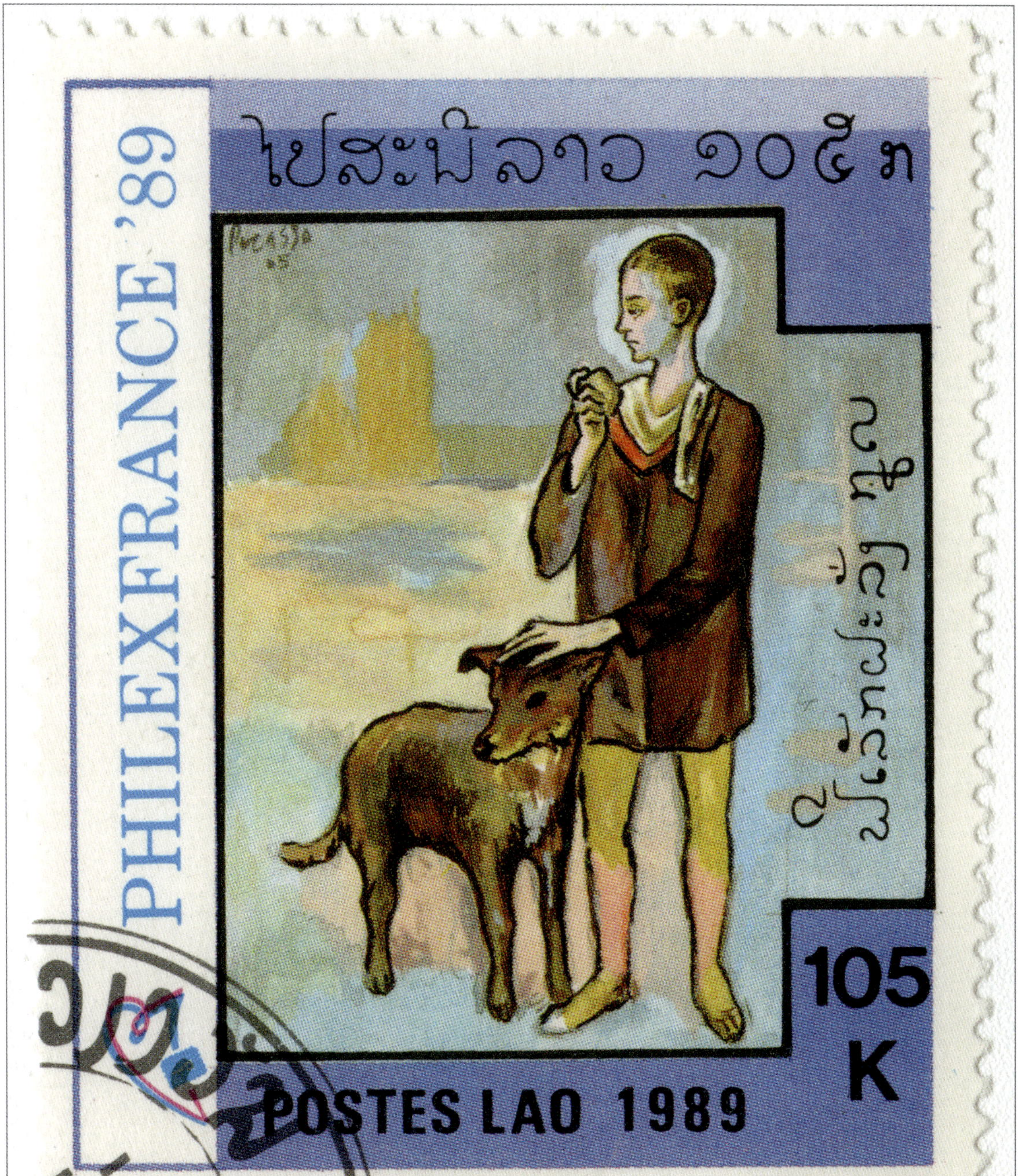

***Boy with a Dog* (1905)** (*Garcon and Chien*) Using this image (*Boy with a Dog*, 1905), the Lao People's Democratic Republic issued this 105-kip stamp on July 17, 1989, to honor the PHILEXFRANCE '89 event.

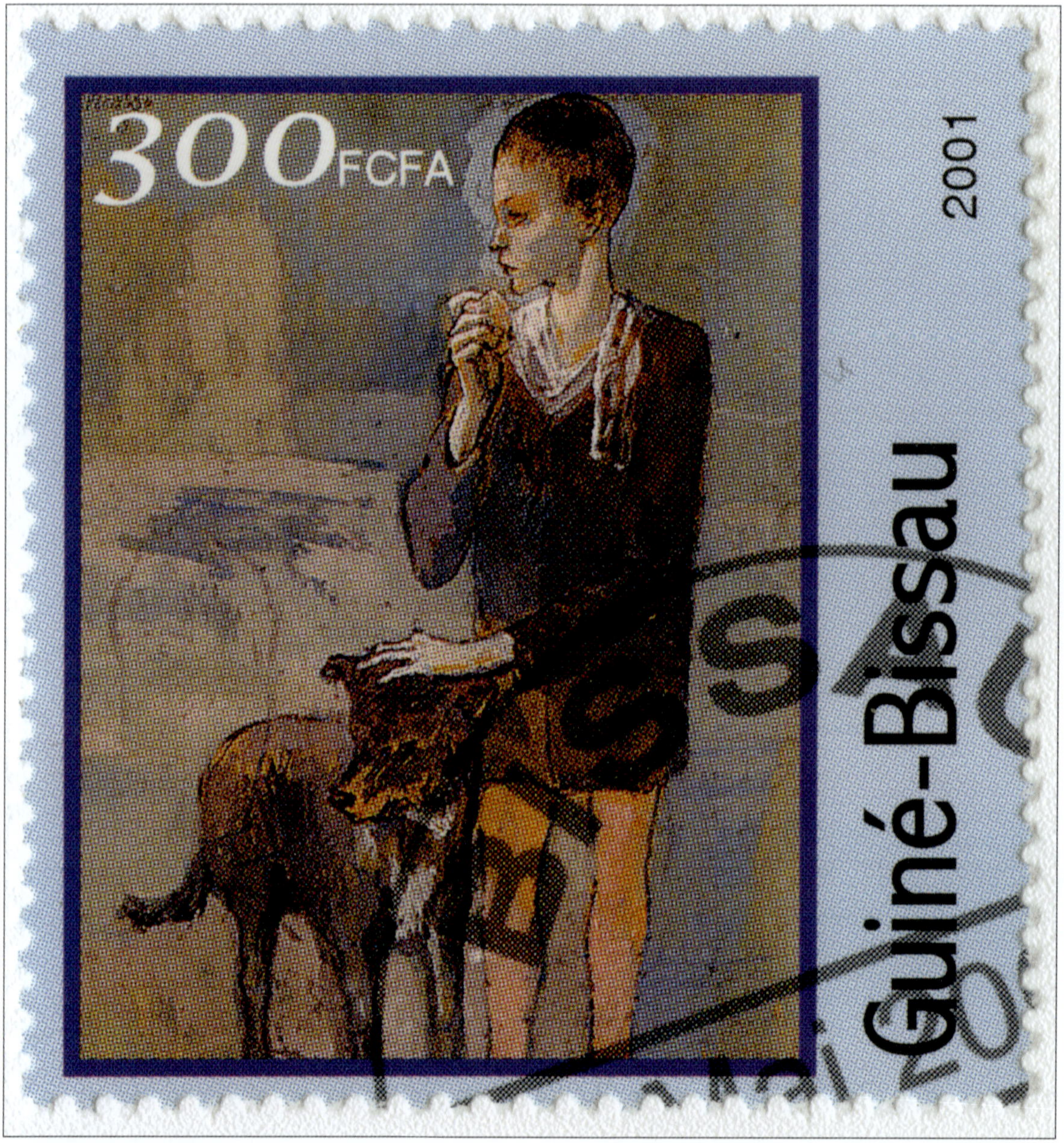

Boy with a Dog (1905) The Republic of Guinea-Bissau, a sovereign state in West Africa, used this image (*Boy with a Dog*, 1905) to issue this 300-franc stamp in 2001.

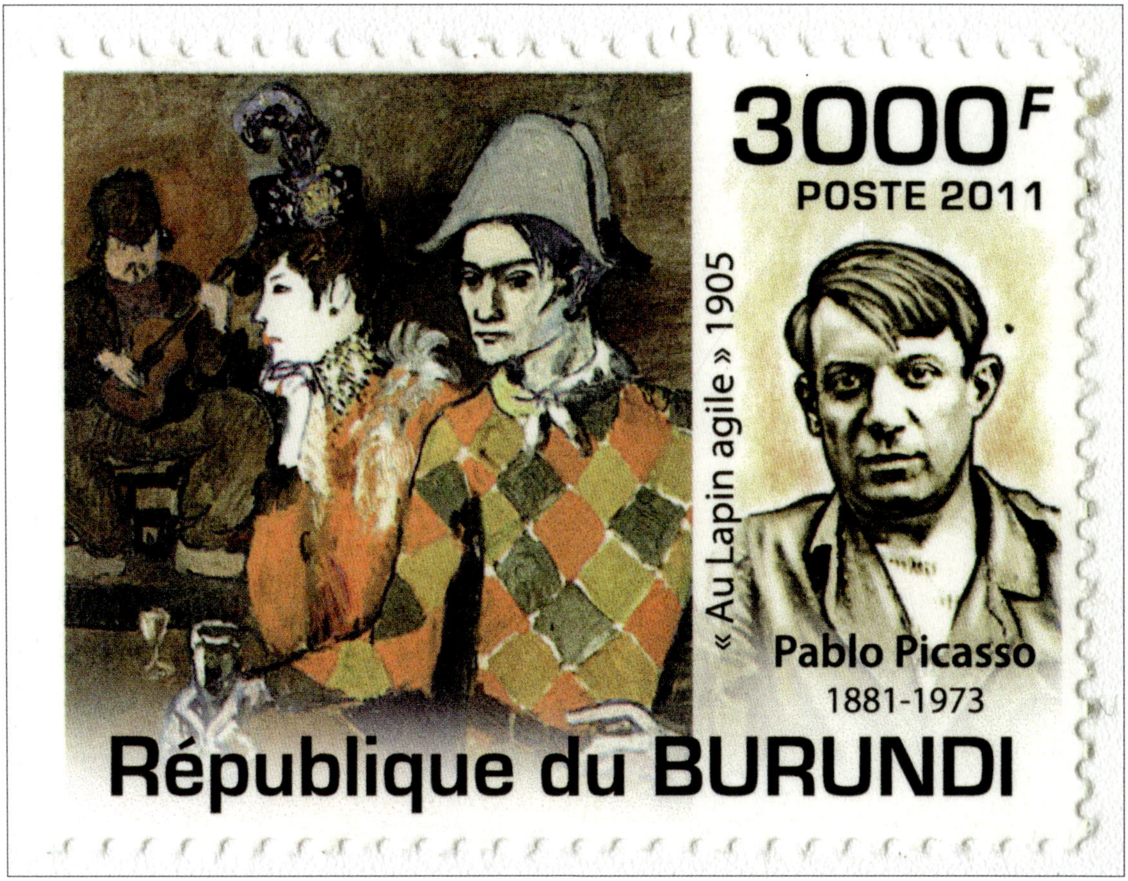

***Harlequin with Glass* (1905)** This is one of several paintings in which Picasso documented the life of the performers in circuses and carnivals that he frequently visited from time to time. Leaving behind the joyless world of the "Blue Period," Picasso now arrived at the new colors that characterize *Harlequin with Glass*. No longer so pessimistic about life, for the first time he began to celebrate it. In 2011 the Republic of Burundi issued a stamp containing this image to honor the 130th anniversary of the birth of Picasso. The stamp also included a self-portrait of Picasso.

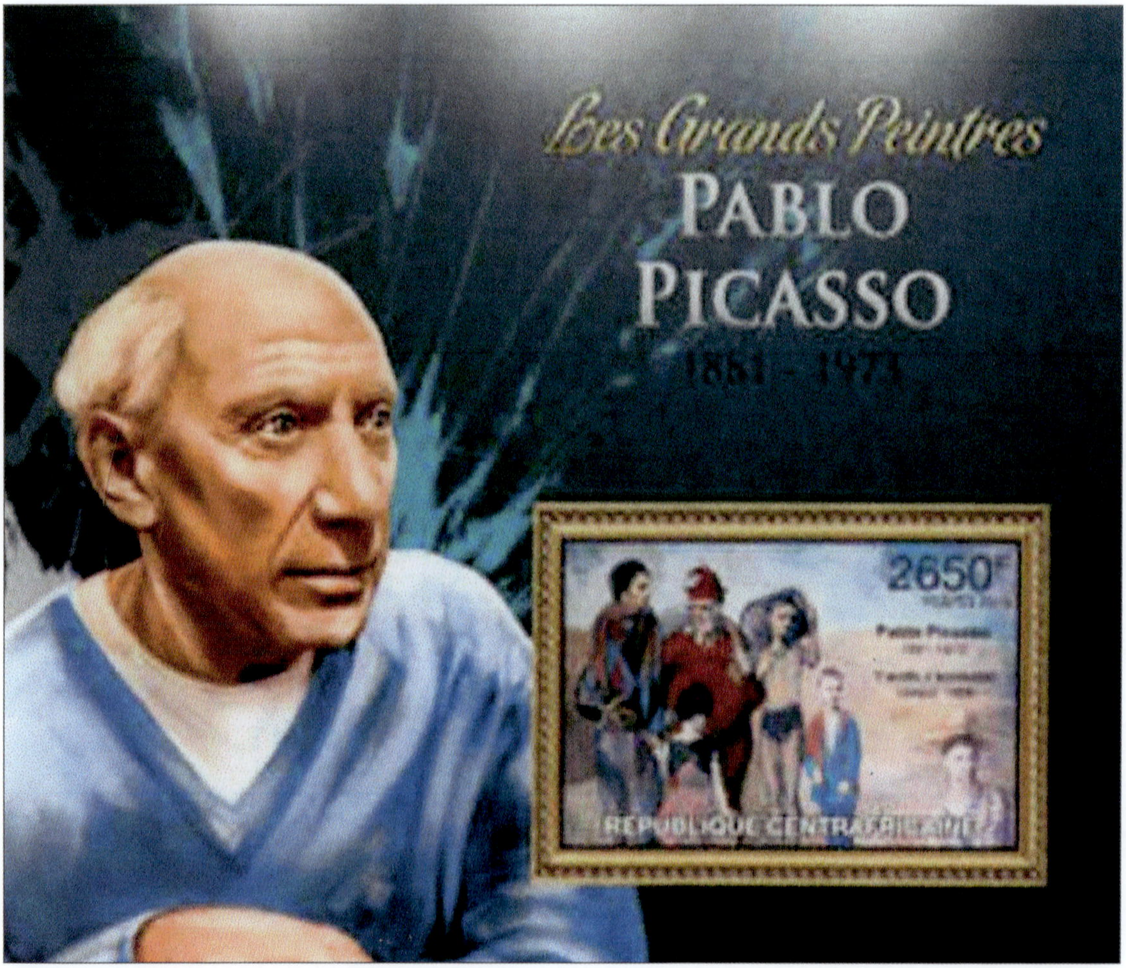

***Family of Traveling Entertainers* (1905)** This large composition required a long period of preparation. It was Picasso's main work of 1905 and marks a transition to his "Rose Period," perhaps his most important work in this period. Picasso at this time lived not very far from the Paris circus and it deeply impressed him. The gentleness of these people disclosed new aspects of human society to him. The oil on canvas painting is in the National Gallery of Art in Washington, DC. This Republic of Central Africa souvenir sheet shows an image of Picasso and a stamp containing an image of *Family of Traveling Entertainers*.

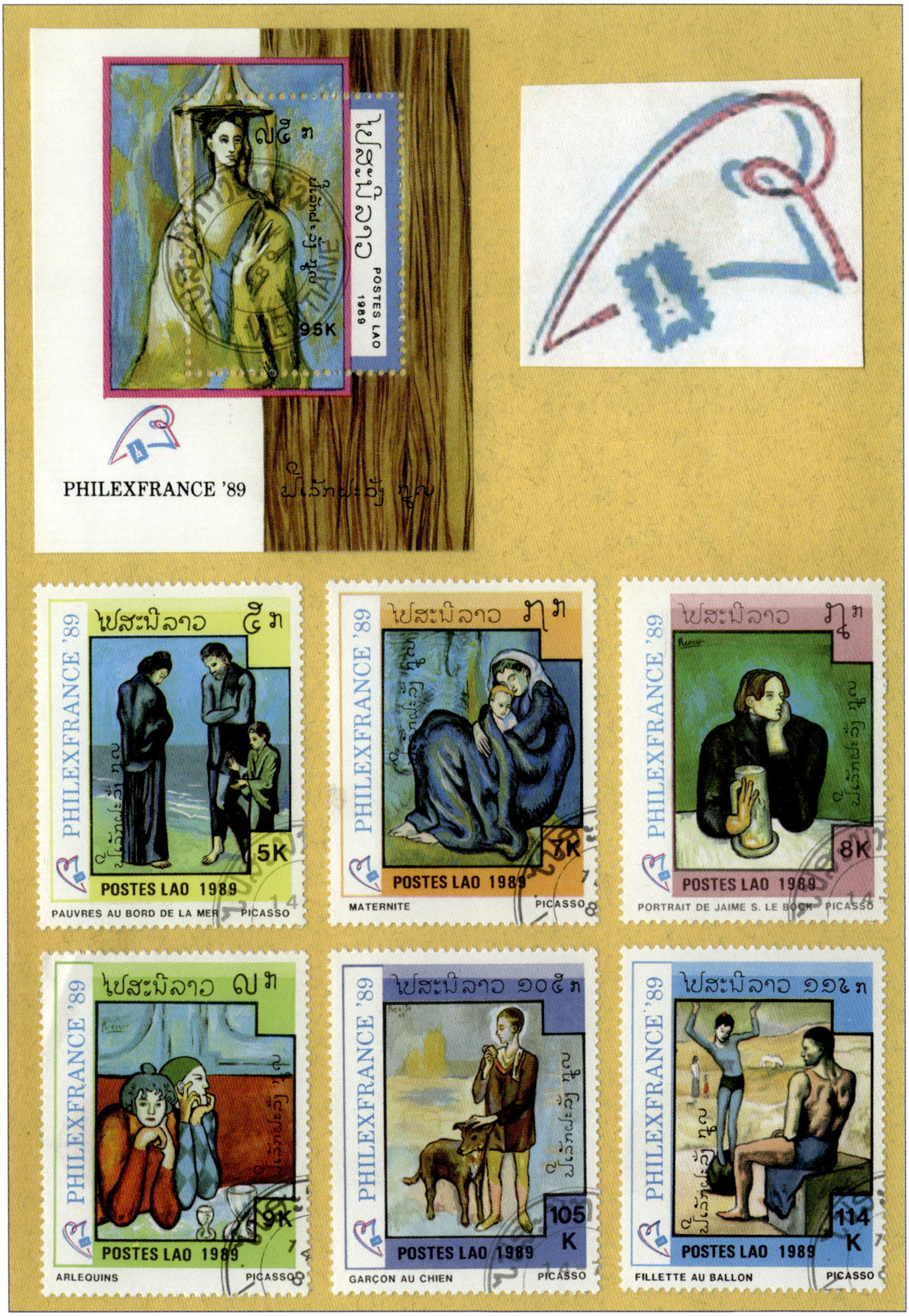

***Spanish Woman from Majorca* (1905)** This gouache and watercolor on cardboard painting (*Spanish Woman from Majorca*, 1905) is in the Pushkin Museum in Moscow, Russia. On July 17, 1989, the Lao People's Democratic Republic issued a souvenir sheet containing an image of this painting.

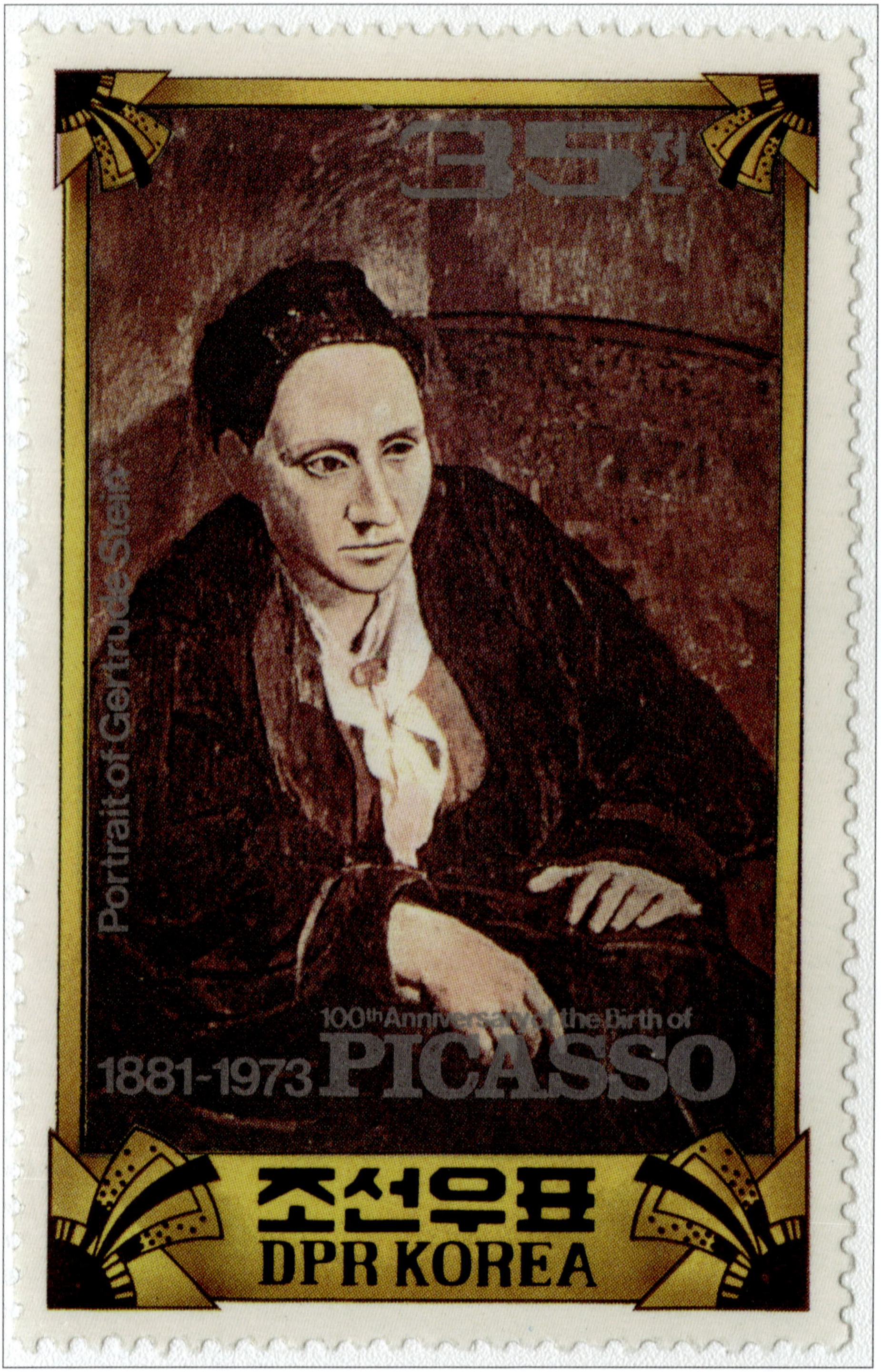

This work (***Portrait of Gertrude Stein***, 1906) ushered in a new phase in Picasso's art. It also represented a gesture of friendly gratitude to one of his earliest patrons and purchasers, a tribute to Miss Stein's imposing personality. Gertrude Stein and her brother Leo belonged to the first generation of Americans who took an active part in the twentieth century's artistic

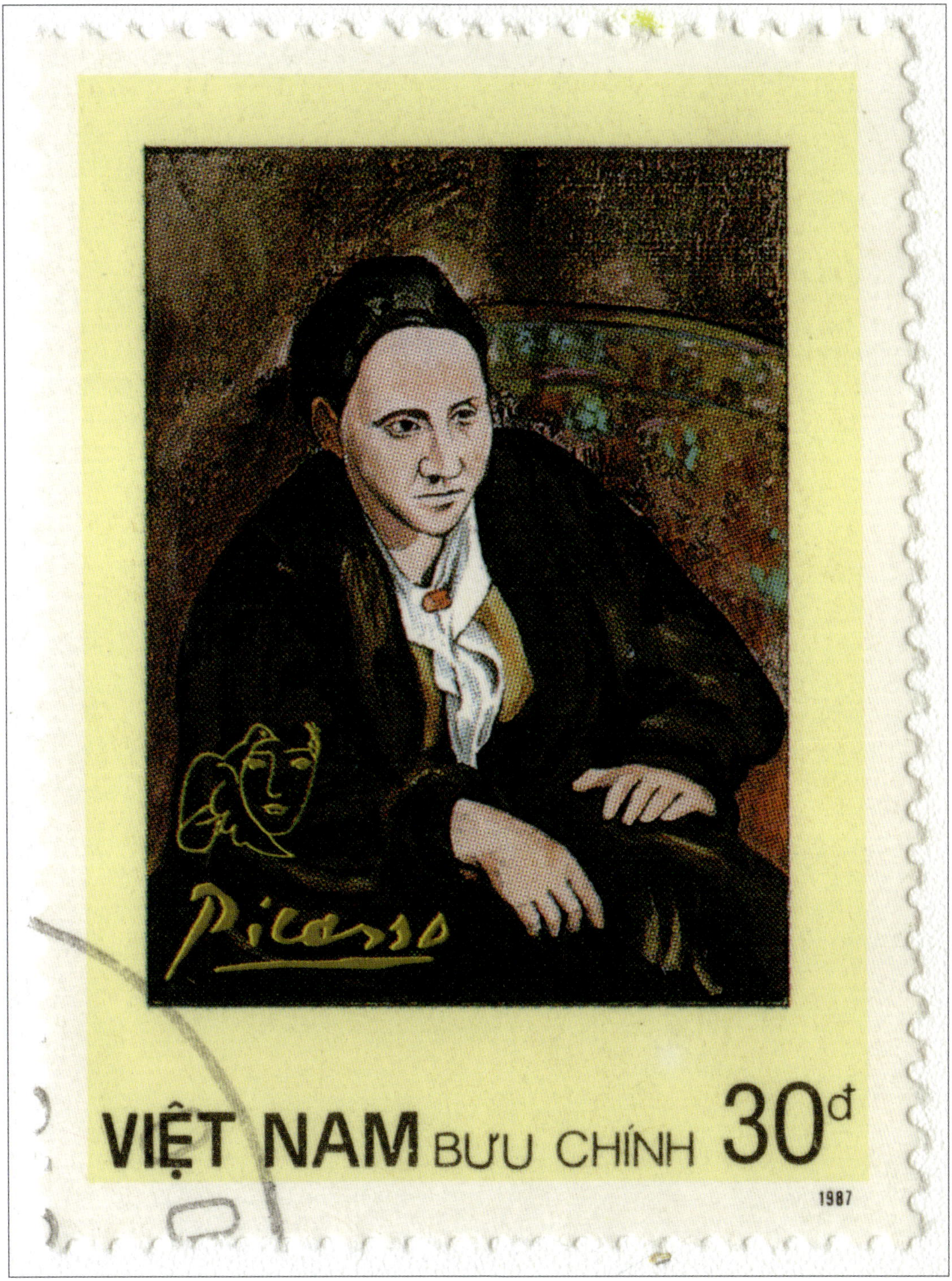

revolutions in Europe—especially in Paris. The painting is in the Metropolitan Museum of Art in New York. These two stamps used the image of this painting. On the left is a stamp issued on March 30, 1982, by North Korea (DPR Korea), honoring the 100th anniversary of the birth of Picasso. The stamp on the right was issued on December 30, 1987, by the Socialist Republic of Vietnam.

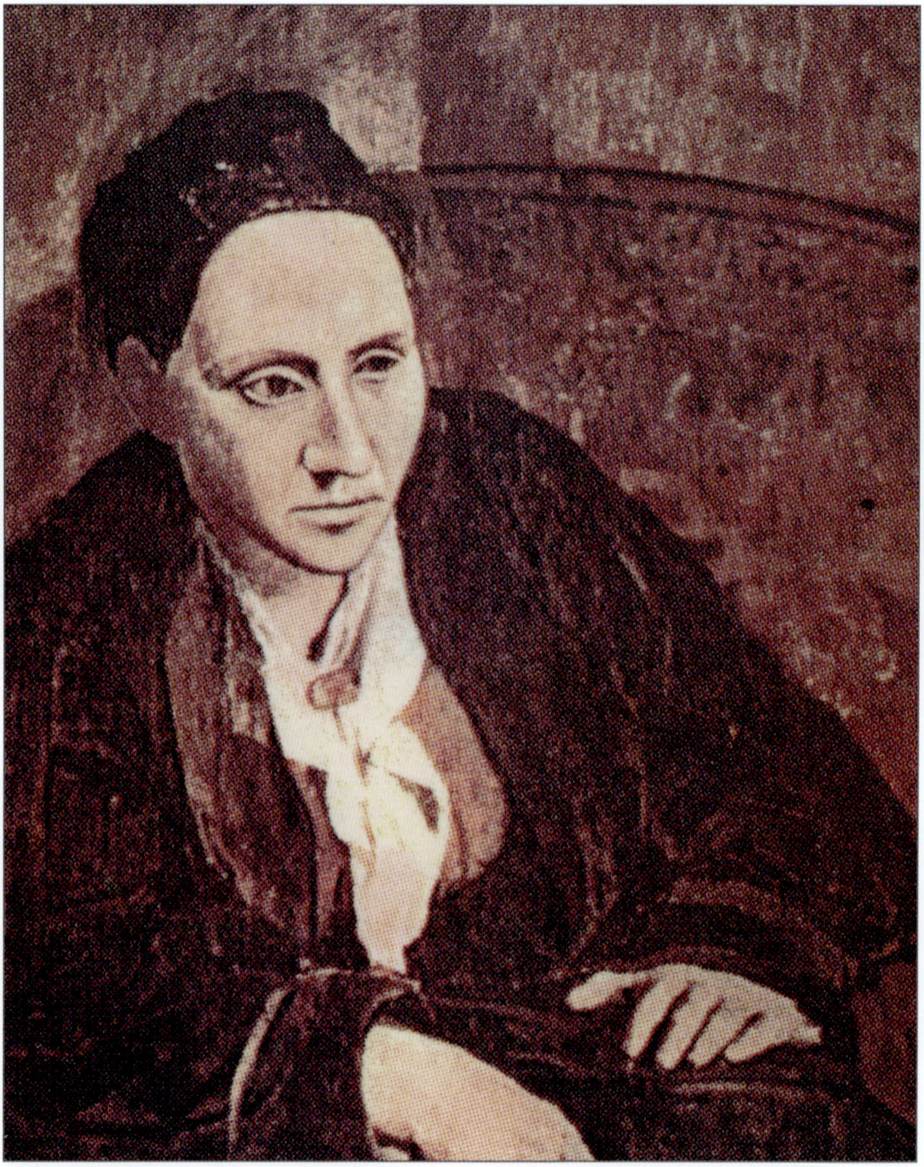

Detail of ***Portrait of Gertrude Stein*** (1906)

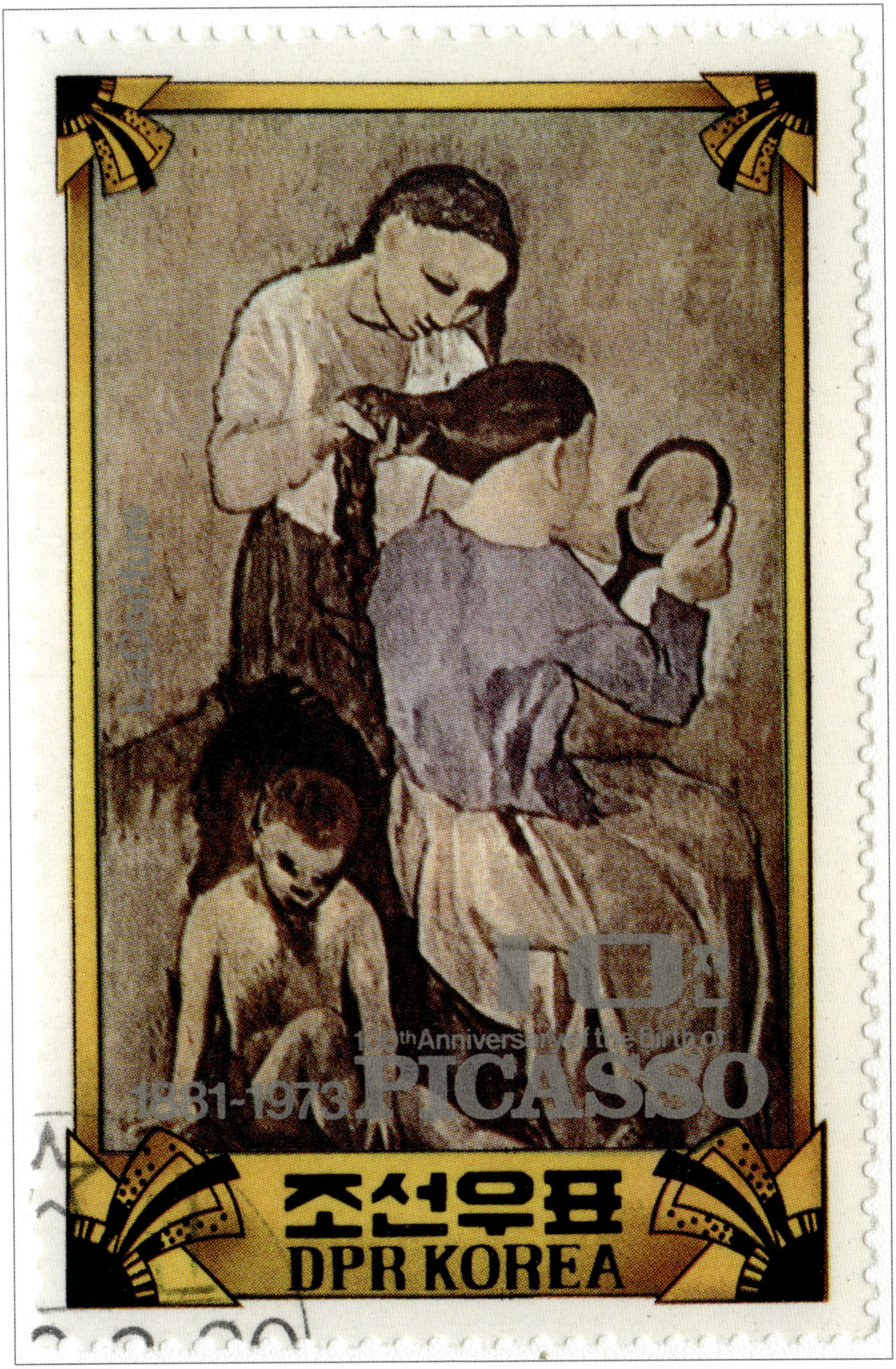

***La Coiffure* (1906)** The three figures form a pyramid, in keeping with the concept of figure composition that had been current in classical painting since Leonardo da Vinci. This rigorously ordered work (*La Coiffure*, 1906) may have been inspired by Picasso's study of classical painting in the Louvre. The oil painting is in the Museum of Modern Art in New York. On March 30, 1982, North Korea (DPR Korea) issued a stamp featuring the painting to honor the 100th anniversary of the birth of Picasso.

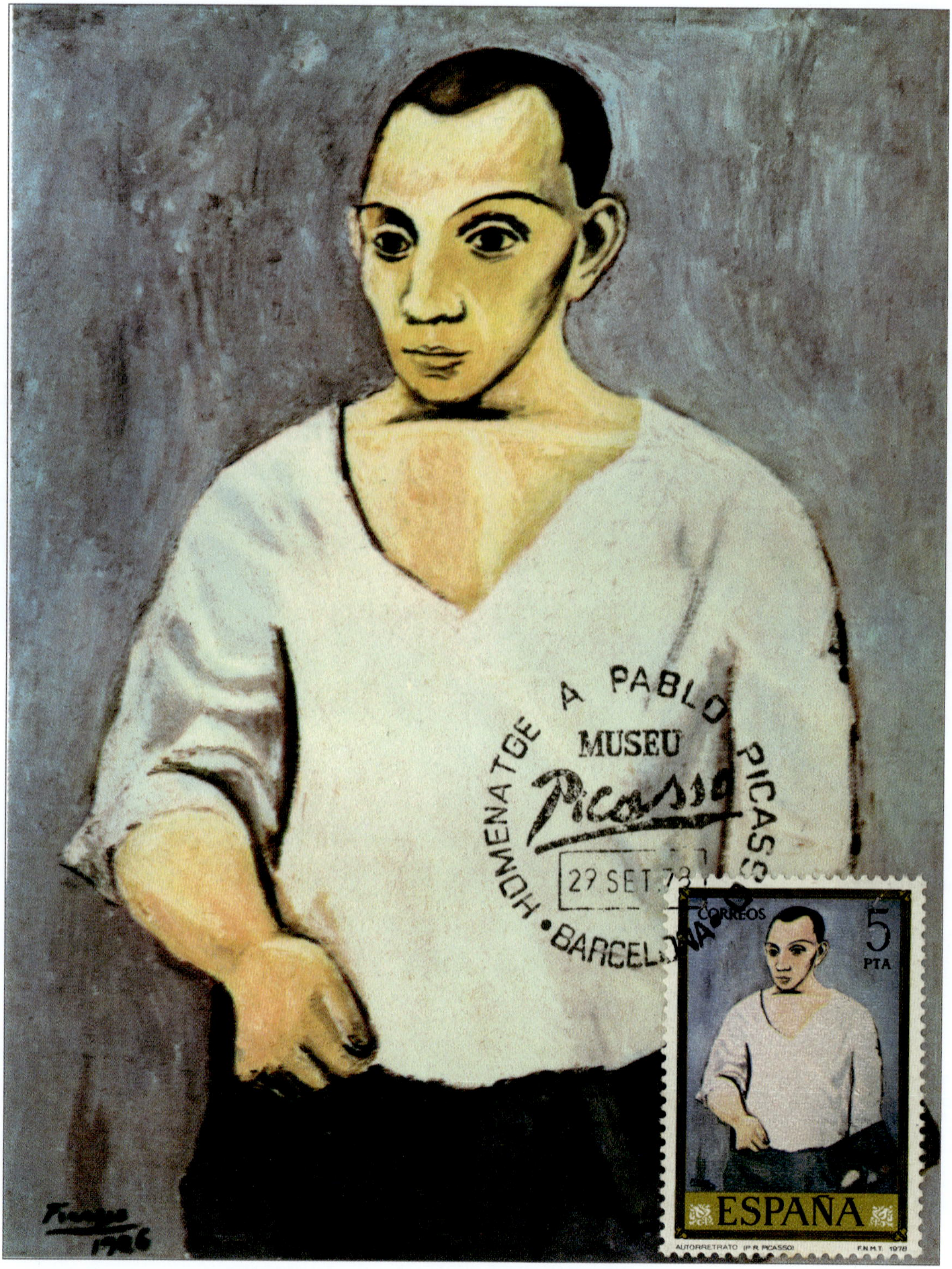

Pablo Picasso *Self-Portrait* (1906) This oil-on-canvas painting (*Self-Portrait*, 1906) is in the Philadelphia Museum of Art. The maximum card (maxicard) and stamp showing the painting were issued in Barcelona, Spain, on September 29, 1978 (Pablo Picasso Stamp Day, 1978).

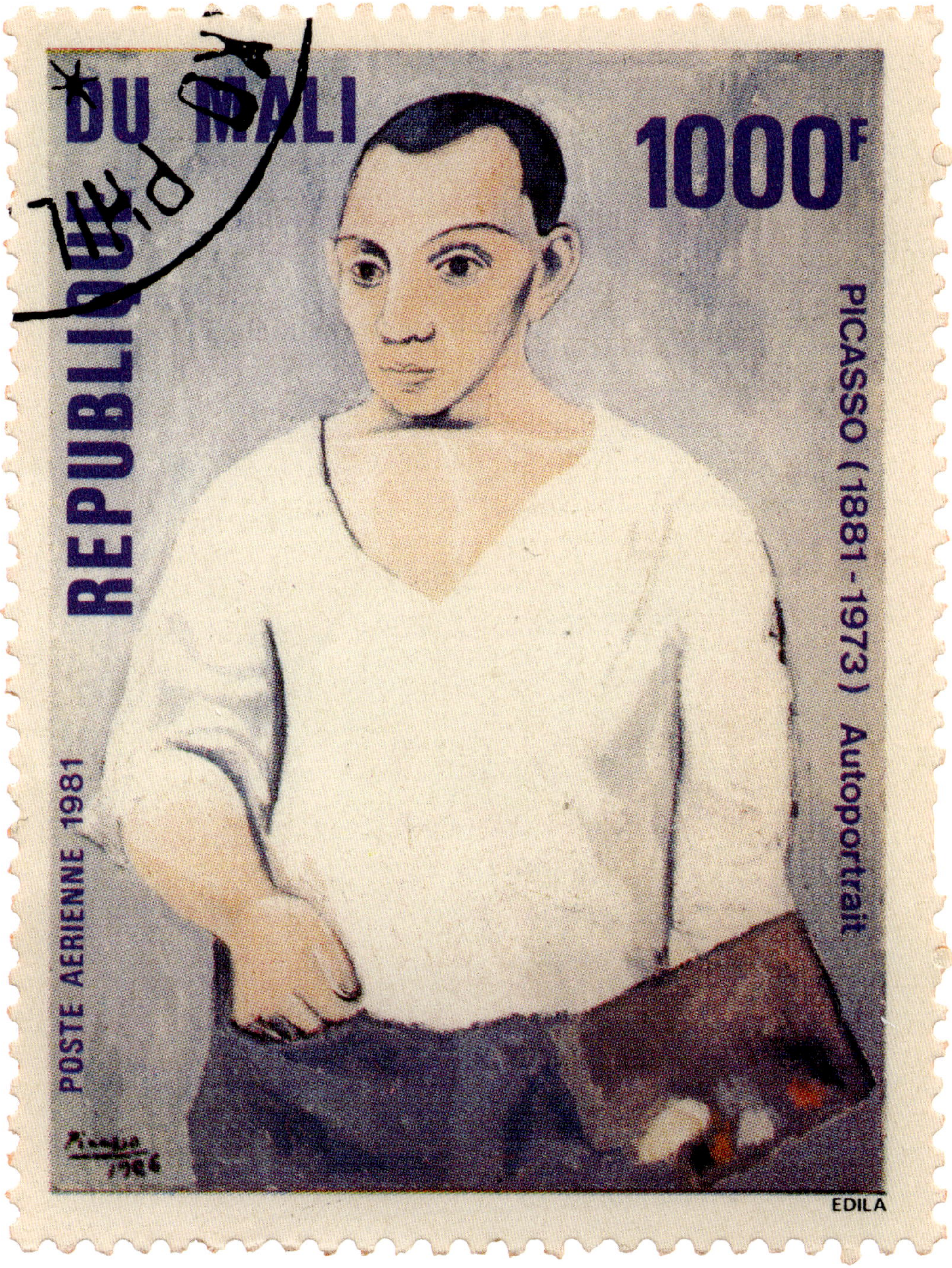

Pablo Picasso *Self-Portrait* (1906) This 1000-franc stamp was issued on January 26, 1981 by the Republic of Mali, a sovereign state in West Africa. The stamp contained the 1906 self-portrait of Picasso.

1907–1916

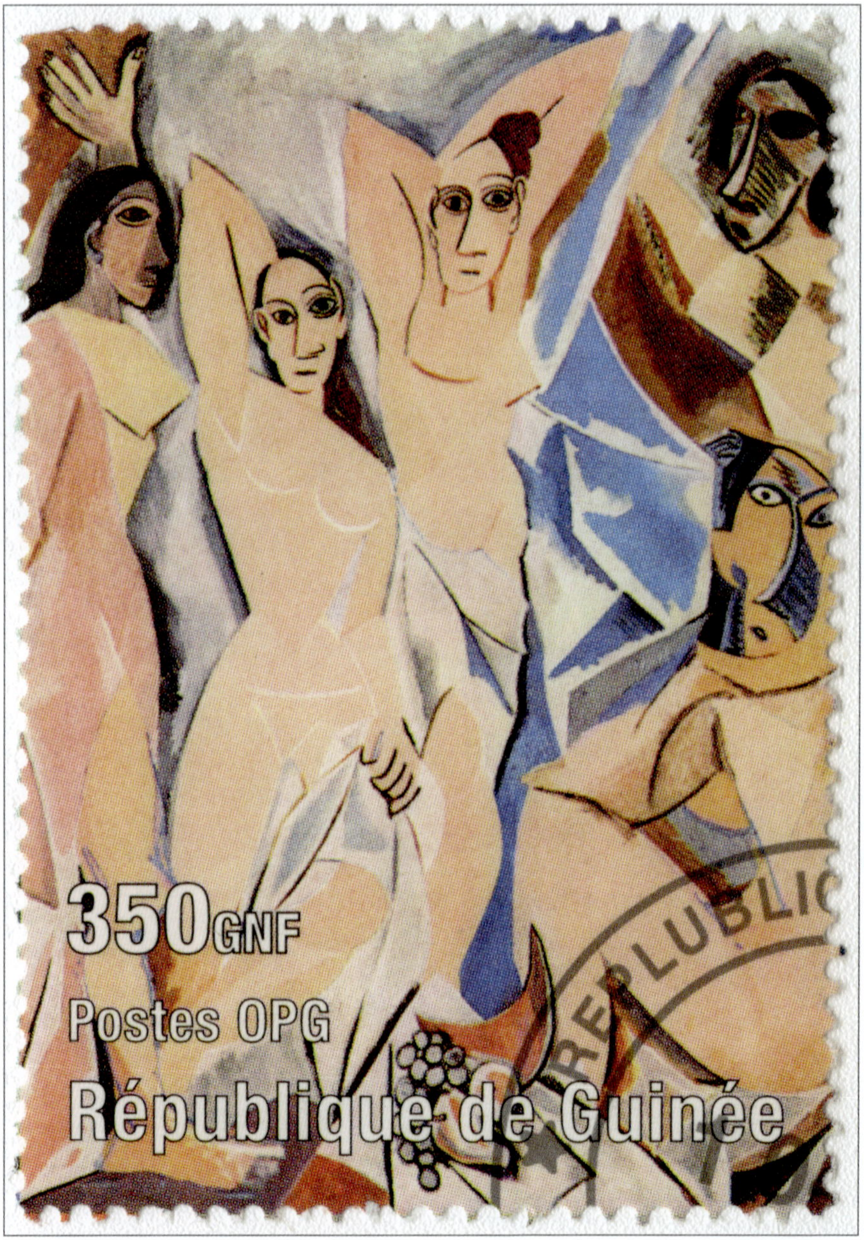

***Les Demoiselles d'Avignon* (1907)** This is one of the most exemplary modes of art history's greatest rule breakers. The style is derived from the African art Picasso saw in Paris and is considered one of the most famous Picasso paintings. This stamp, which illustrates the famous painting (*Les Demoiselles d' Avignon*, 1907), was issued on April 1, 1998, by the Republic of Guinea, a country on the western coast of Africa.

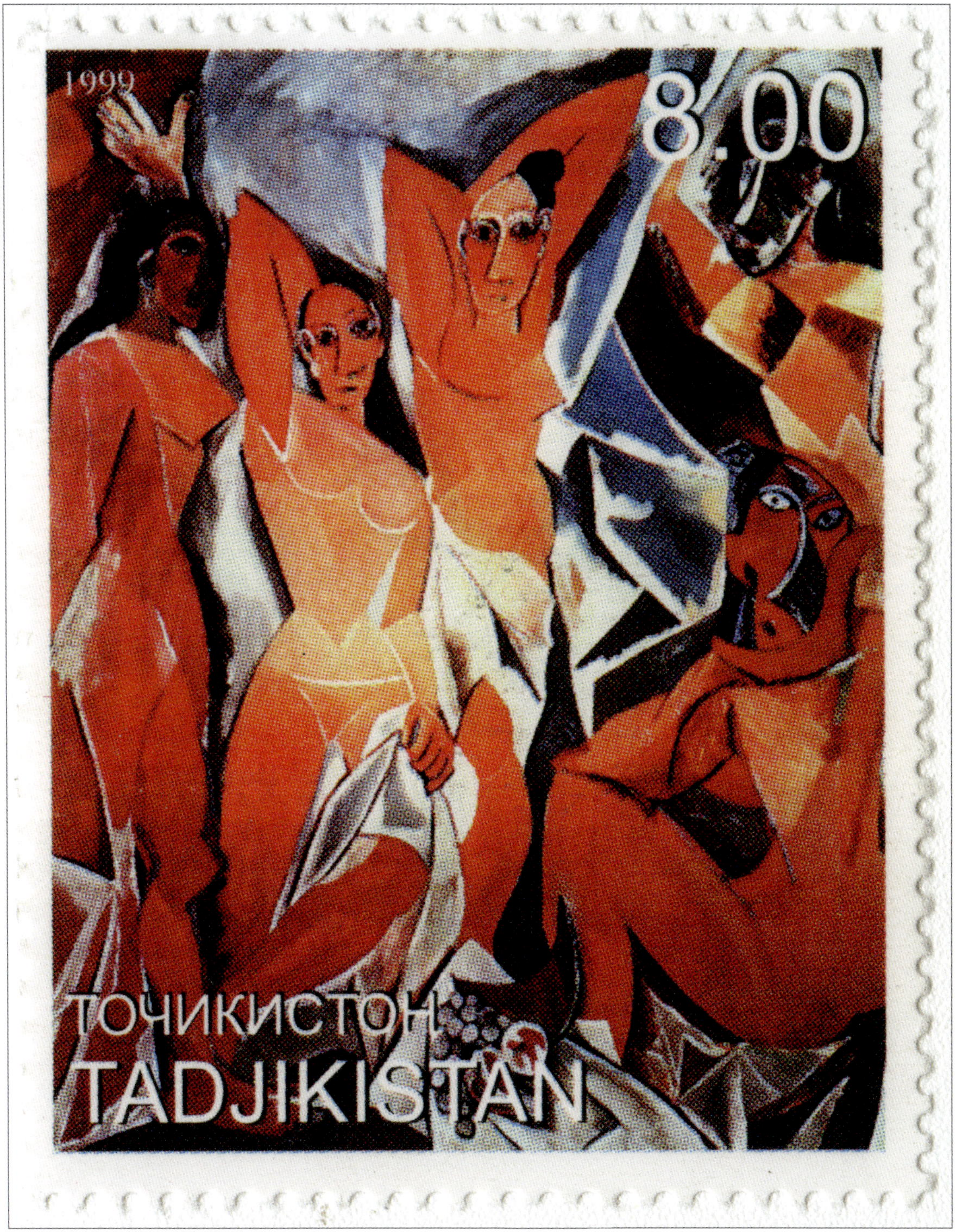

***Les Demoiselles d'Avignon* (1907)** This eight-ruble stamp (*Les Demoiselles d' Avignon*, 1907) was issued, possibly in 1999, in the name of the Republic of Tajikistan, a sovereign state in central Asia.

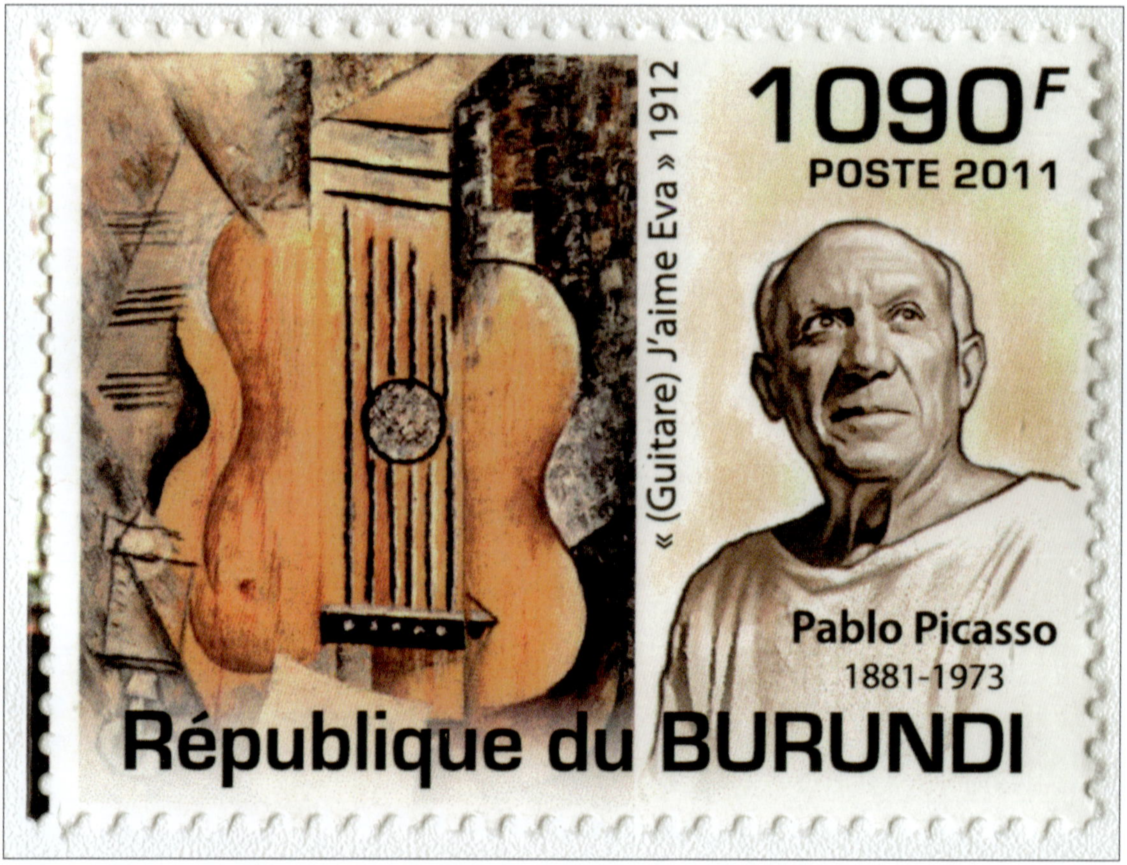

***(Guitare) J'aime Eva* (1912)** In 2011, the Republic of Burundi used this painting (*Guitare J'aime Eva*, 1912) when producing a stamp celebrating the 130th anniversary of the birth of Pablo Picasso. The stamp also includes a *Self-Portrait* of Picasso.

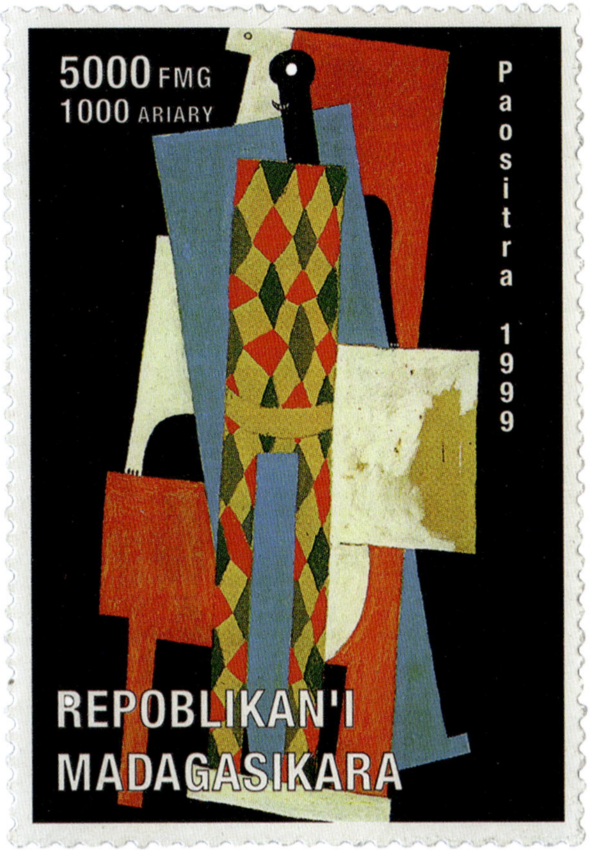

***Harlequin* (1915)** This oil on canvas painting is in the Museum of Modern Art in New York. This 5,000-franc or 1,000-ariary stamp was issued, possibly in 1999, in the name of the Republic of Madagasikara.

1917–1935

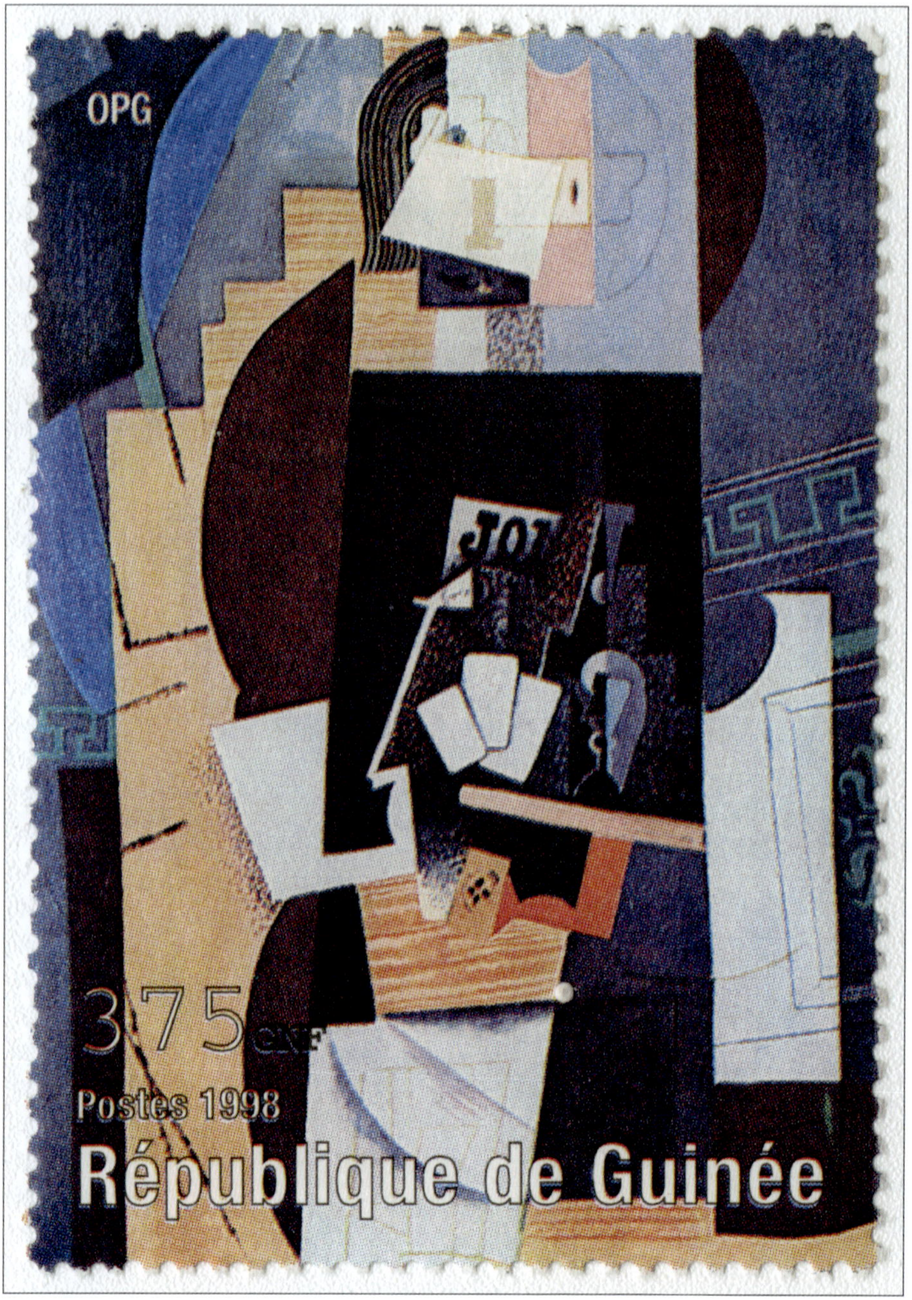

***Card Player* (1914)** This oil painting (*Card Player*, 1914) is in the Museum of Modern Art in New York. The Republic of Guinea used the painting in 1998 when they released this stamp honoring the twenty-fifth anniversary of the death of Picasso.

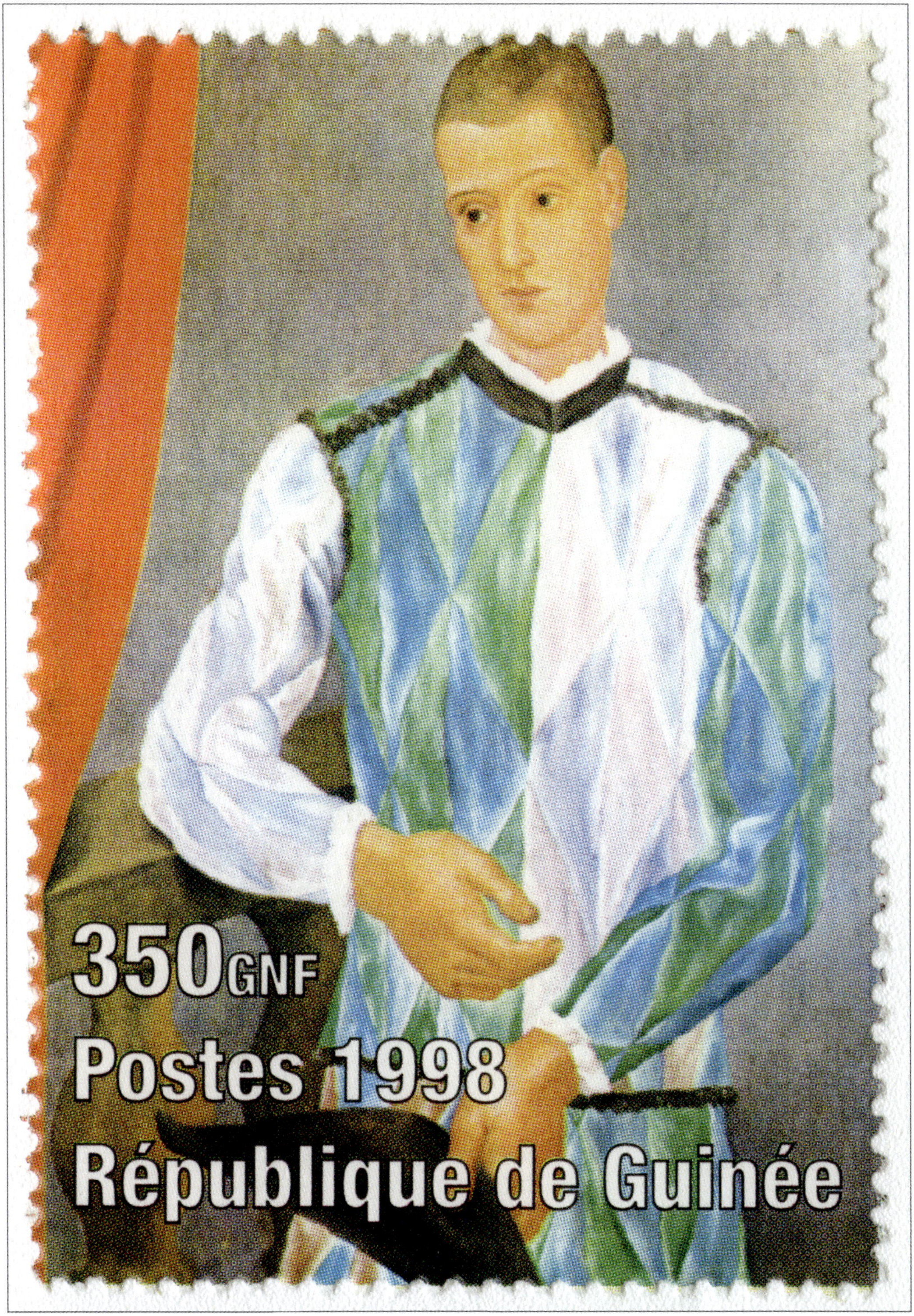

***Harlequin* (1917)** This oil-on-canvas painting (*Harlequin*, 1917) is in the Picasso Museum in Barcelona, Spain. On April 1, 1998, the Republic of Guinea issued this stamp using an image of the painting.

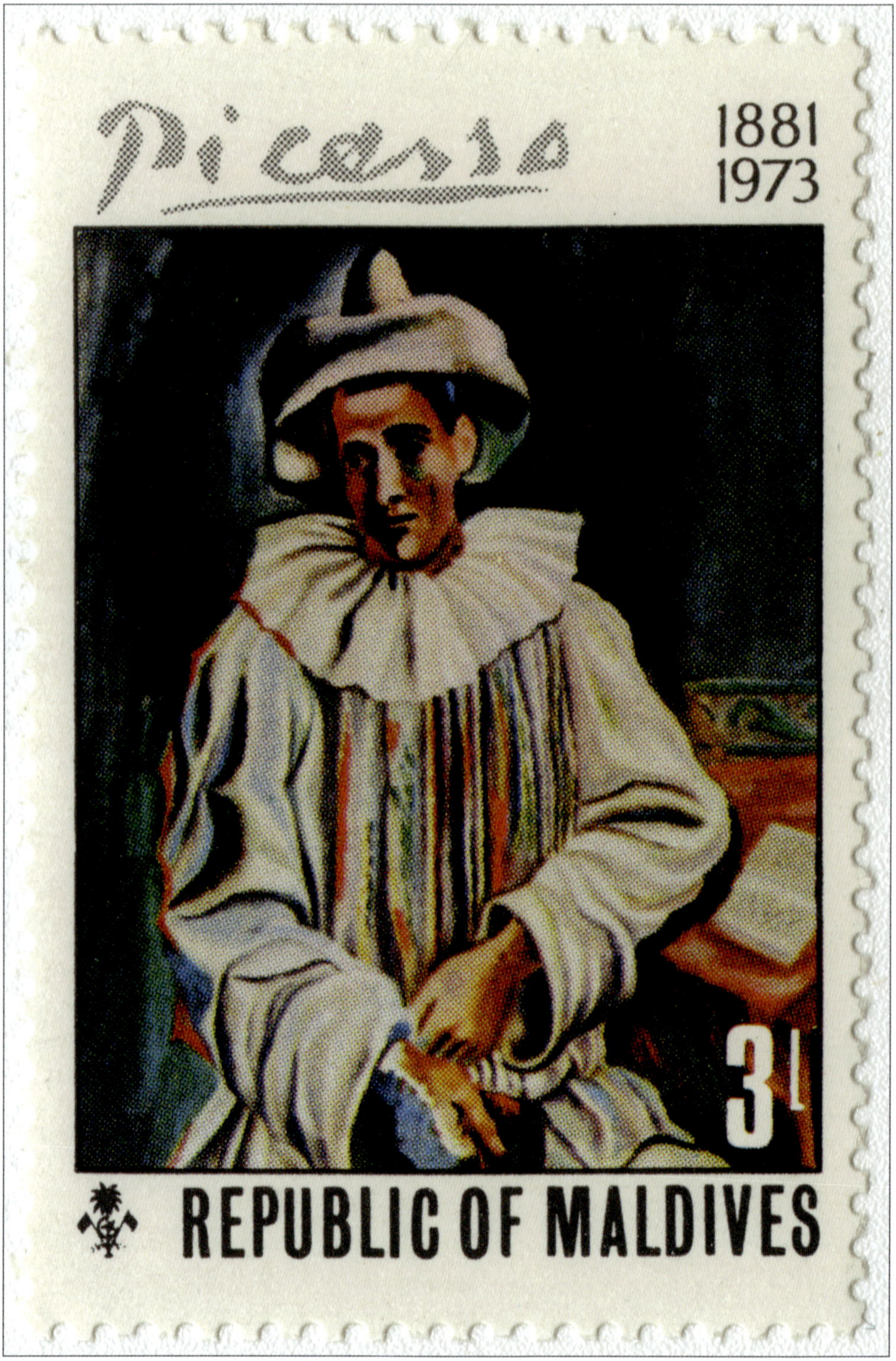

Pierrot Seated (1918) This painting (*Pierrot Seated*, 1918) is in the Museum of Modern Art in New York. The stamp using this image was issued in the name of the Republic of Maldives, a South Asian island country.

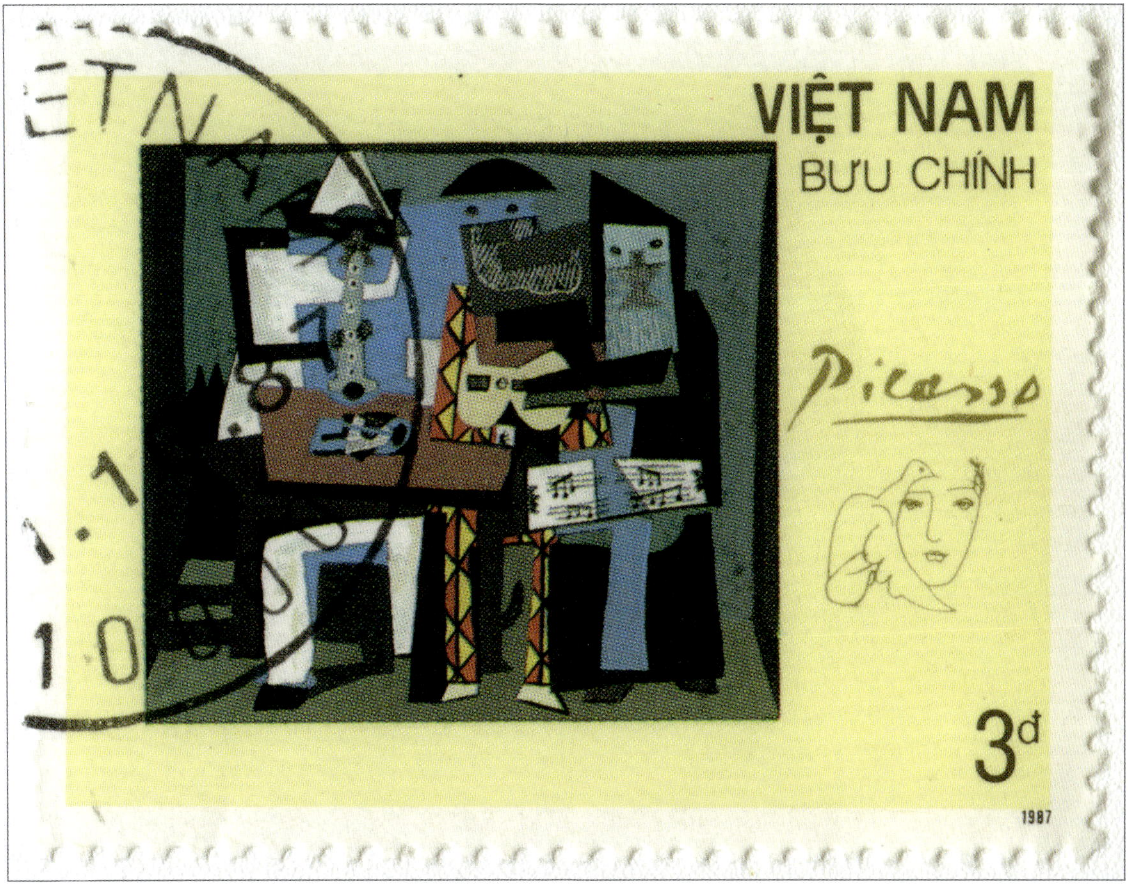

***Three Musicians* (1921)** Picasso painted several different versions of some of his paintings, giving them the same title. In summer 1921, he painted two great compositions, both of them generally called the *Three Musicians*. In both paintings, three overly life-sized figures are seated at a table: a pierrot, a harlequin, and a monk. In this version a dog lies on the floor beneath the table. This painting is in the Museum of Modern Art in New York. On December 30, 1987, the Socialist Republic of Vietnam, the easternmost country on the Indochinese Peninsula in Southeast Asia, issued a stamp with this image.

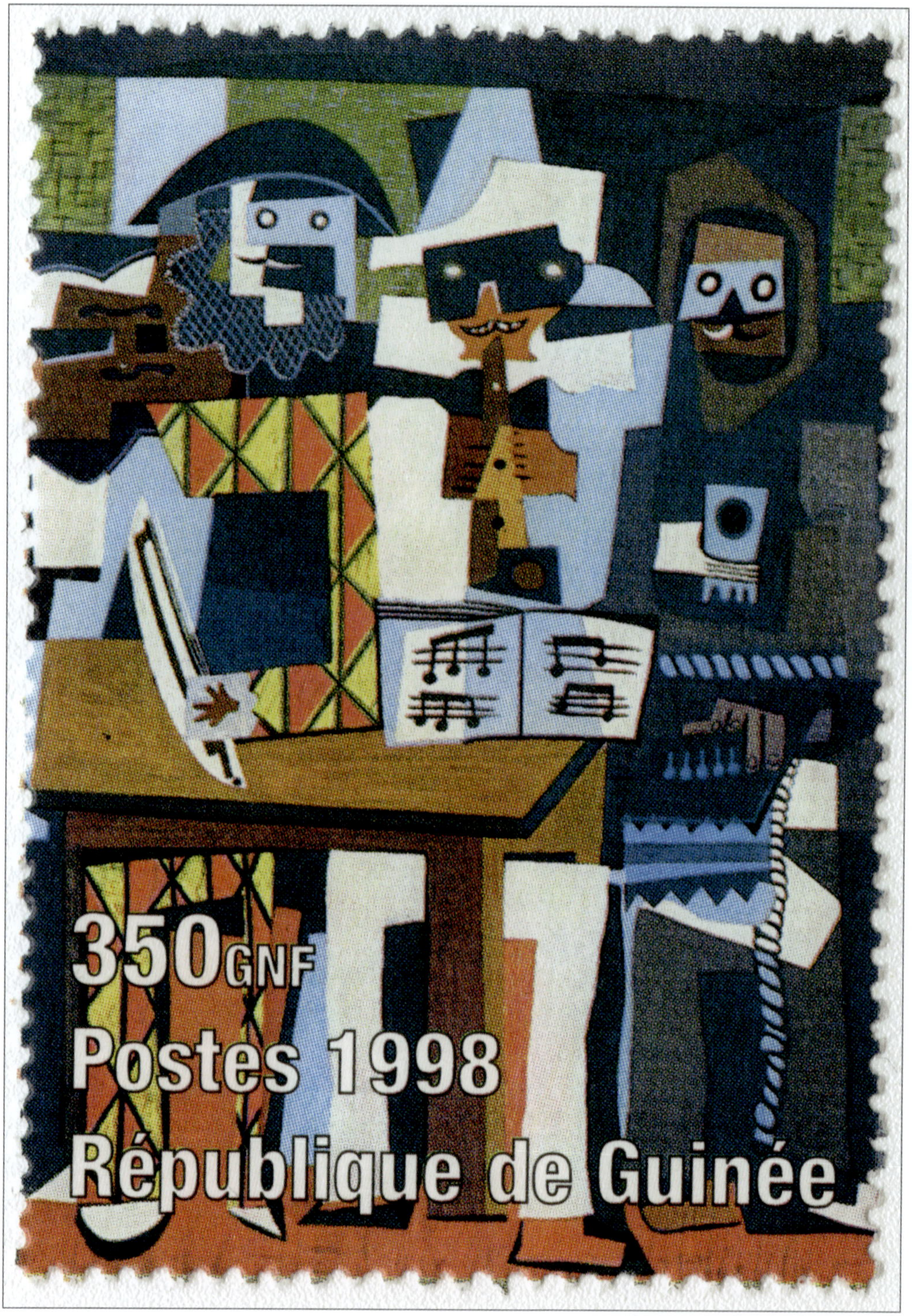

***Three Musicians* (1921)** The second version of this painting (*Three Musicians*, 1921) is more complex in pattern and gayer in color. This bold, large painting is one of the last that Picasso made in the cubist style and is in the Philadelphia Museum of Art. This stamp was issued on April 1, 1998, by the Republic of Guinea, a country on the western coast of Africa.

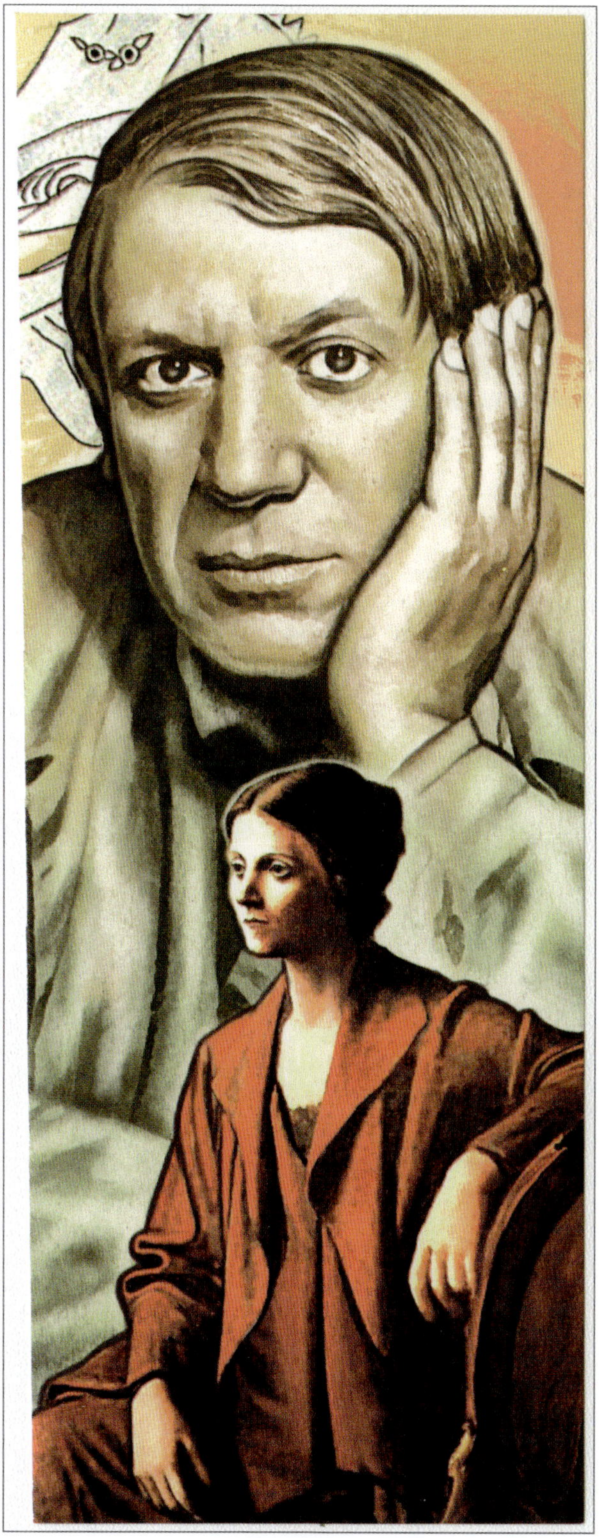

Pablo Picasso and his wife, Olga Koklova

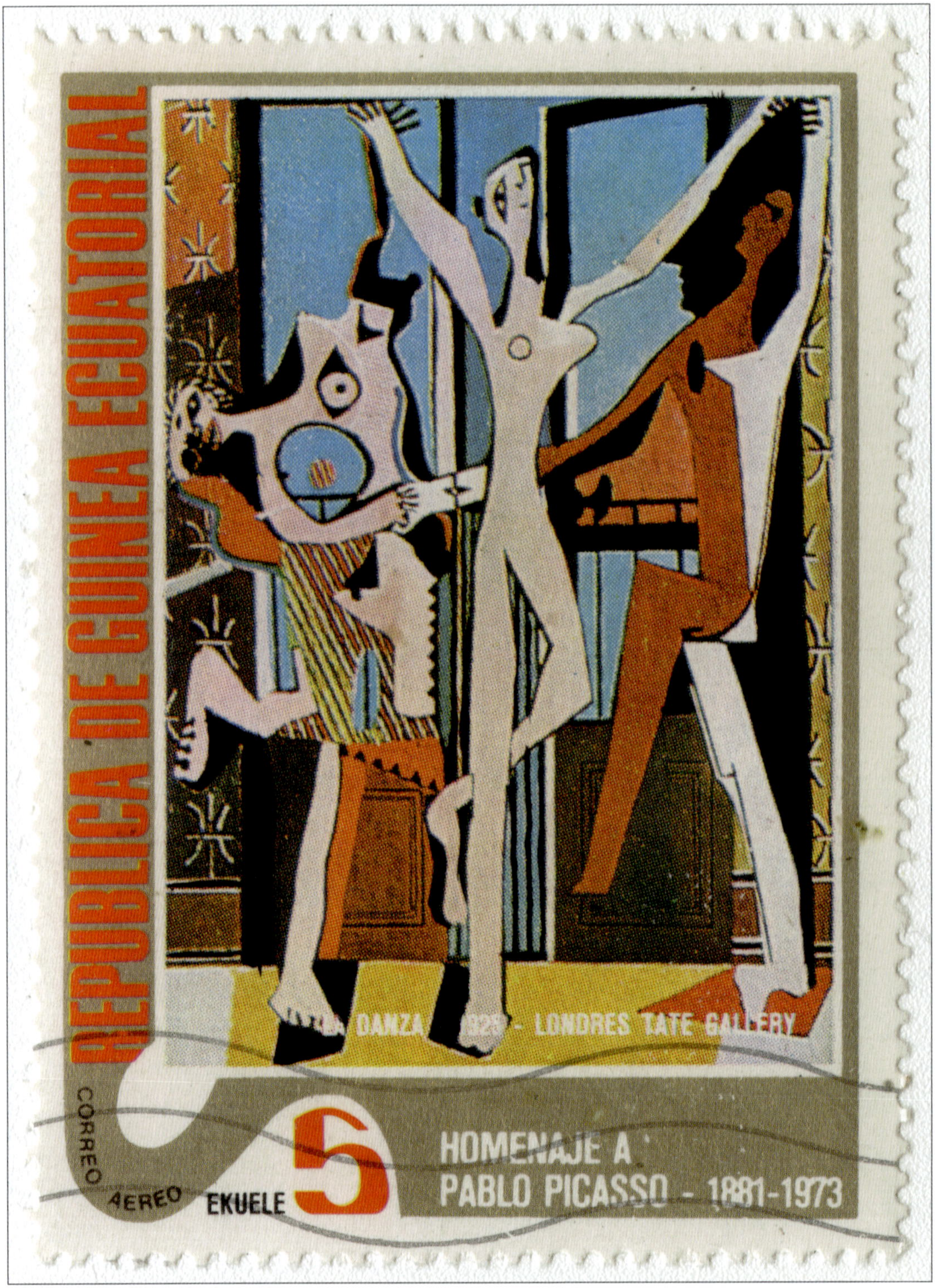

***The Three Dancers* (1925)** Two stamps that used this image (*The Three Dancers*, 1925) were the forty-five-franc stamp on the right, issued in 1988 by the Togolese Republic, and the stamp on the left, issued by Guinea Ecuatorial.

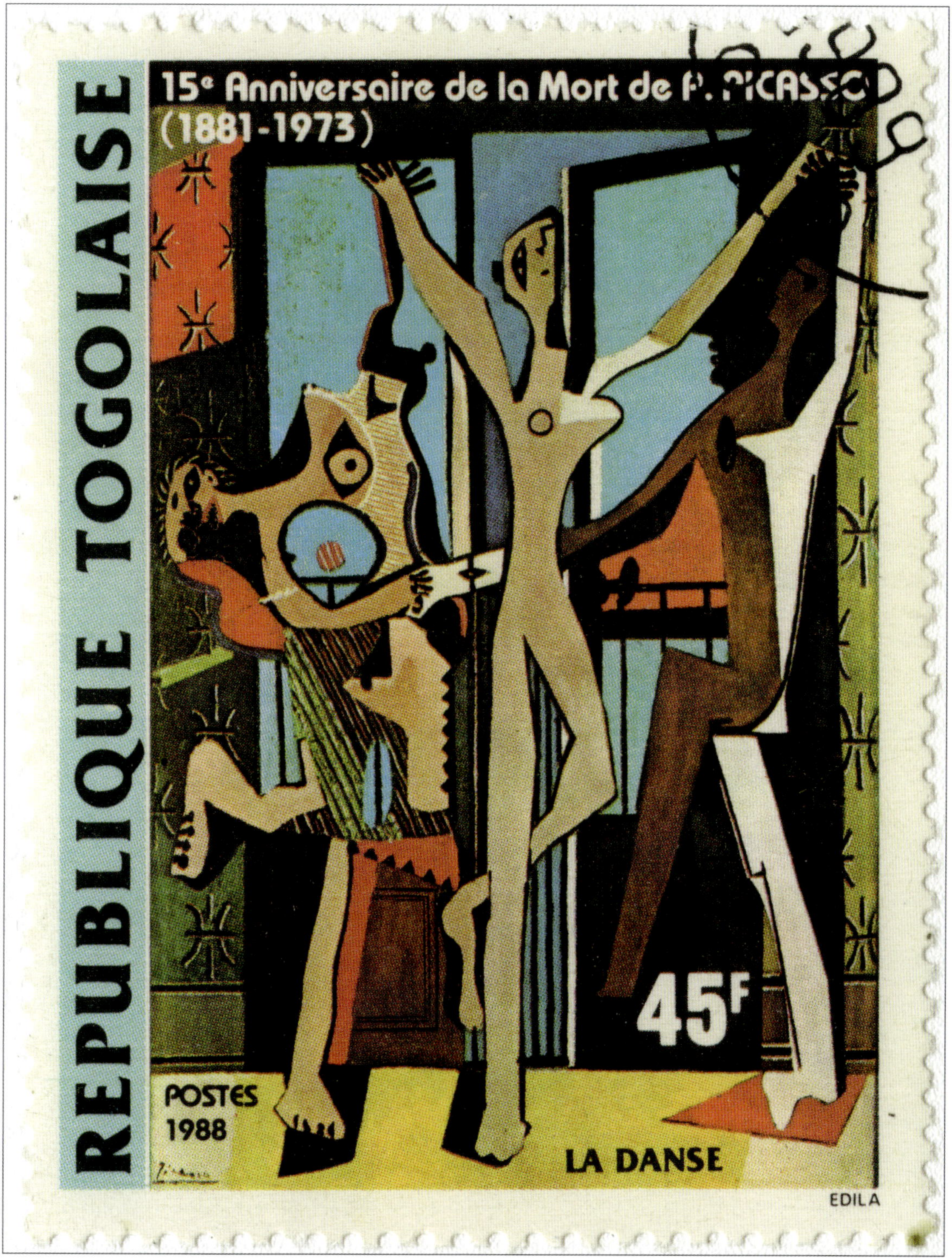
15e Anniversaire de la Mort de P. PICASSO
(1881-1973)
REPUBLIQUE TOGOLAISE
45F
POSTES
1988
LA DANSE
EDILA

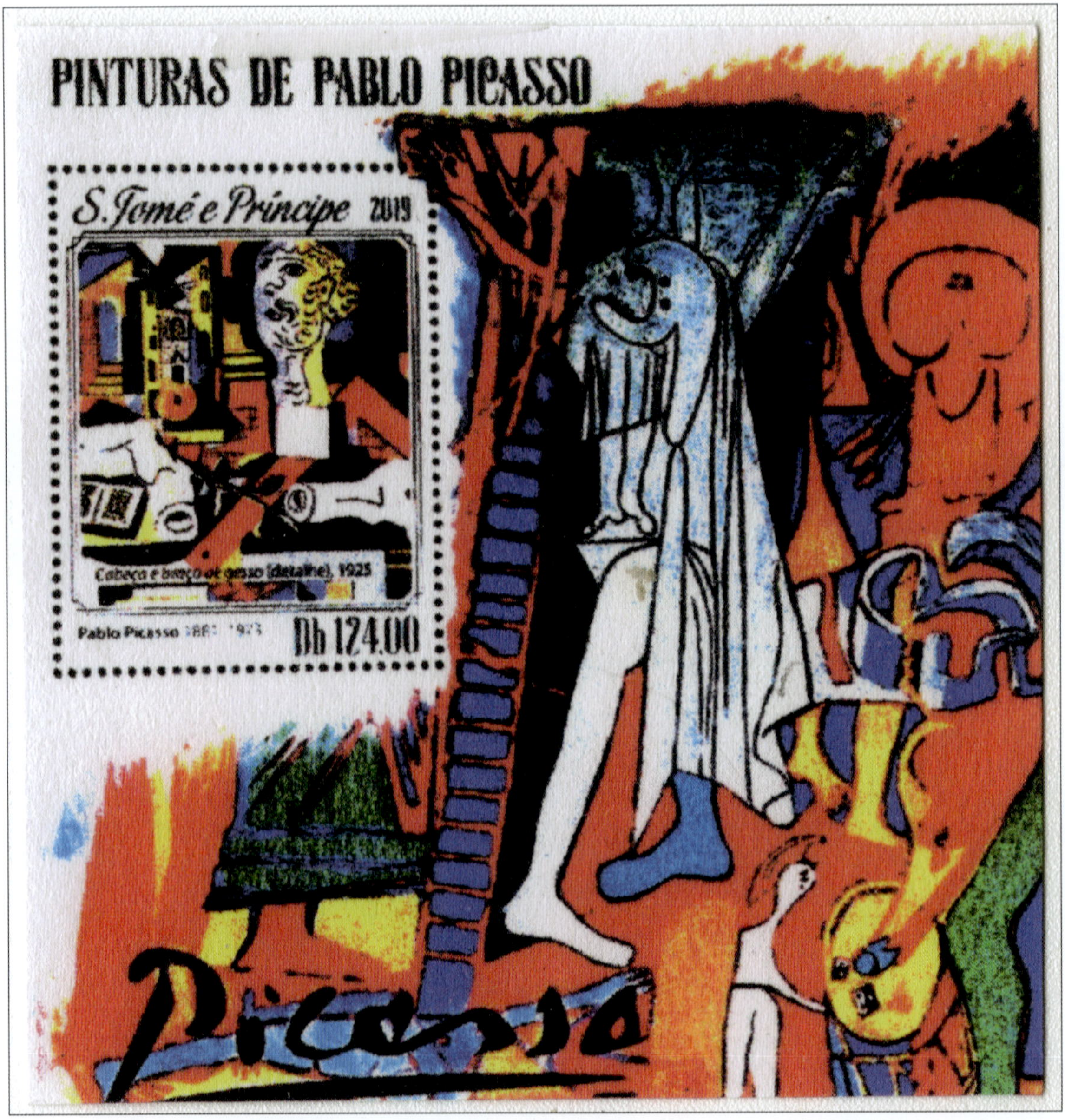

Studio with Plaster Head (1925) This oil-on-canvas painting (*Studio with Plaster Head*, 1925) is in the Museum of Modern Art in New York. This 124-dobra stamp was issued in 2019 by the Democratic Republic of Sao Tome and Principe, an island nation in the Gulf of Guinea. The stamp is in position on a stamp souvenir sheet titled *Pictures of Pablo Picasso*. The souvenir sheet also includes a portion of an image of *Crucifixion*, a painting Picasso created in 1930.

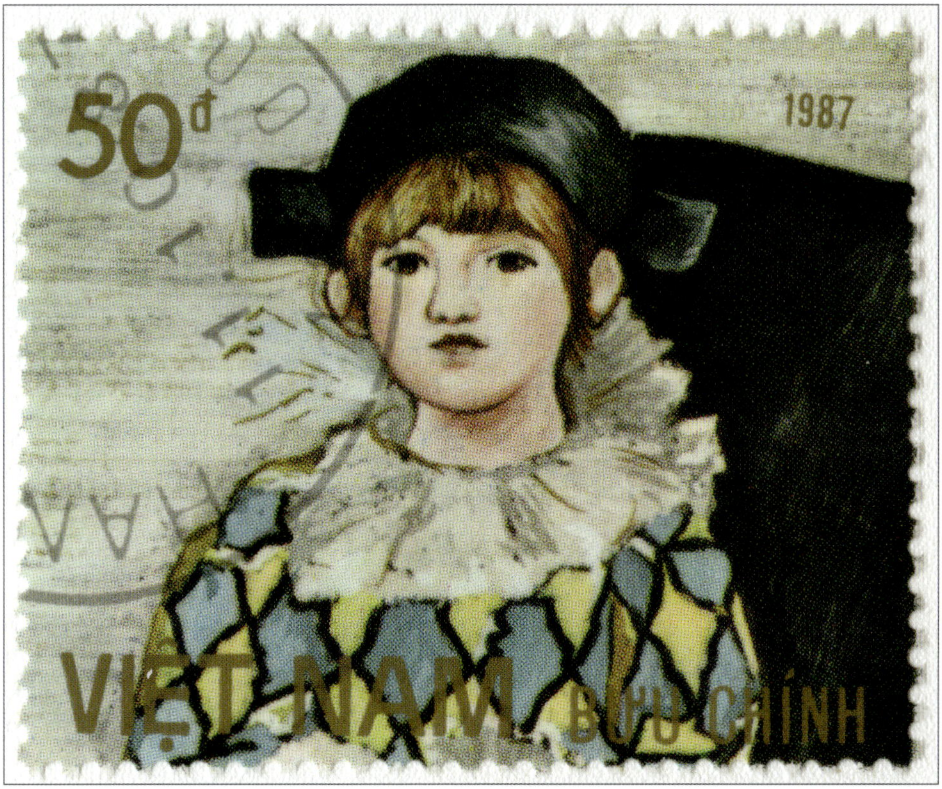

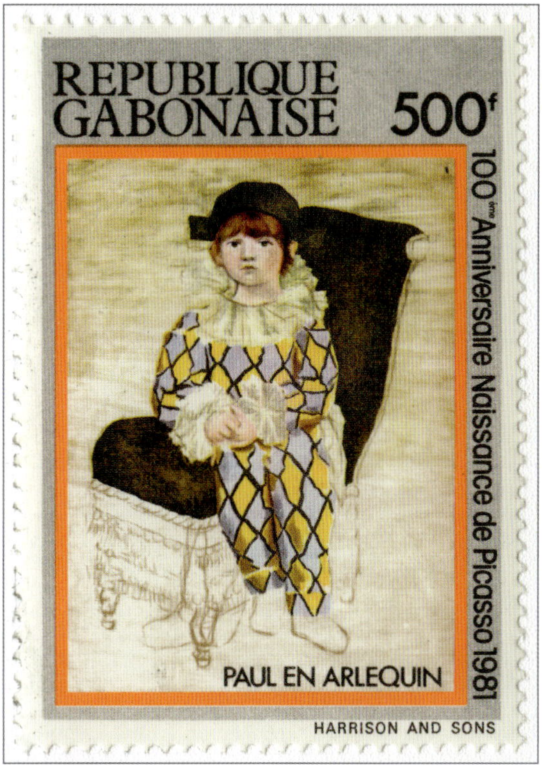

***Paul as Harlequin* (1925)** This oil-on-canvas painting (*Paul as Harlequin*, 1925) shows Picasso's oldest son Paulo (Paul) in pierrot costume, dressed up as a bullfighter, or simply a child playing. The painting is now in the Picasso Museum in Paris. Images of the painting appear on the stamps shown. The top stamp was issued in 1987 by Vietnam. The 500-franc stamp was issued September 25, 1981, by the Gabonese Republic, a sovereign state on the west coast of central Africa.

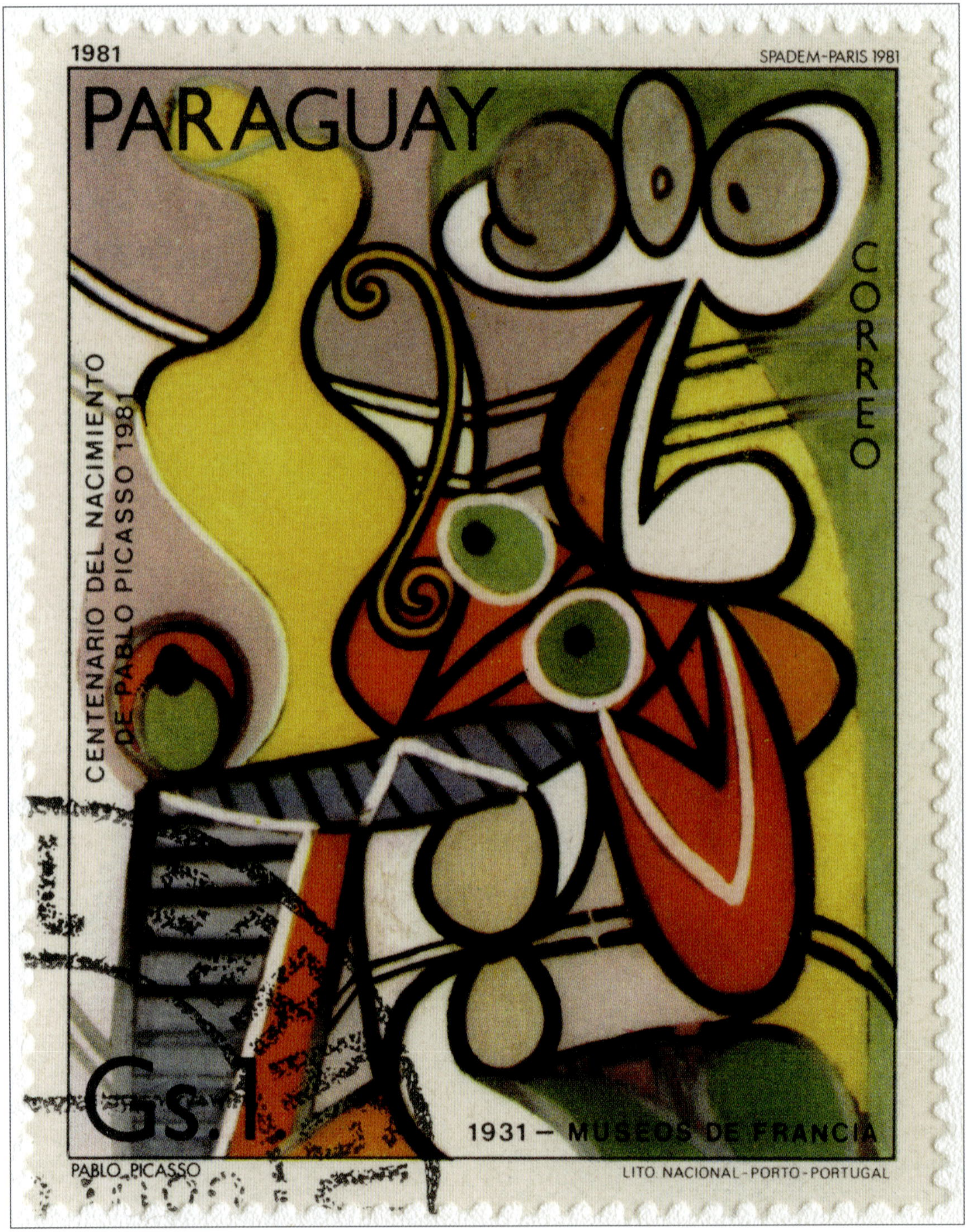

***Still Life on a Pedestal Table* (1931)** This painting (*Still Life on a Pedestal Table*, 1931) is in the Picasso Museum in Paris. On October 19, 1981, the Republic of Paraguay issued a stamp using an image of this oil-on-canvas painting.

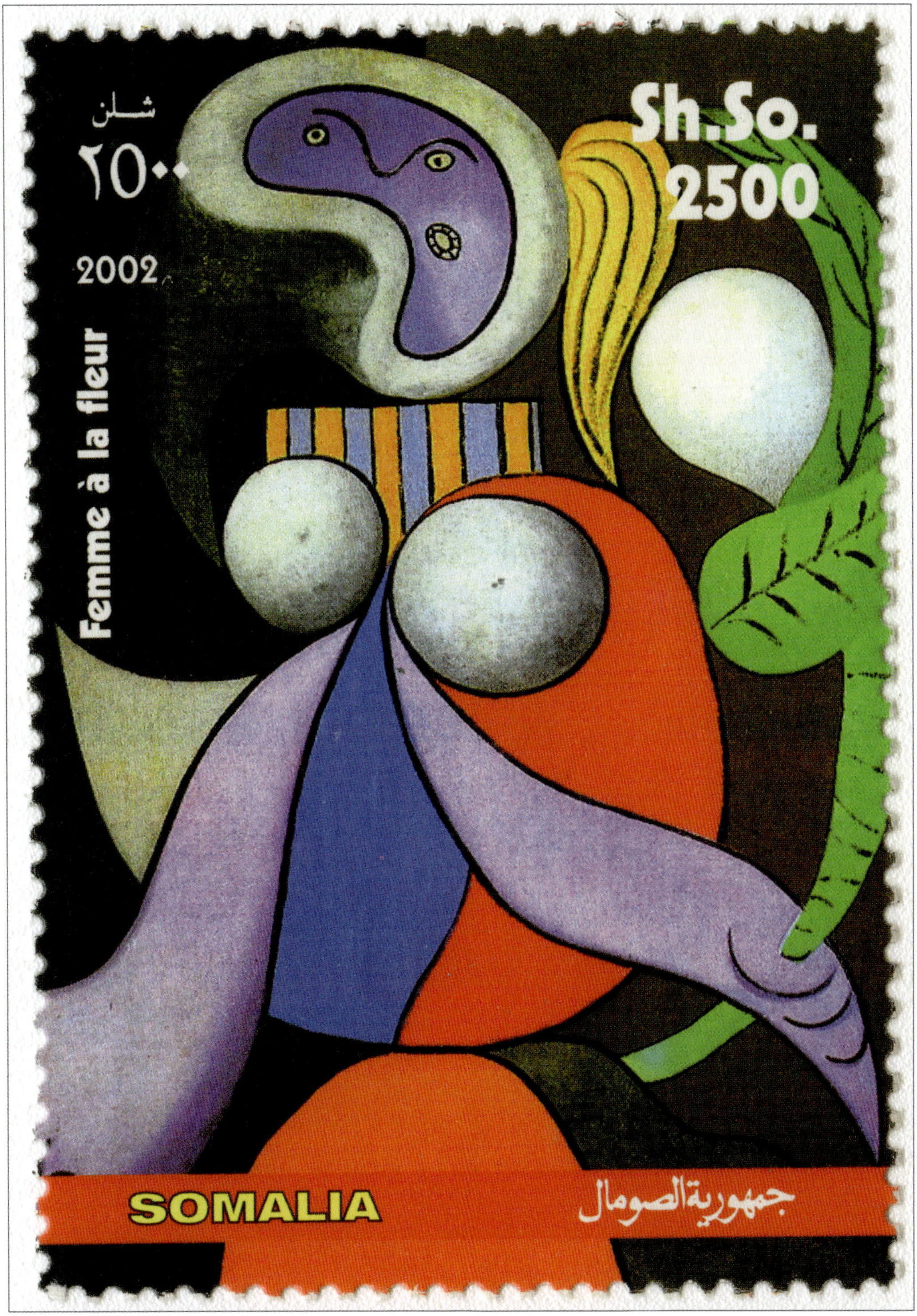

Woman with a Flower (1932) Using this image (*Woman with a Flower*, 1932), a 2,500-shilling stamp was issued, possibly in 2002, in the name of the Federal Republic of Somalia, a country in the Horn of Africa.

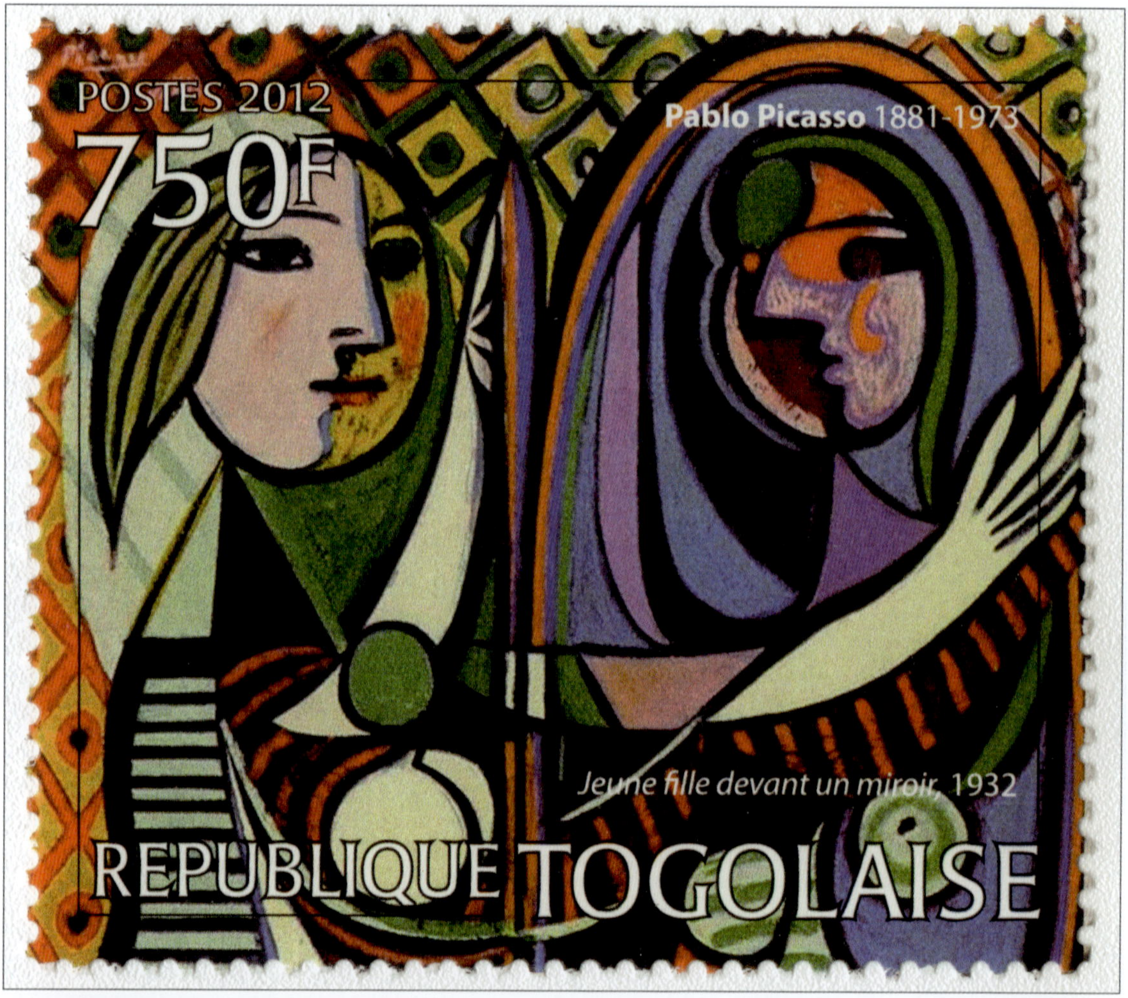

Girl in Front of a Mirror (1932) Part of this painting (*Girl in Front of a Mirror*, 1932) was used on the 750-franc stamp issued in 2012 by the Togolese Republic.

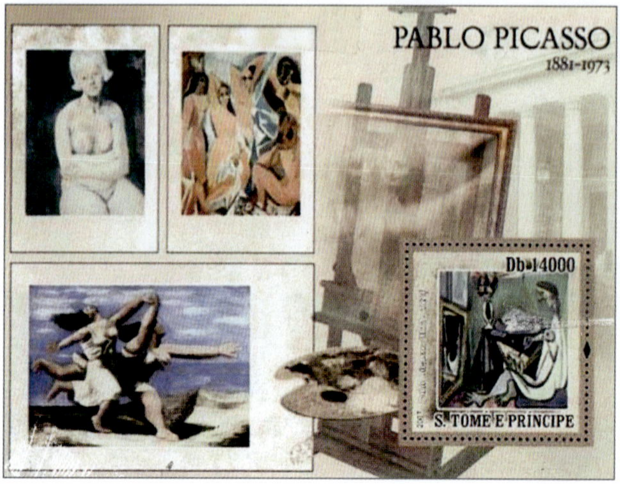

The Muse (1935) A stamp souvenir sheet consisting of one stamp and three paintings illustrating Picasso artwork was issued by St. Thomas & Prince Islands in 2007. In addition to *The Muse*, three of the paintings shown on the souvenir sheet are *La Belle Hollandaise* (Dutch Girl, 1905), *Les Demoiselles d'Avignon* (The Young Ladies of d'Avignon, 1907), and *Women Running on the Beach* (1922).

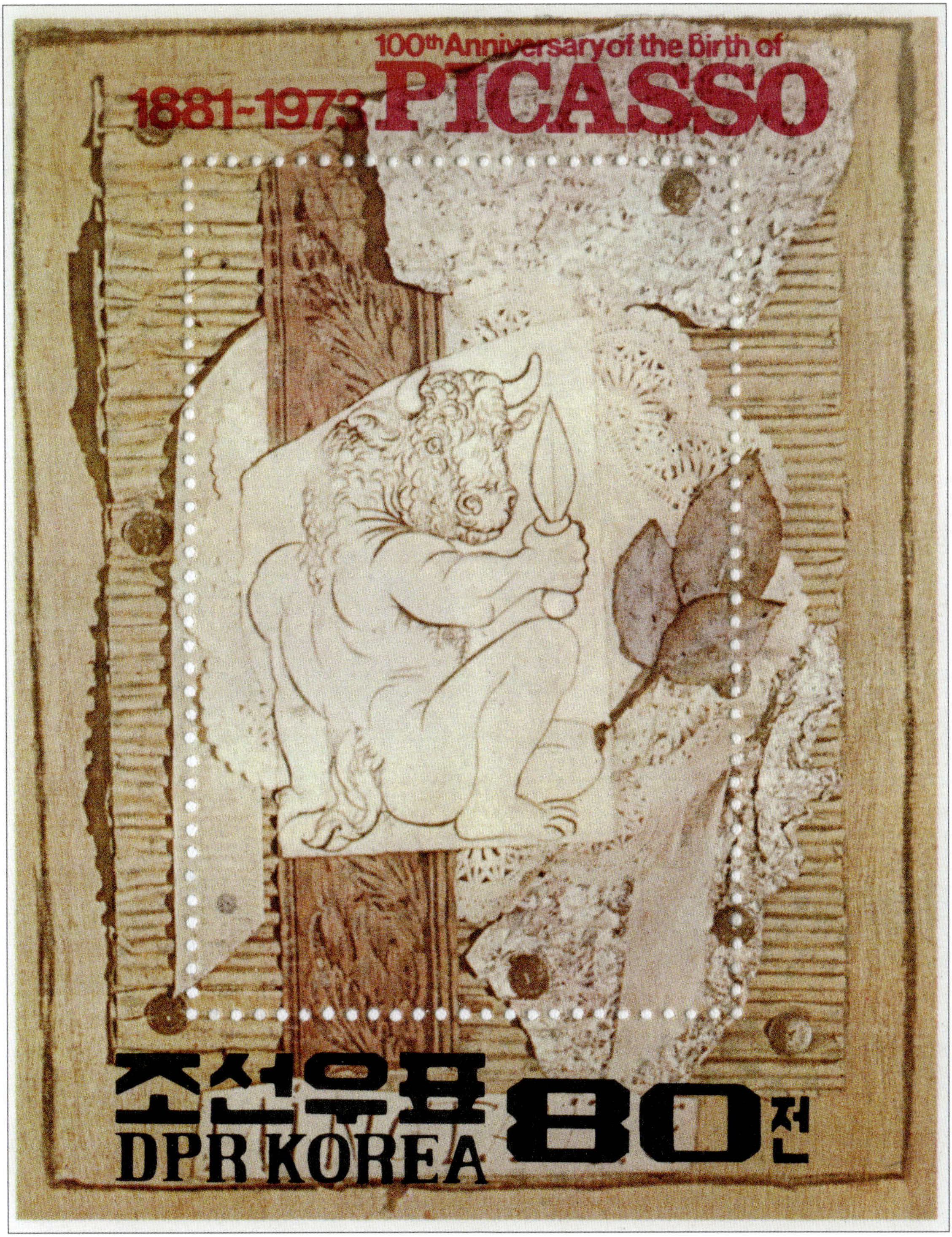

***Minotaur* (1934)** This painting (*Minotaur*, 1934) is in the Museum of Modern Art in New York. On March 30, 1982, to celebrate the 100th anniversary of the birth of Picasso, North Korea (DPR Korea) issued a stamp featuring this painting.

1936–1945

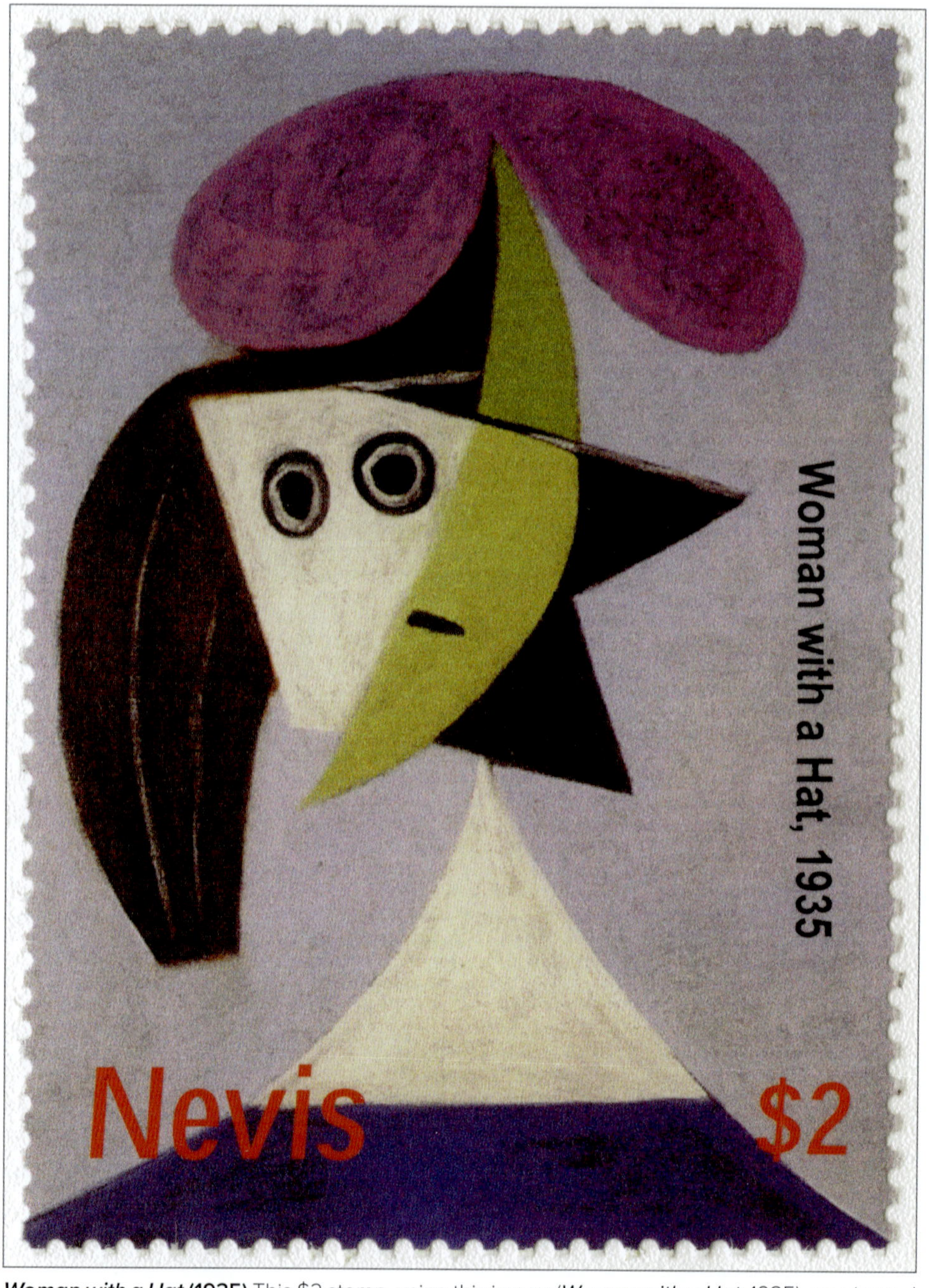

Woman with a Hat **(1935)** This $2 stamp, using this image (*Woman with a Hat*, 1935), was issued on March 4, 2004, by the Federation of St. Kitts and Nevis, honoring Picasso's thirtieth memorial anniversary.

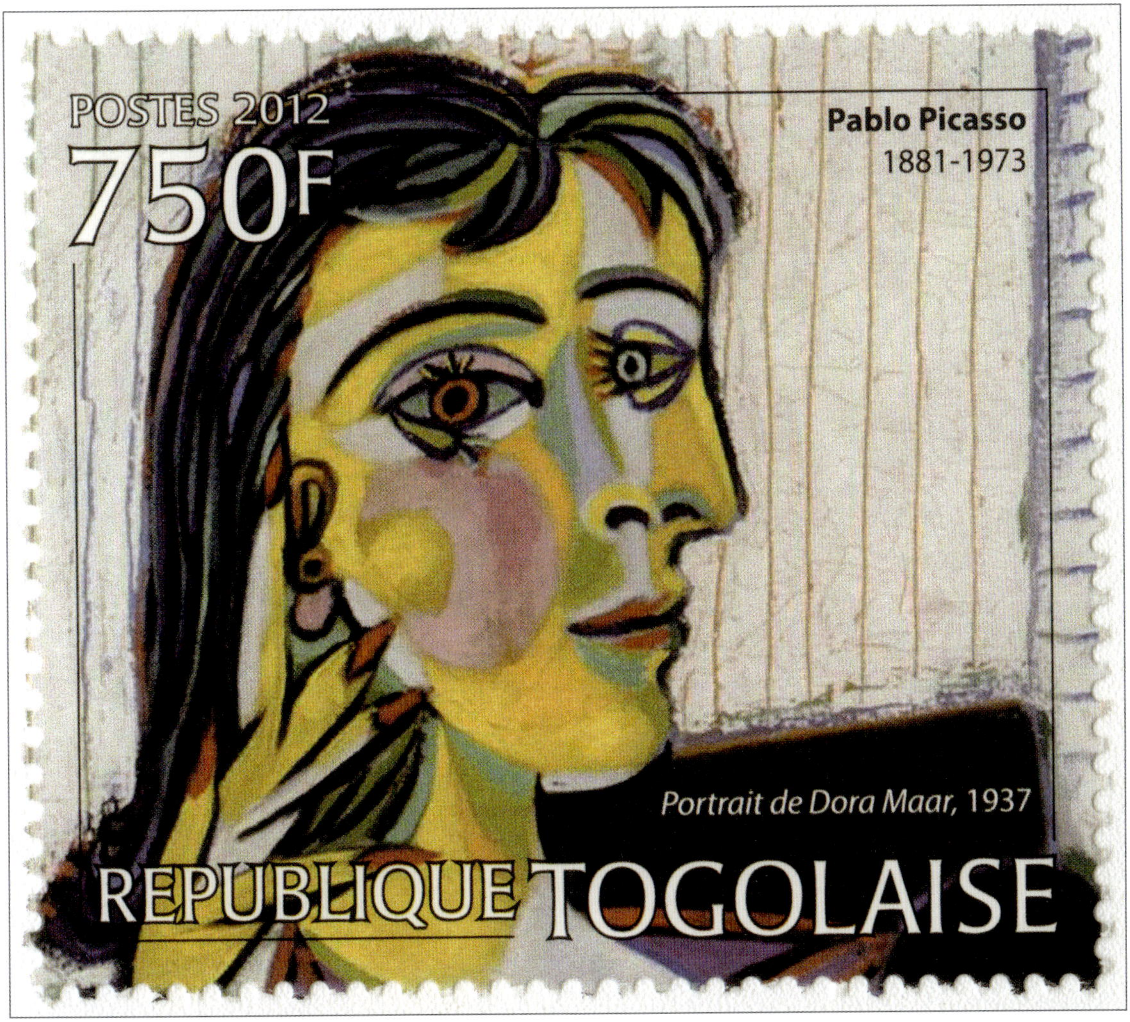

***Portrait of Dora Maar* (1937)** Part of the Dora Maar painting (*Portrait of Dora Maar*, 1937) was used on this 750-franc stamp, issued possibly in 2012 in the name of the Togolese Republic.

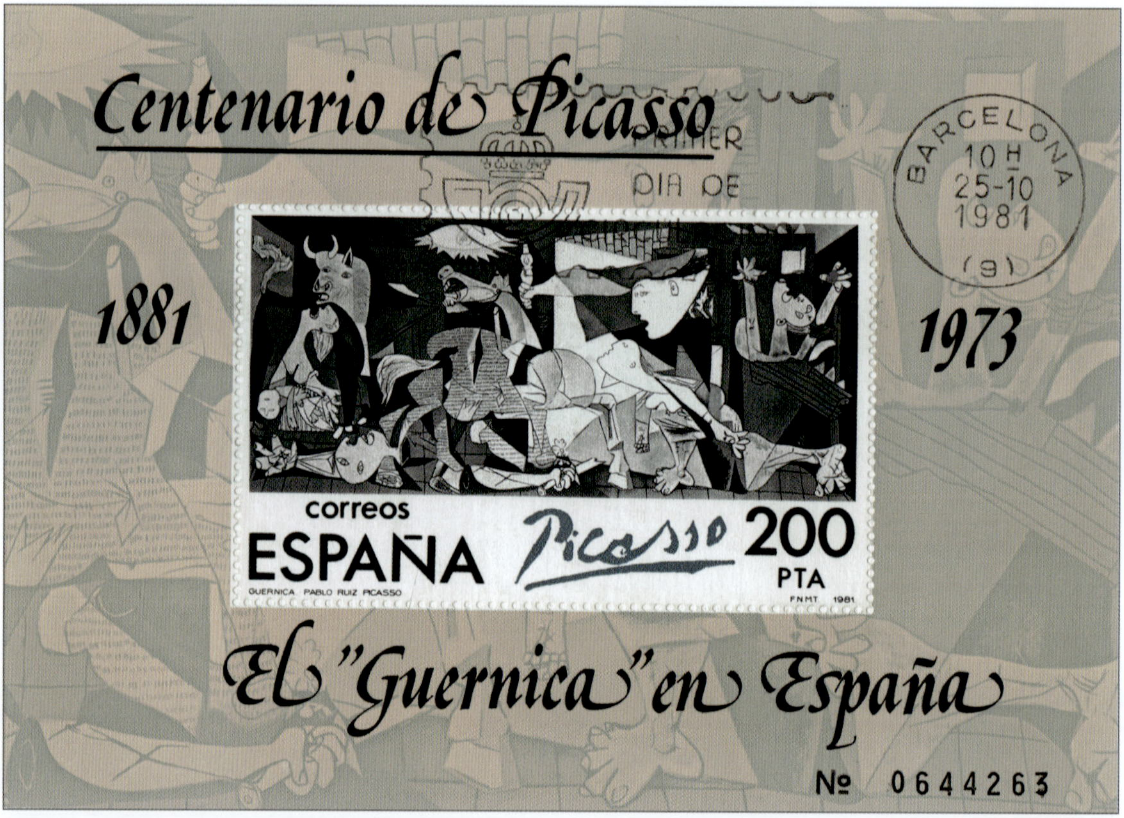

Guernica* (1937)** This maximum card containing Picasso's ***Guernica was issued in Barcelona, Spain, on October 25, 1981.

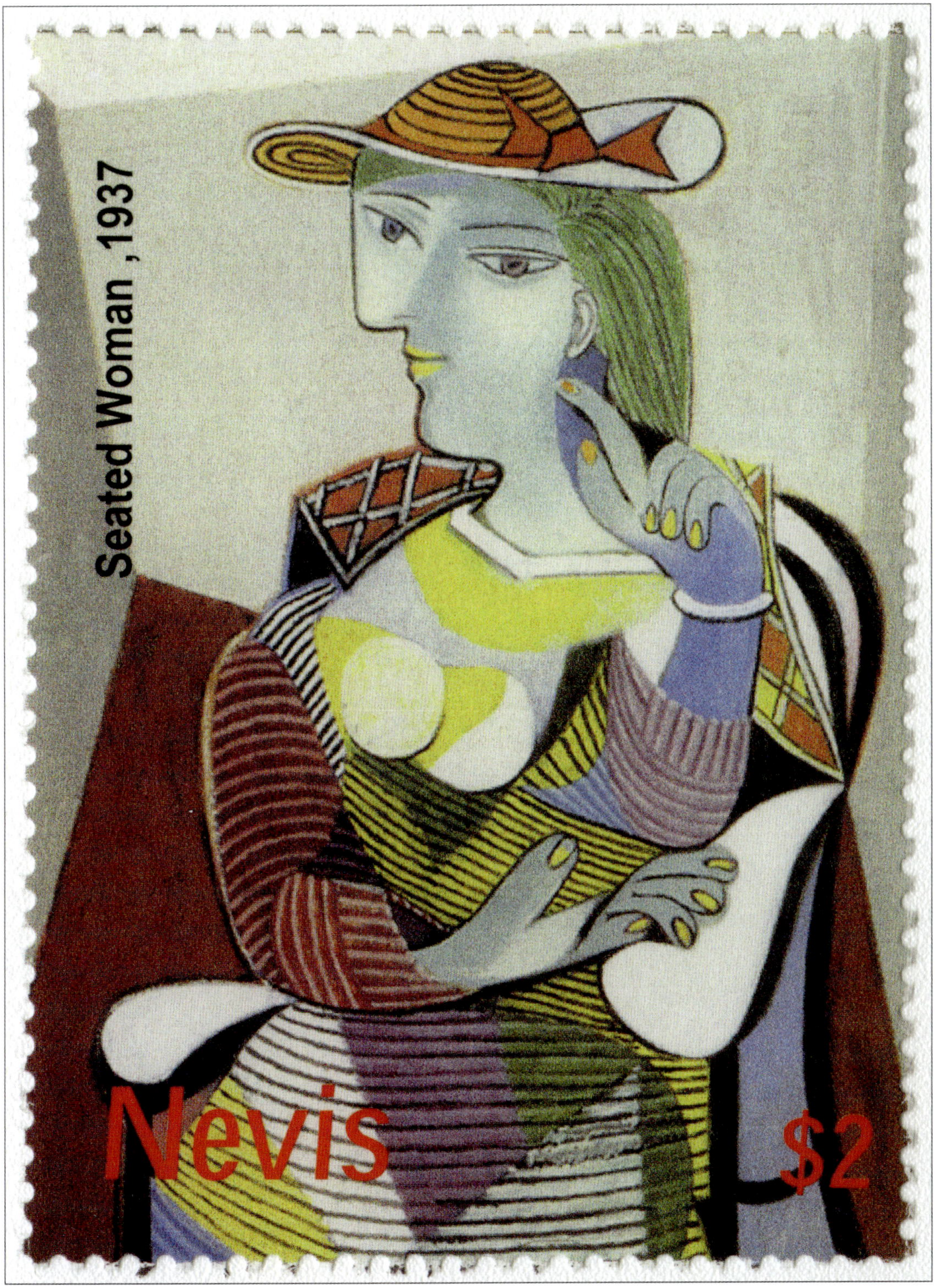

***Seated Woman* (1937)** This $2 stamp (*Seated Woman*, 1937), issued on March 4, 2004, by the Federation of St. Kitts and Nevis, honors Picasso's thirtieth memorial anniversary.

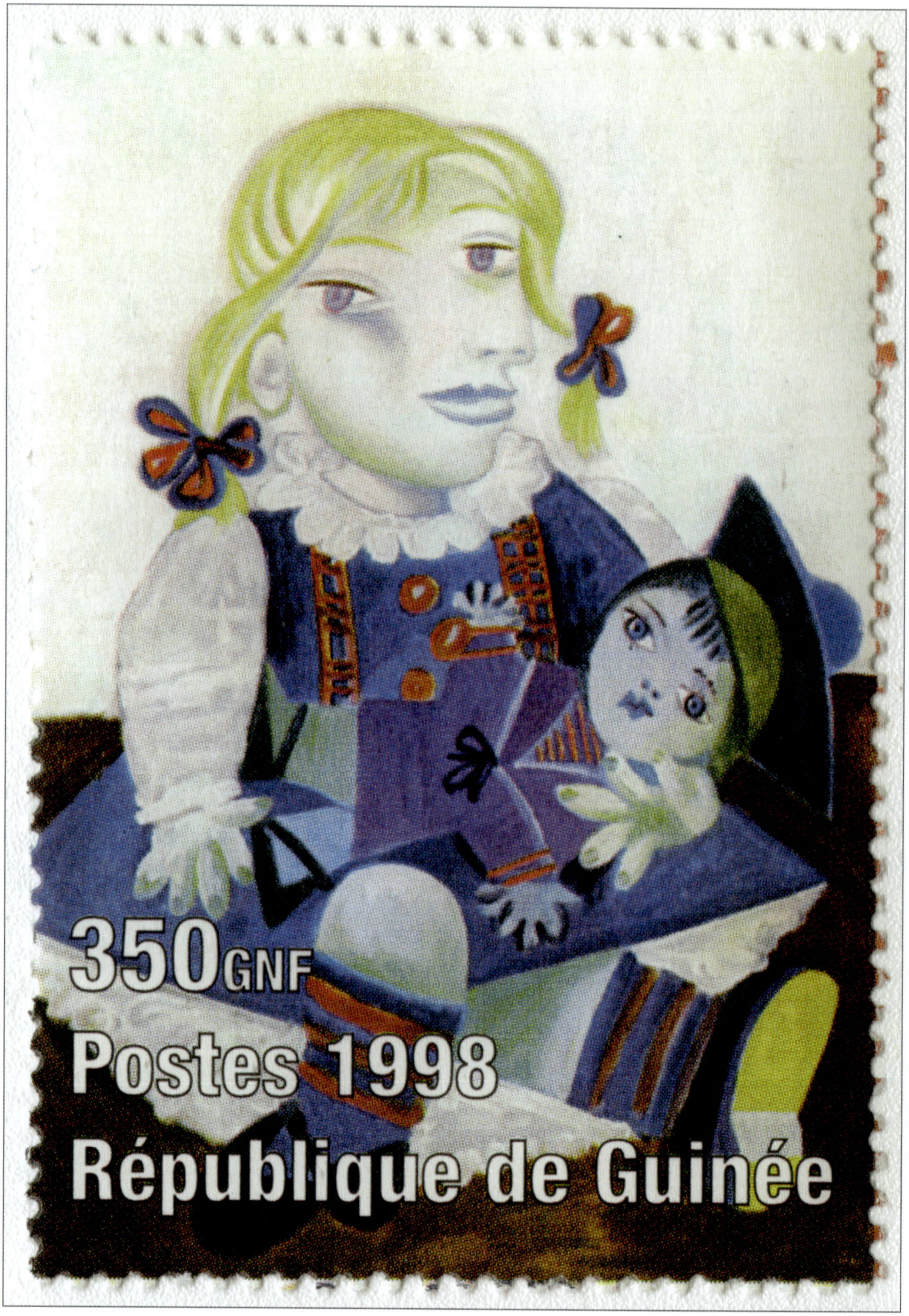

***Portrait of Maya with Her Doll* (1938)** This oil-on-canvas painting (*Portrait of Maya with Her Doll*, 1938) is in the Picasso Museum in Paris. It was used by the Republic of Guinea to issue this stamp on April 1, 1998.

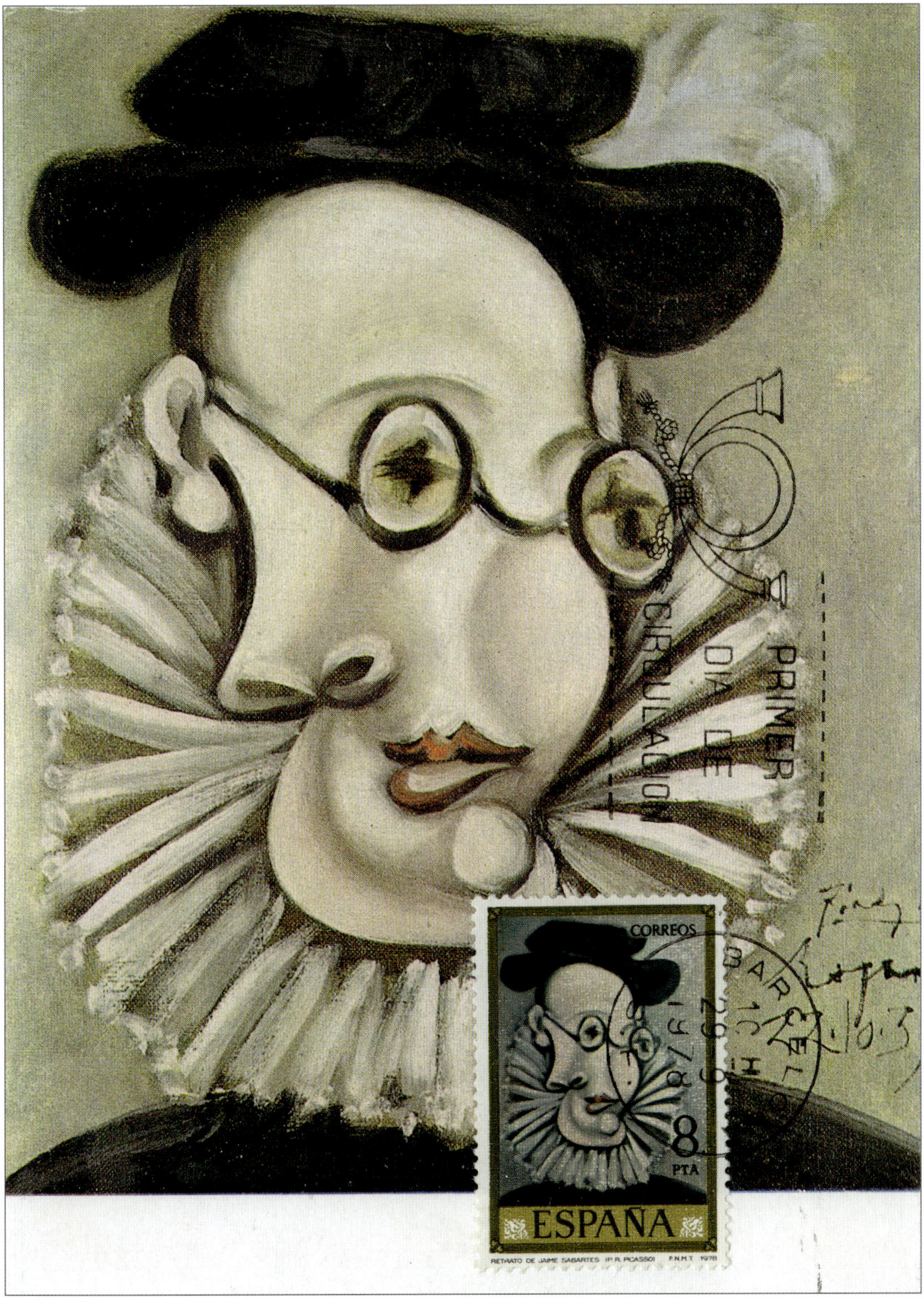

***Portrait of Sabartes* (1939)** This oil-on-canvas painting (*Portrait of Sabartes*, 1939) is in the Picasso Museum in Paris. The maximum card (maxicard) and stamp were issued on September 29, 1978, in Barcelona, Spain.

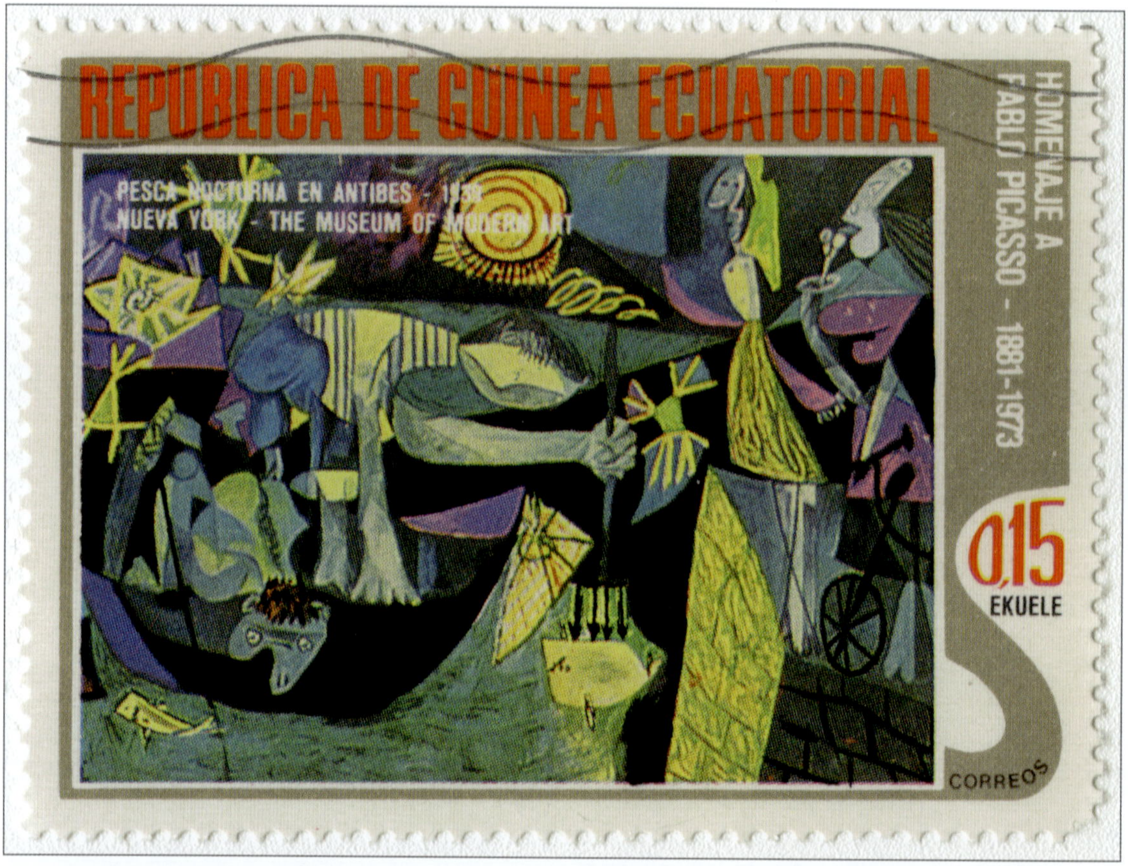

***Night Fishing at Antibes* (1939)** An oil-on-canvas painting (*Night Fishing at Antibes*, 1939), it is in the Museum of Modern Art in New York. This painting was used on a stamp issued by the Republic of Guinea Ecuatorial.

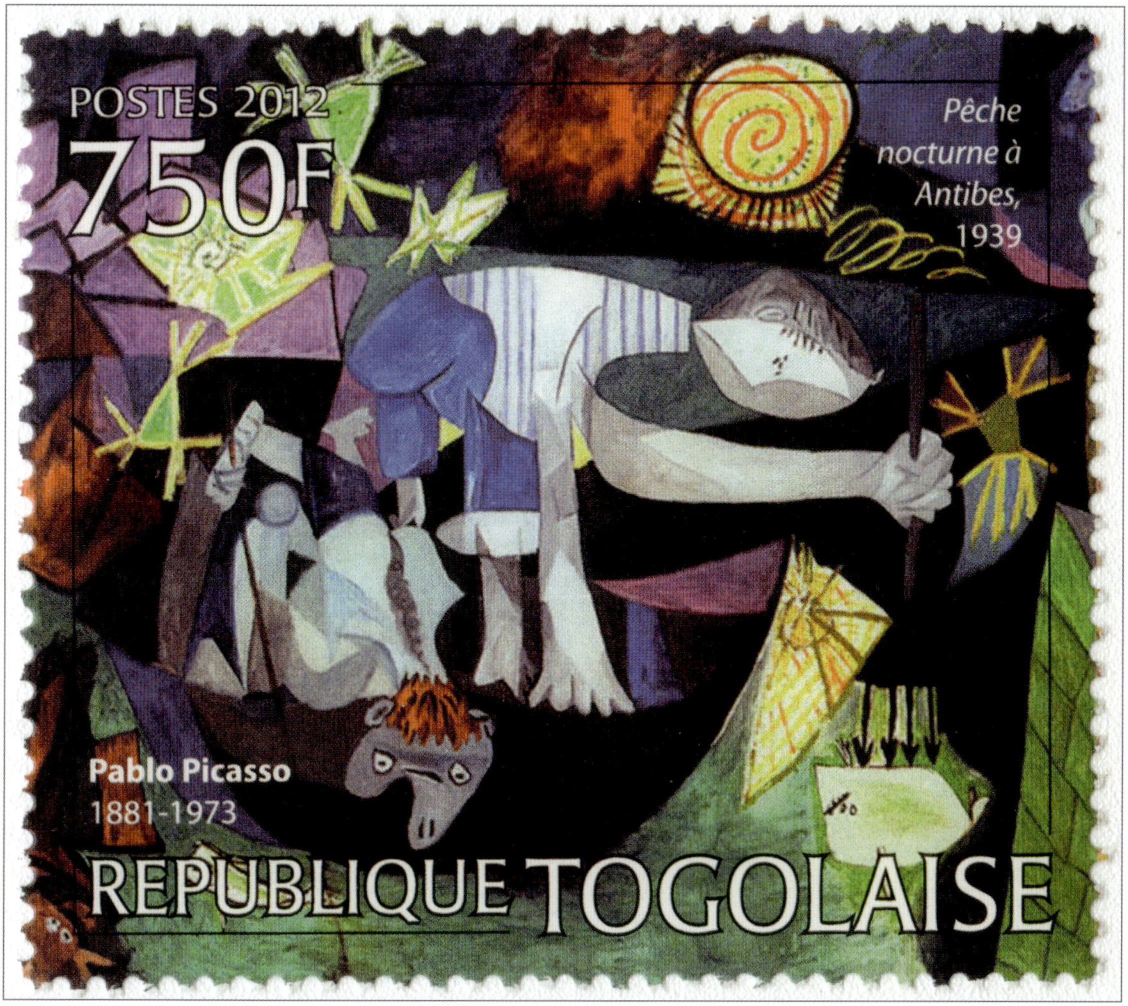

***Night Fishing at Antibes* (1939)** Part of this painting (*Night Fishing at Antibes*, 1939) was used on a 750-franc stamp issued in 2012 by the Togolese Republic, a sovereign state in West Africa.

1946–1954

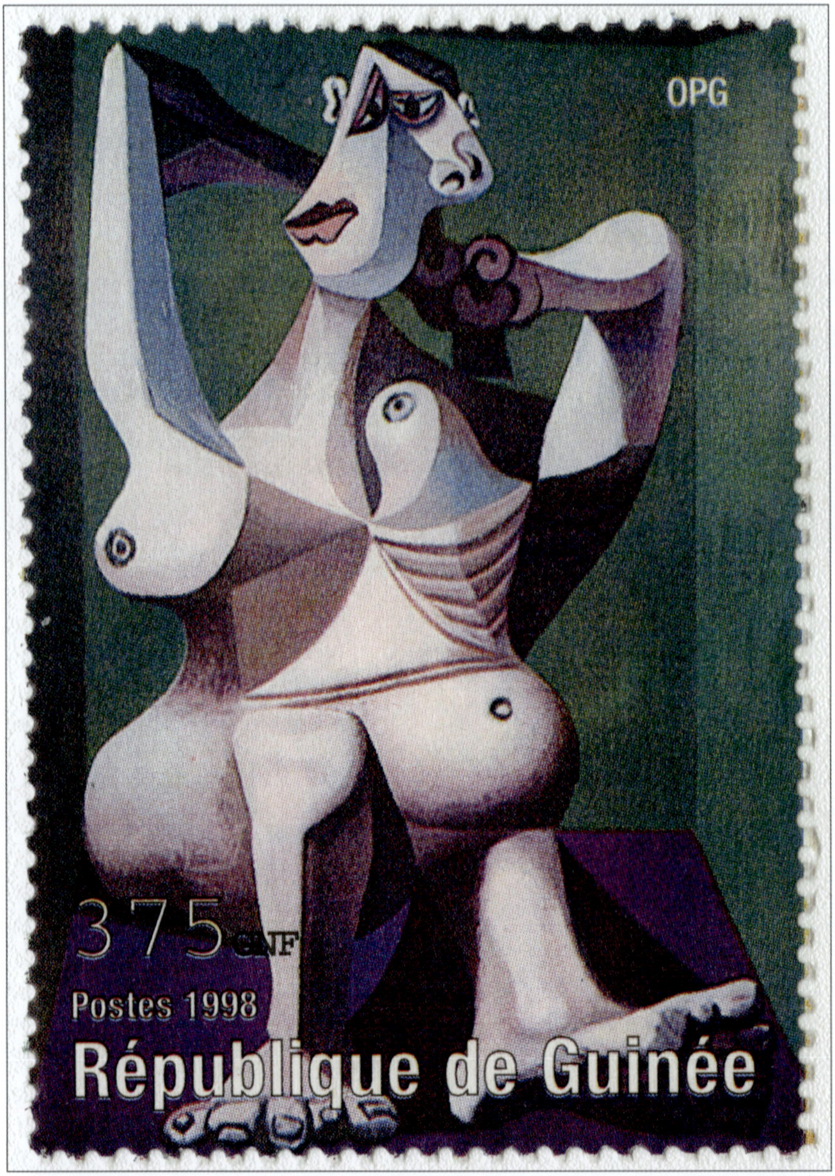

Woman Dressing Her Hair **(1940)** This portrait (*Woman Dressing Her Hair*, 1940) of a seated, naked woman, Dora Maar, tidying her hair with her hands, represents a high point in Picasso's wartime paintings. The distorted painting expresses the sense of menace Picasso felt at a time when the political situation across Europe grew darker day by day. The painting is in the Museum of Modern Art in New York. In 1998 the Republic of Guinea used this painting on a stamp that was issued to honor the twenty-fifth anniversary of the death of Picasso.

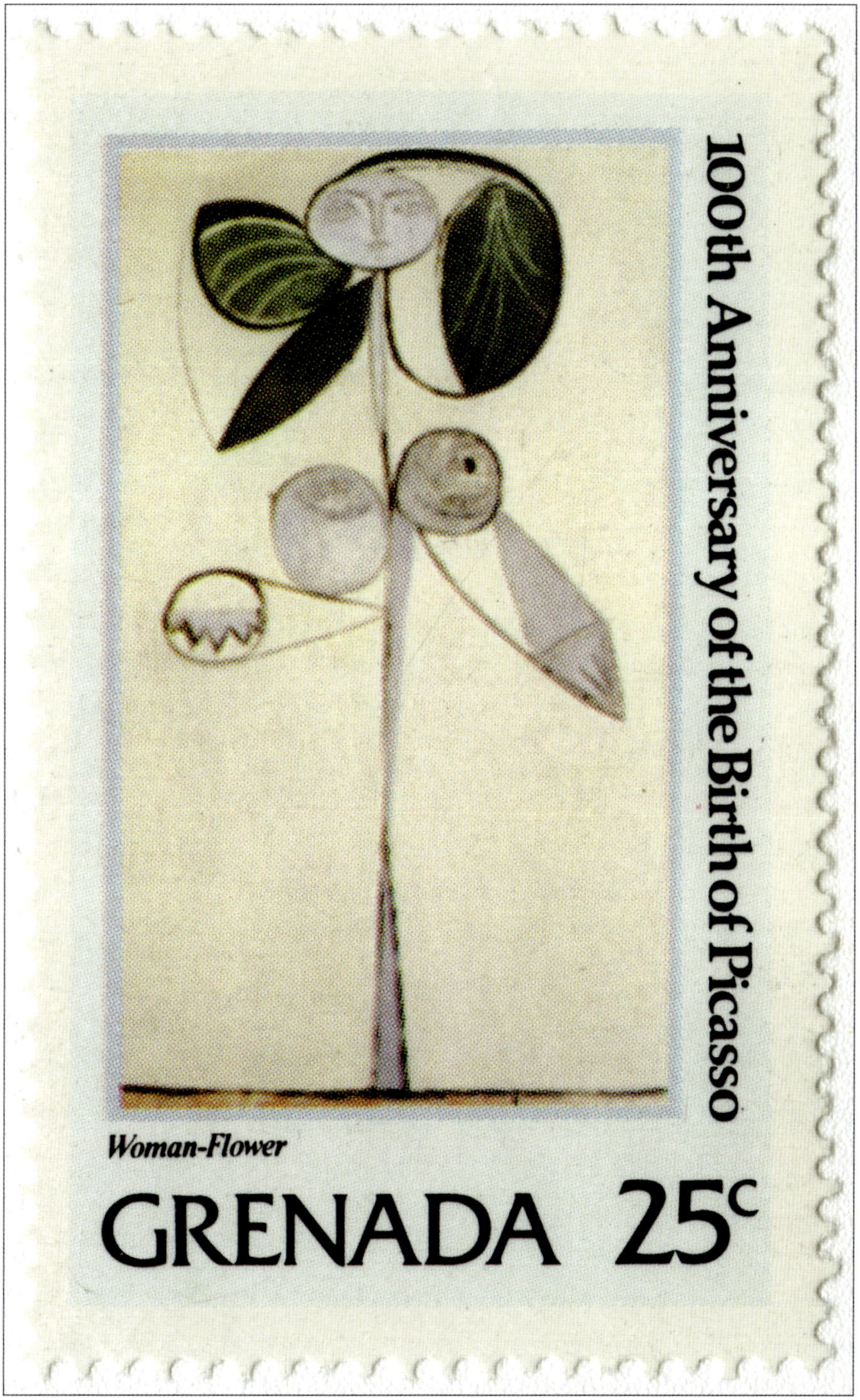

***Françoise as a Flower* (1946)** This oil-on-canvas painting of Françoise Gilot (*Françoise as a Flower*, 1946) was used on this twenty-five-cent stamp. It was issued on April 28, 1981, by Grenada, a sovereign state in the southeastern Caribbean Sea consisting of the island of Grenada and six smaller islands in the Grenadines island chain. The stamp honored the 100th anniversary of the birth of Picasso.

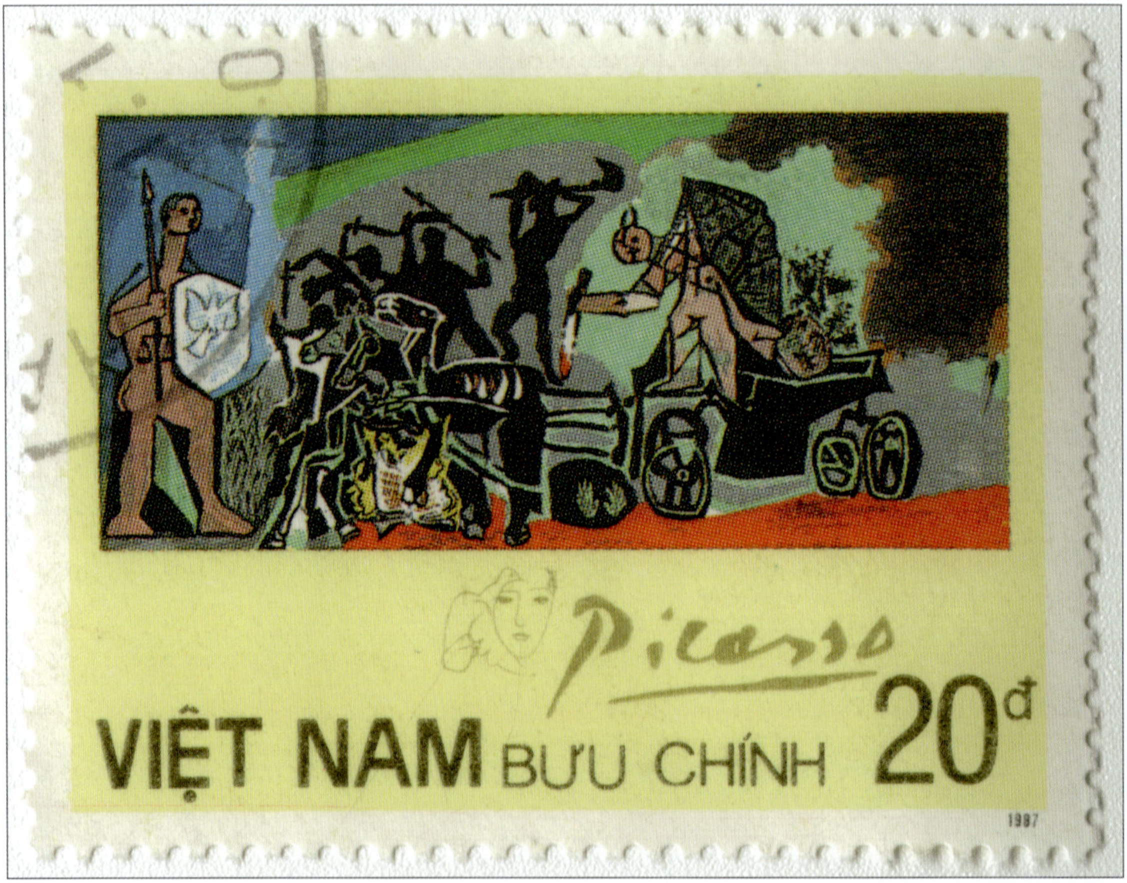

***War* (1952)** The Socialist Republic of Vietnam used this painting (*War*, 1952) on a stamp issued December 30, 1987.

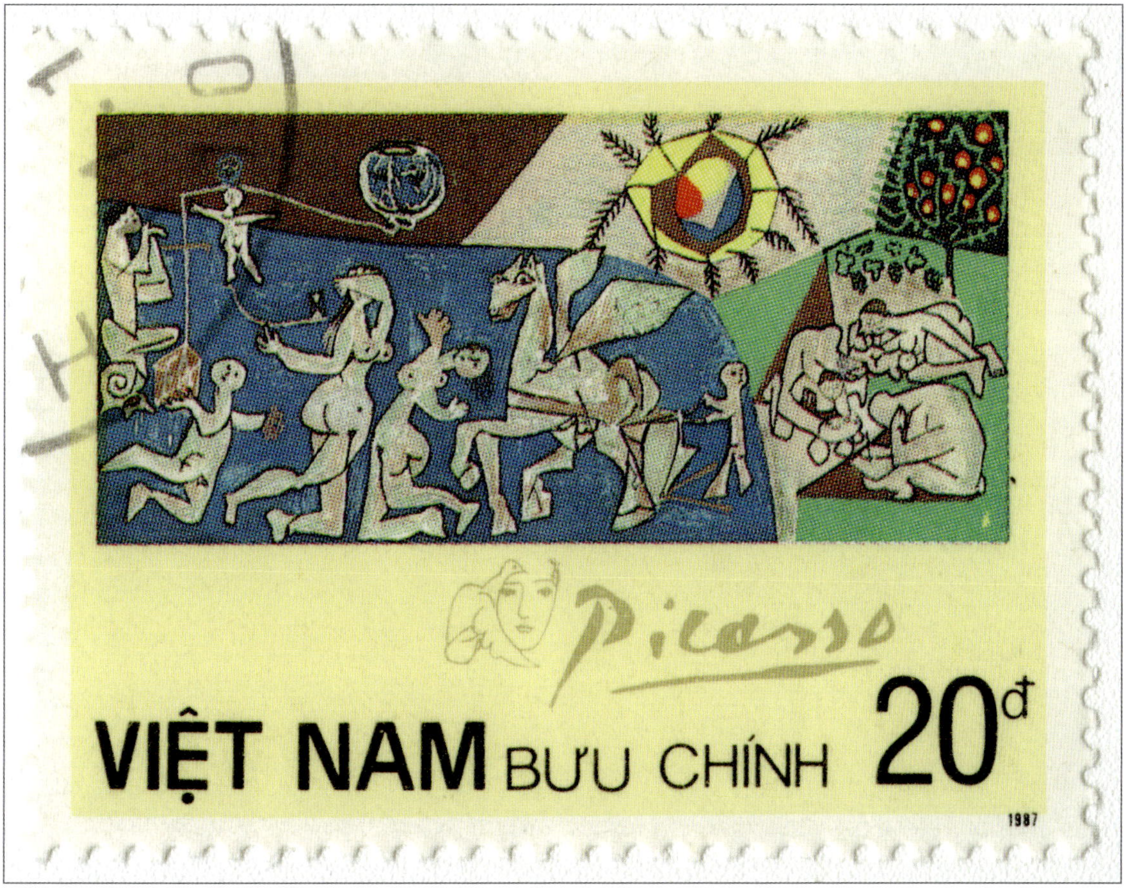

***Peace* (1952)** In 1952 Picasso painted one of his last major works on a theme of his own. Since then, most of his paintings have been based on other artists' pictures. This work (*Peace*, 1952) consisted of two large panels: *War* and *Peace*. On December 30, 1987, the Socialist Republic of Vietnam used the image of *Peace* on a stamp.

1955–1972

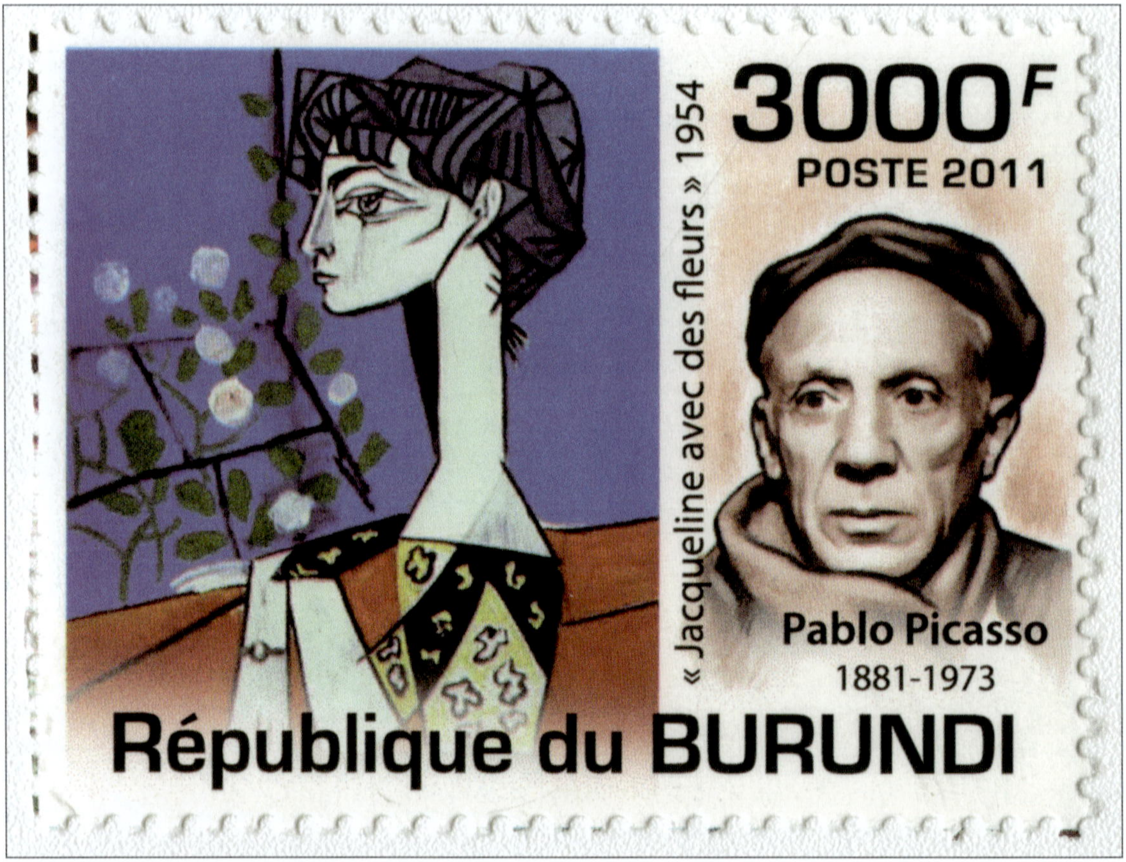

Jacqueline with Flowers* (1954)** Jacqueline Rogue, Picasso's second wife, was one of his favorite subjects later in life. In fact, in just one year (1963) he painted 150 portraits of her. They often went to the bullfights in Spain. In many of Picasso's portraits of women, he changed their shapes so much it is hard to recognize them as people. He liked the idea of making them look strange or dreamlike, and thus more interesting. Sometimes the distortions look cruel, as in the portrait of Dora Maar, ***Weeping Woman. The Republic of Burundi issued a stamp in 2011 that included this painting of Jacqueline (*Jacqueline with Flowers*, 1954). The stamp celebrated the 130th anniversary of the birth of Picasso.

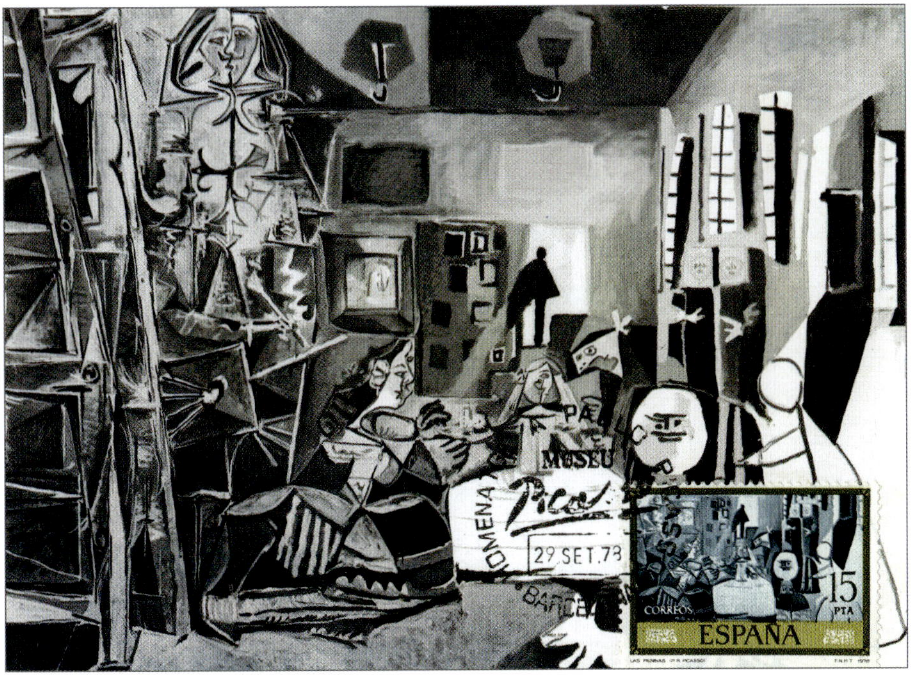

***La Meninas* (1957)** Diego Velázquez was a great Spanish artist with whom Picasso had studied at art school. At the end of his life, Picasso decided to do his own version of one of Velázquez's greatest works, *La Meninas*. He studied the original closely, doing many paintings and drawings of it in his own style. Picasso worked on his version from August 17 to December 30, 1957. His version of this painting got its effect from the contrast of gray and black areas. This oil-on-canvas painting is in the Picasso Museum in Barcelona, Spain. The maximum card (maxicard) and stamp were issued in Barcelona on September 29, 1978.

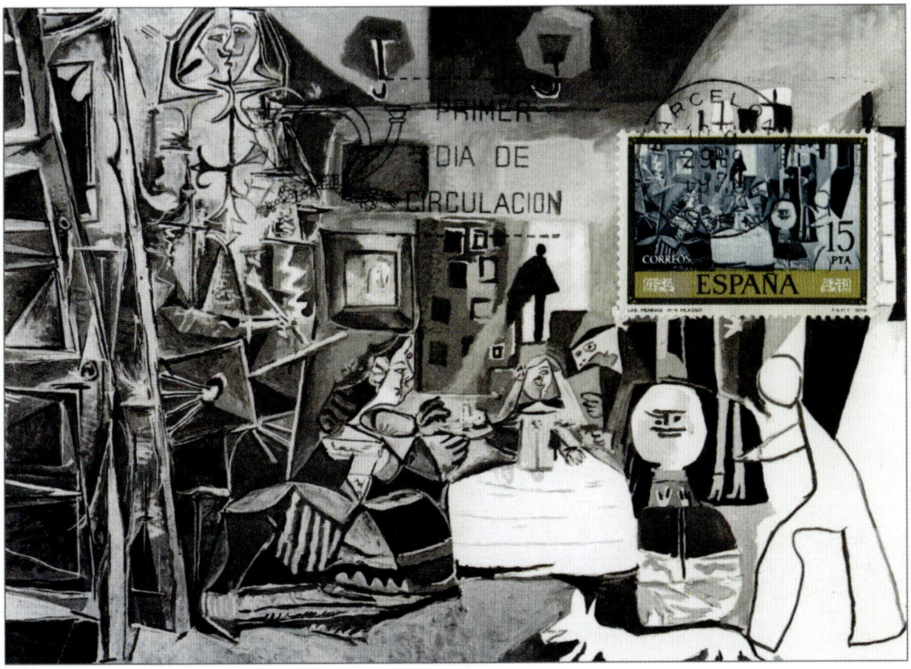

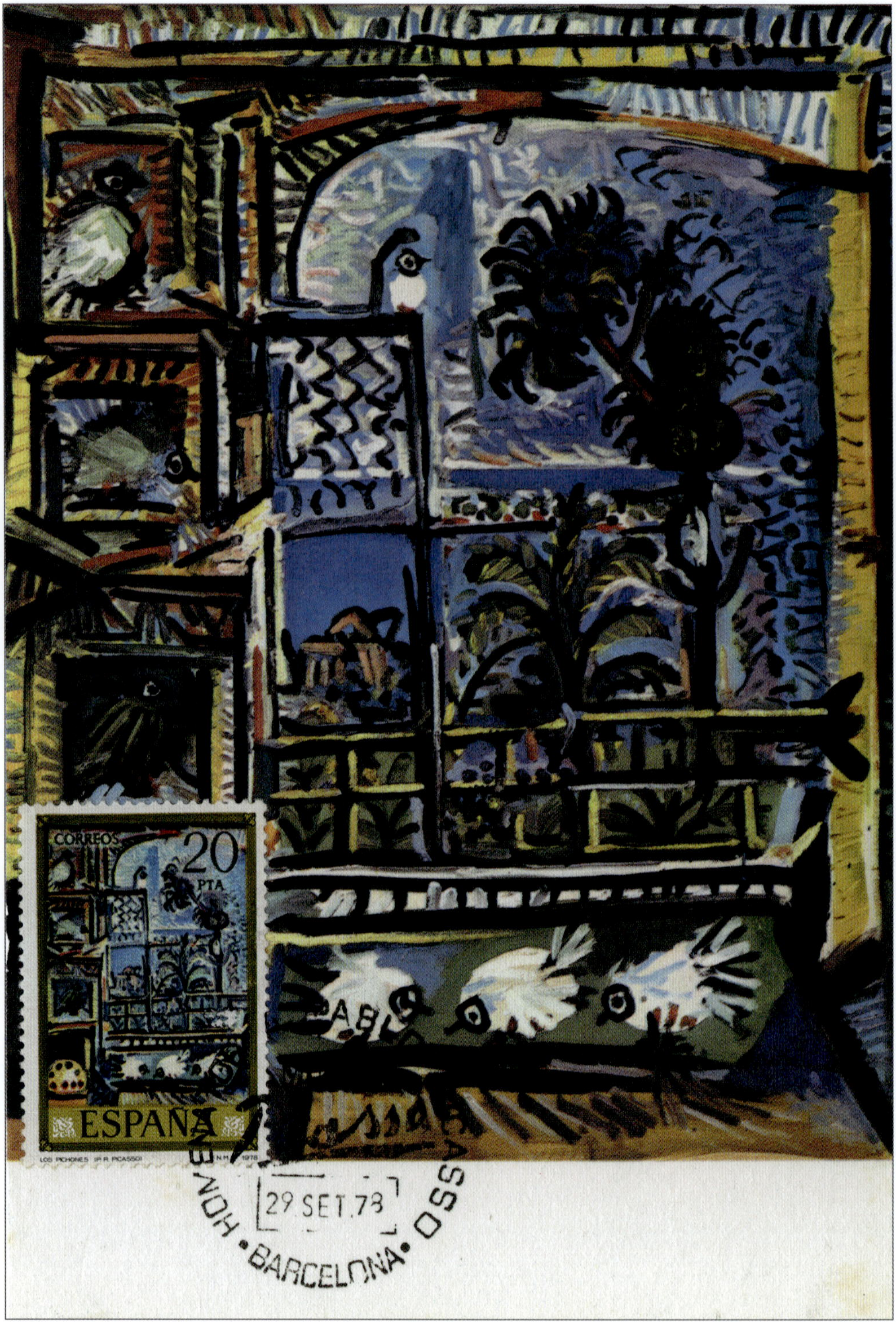

***The Pigeons* (1957)** Picasso painted the oil-on-canvas *The Pigeons* on September 11, 1957. The painting is now in the Picasso Museum in Barcelona. The image was used on a maximum card (maxi-card) and stamp issued on September 29, 1978, in Barcelona, Spain.

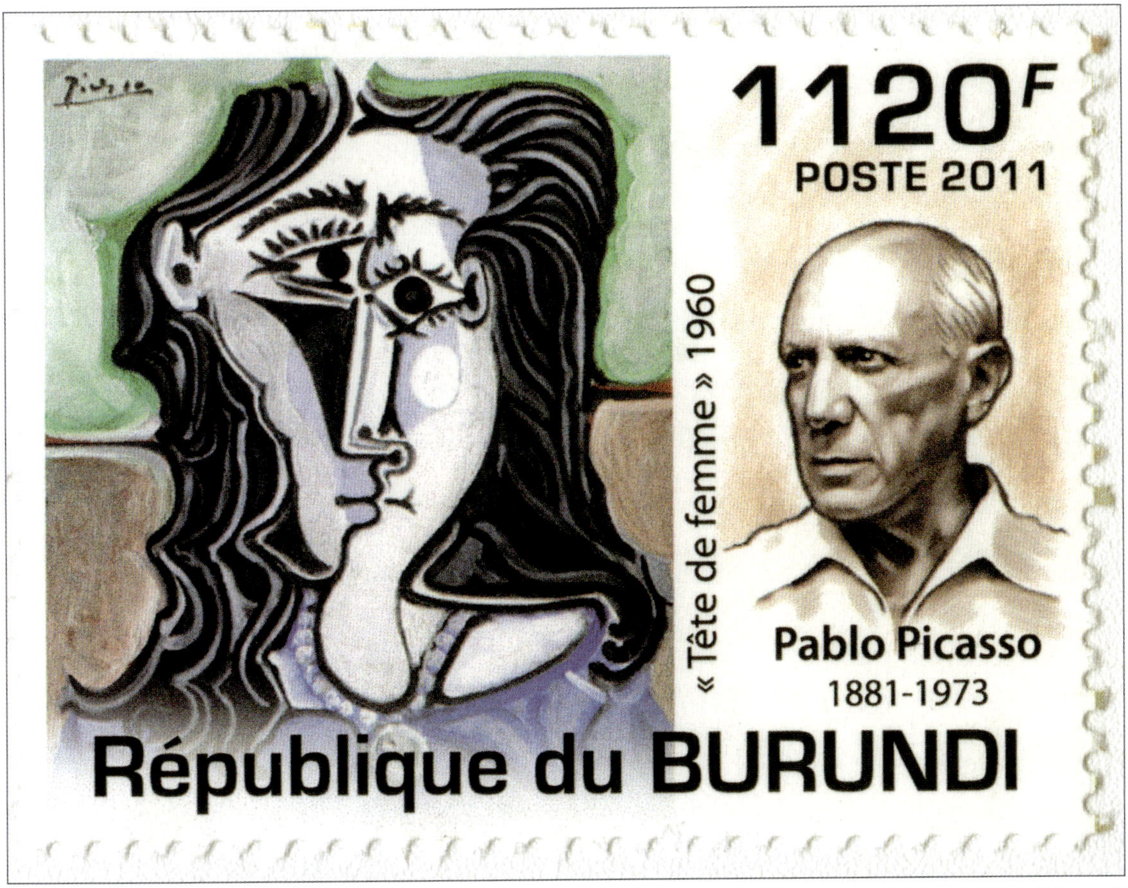

***Tête de Femme* (1960)** In 2011, celebrating the 130th anniversary of the birth of Picasso, the Republic of Burundi issued a stamp using this image (*Tête de Femme*, 1960).

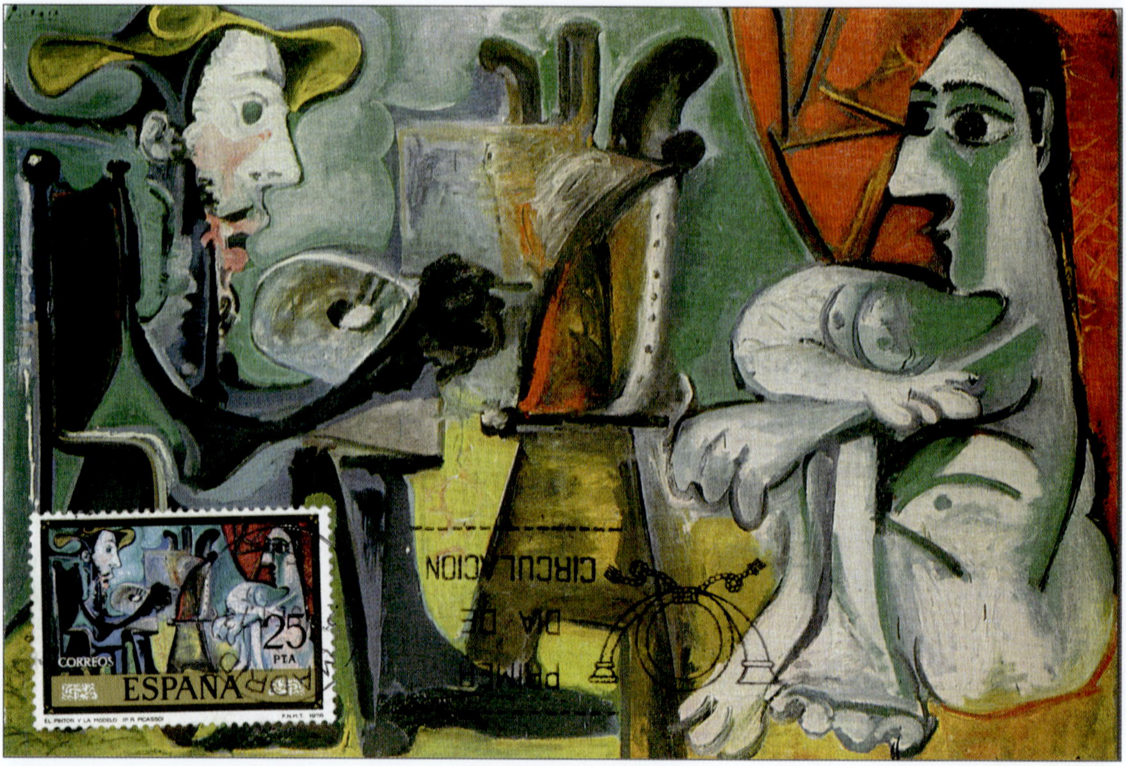

The Artist and His Model (1963) This maximum card (maxicard) and stamp were issued on September 29, 1978, using *The Artist and His Model* (1963), and canceled in Madrid, Spain.

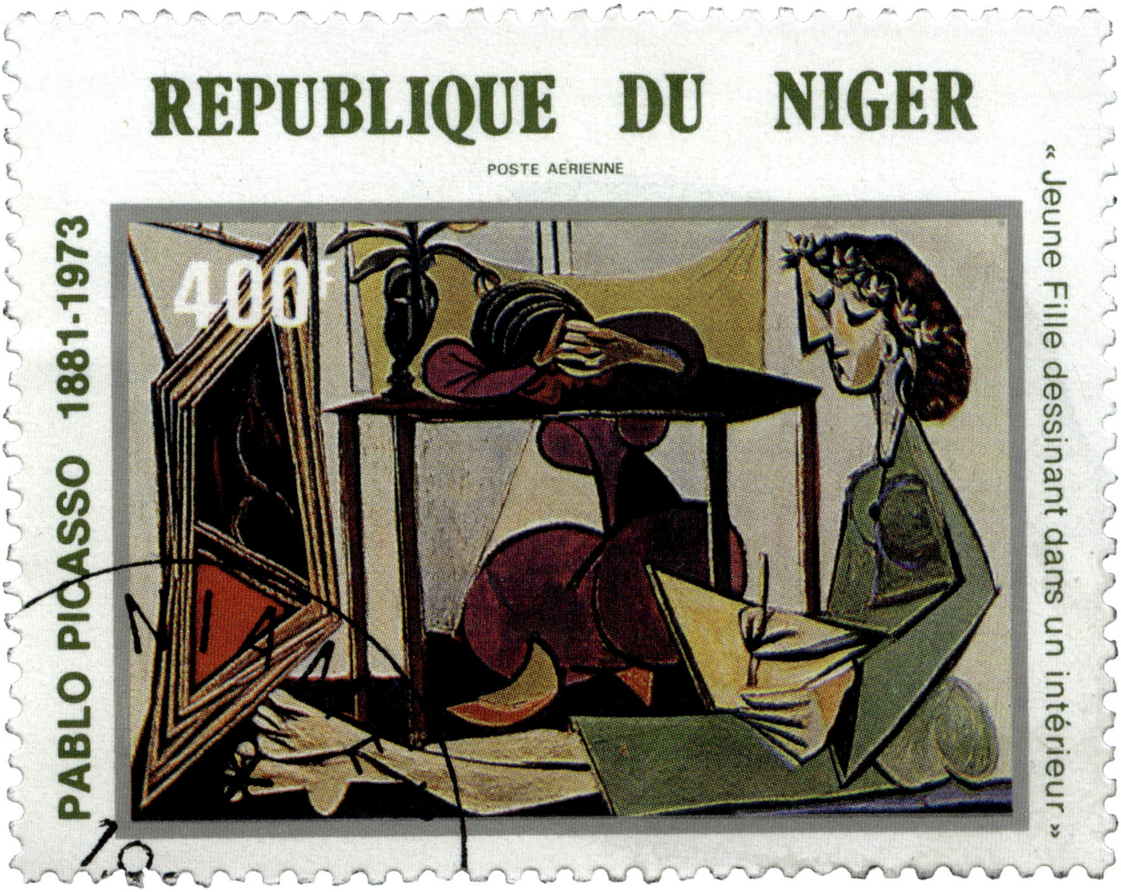

***Interior With A Girl Drawing* (1935)** An oil on canvas portrait of Marie-Therese Walker, Picasso's mistress. The painting is in the Museum of Modern Art in New York City, NY. This 400-franc stamp was issued on June 25, 1981 by the Republic of Niger a sovereign state in Western Africa.

GLOSSARY

abstract art: Art that has no recognizable subject matter but is an art arrangement of shapes and colors

art: The expression or application of human creative skill and imagination, typically in a visual form such as painting or sculpture, producing works to be appreciated primarily for their beauty or emotional value

artist: A person engaged in an activity related to creating art

block of stamps: Consists of four or more connected or unsevered stamps, with at least two stamps vertically and two horizontally (which would be called a block of four)

booklets: Refers to stamps arranged in booklet format and secured with staples for easy carrying

bourse: Usually a bourse is considered a marketplace where one can buy, sell, or trade stamps, etc.

Braque, Georges: French painter (1882–1963)

cachet: A printed design usually on the front left side of an envelope, with design and wording appropriate to a stamp being issued for the first time, or to commemorate an important event

cancellation: A mark of obliteration or canceling the stamp to show that it is no longer valid for postal duty

canvas: Fabric stretched over a wooded frame to paint on

centennial: The name of a one hundredth anniversary of an important event

ceramics: Artworks created by baking clay

collage: A picture made by gluing together newspaper clippings, photographs, scraps of fabric, wallpaper, cut-up pictures, and more

composition: The way in which the different parts of a picture are arranged

counterfeits: Refers to bogus or fake stamps made to defraud governments, as well as stamp collectors. There are known fake stamps of many famous painters, including Picasso.

covers: An entire envelope with stamp or cancellation (or both), commemorative or regular issue

cubism: The name of an art movement evolving in Paris, France, around 1907, led by Pablo Picasso and fellow painter Georges Braque. The cubists painted multiple angles of an object or person so they were all seen at once.

distortion: Changing the usual shape of an object

etching: A print on paper made from an engraved metal plate

fake: A deliberate forgery of a work of art, stamps, or other items. Several fake Picasso paintings and Picasso stamps have been identified. Picasso's global reach and the internet have created a made-to-order business of knockoff paintings and stamps.

fine art: Art appealing to a sense of beauty

first-day cover: A cover bearing a new stamp and canceled with the first day of use, usually at an officially designated location

first word: Picasso's first word as a child was "piz," meaning "pencil."

gouache ("gwash"): A form of watercolor based on opaque pigments or on the addition of white to produce opacity

image: Any picture, drawing, photograph, sculpture, or other form that creates a likeness or representation of an object

imagination: A particularly human trait of being able to think up ideas and dreams and transform them into art. Pablo Picasso was very imaginative.

imperforate: When a stamp has to be cut from a sheet or has no perforations, it is known as imperforate.

impressionism: The first major avant-garde art movement, formed in the 1860s. Its members, including Picasso, wanted to paint outdoors and study the changing effects of natural light.

Koklova, Olga: A Russian ballerina who in 1918 became Picasso's first wife. Their marriage introduced Picasso to the high circles of society—his bohemian life was now over.

landscape: An artwork where the features of the land are the most important subject: trees, rivers, mountains, etc.

Louvre Museum: A famous museum in Paris where many of the greatest works of art by the greatest painters of all time are held and displayed

maximum card: A philatelic term that refers to the artistic postcard and also a stamp and a postmark on which there are different but very alike images, seeking to maximize the best match of all three elements. A maximum card is also called a maxicard. A maximum card or maxicard is a postcard with a postage stamp placed on the picture side of the card. Ideally, the theme of the postage stamp and the theme of the postcard match. In most cases the cancel also is related to the theme.

medium: The means by which an artist (or person) chooses to communicate

mint: When a stamp is referred to as mint, it is mainly with full gum on the back and, of course, uncanceled.

modern art: Collective term for the various artistic styles since about 1890

Museum of Modern Art (MOMA): An art museum in midtown Manhattan, New York City. The museum contains many Picasso paintings.

naturalism: Factual and realistic representation in art

neoclassical: Describes a style that seeks to revive or develop classical ideas of art

Picasso Museum (Barcelona): This museum features many of Picasso's early works created while he was living in Spain. The museum also has the extensive Picasso collection of Jaime Sabartes, Picasso's close friend and personal secretary.

Picasso Museum (Paris): The elegant Picasso Museum (Musée Picasso) in Paris, in the city's Marais neighborhood, houses the world's largest public collection of Picasso paintings.

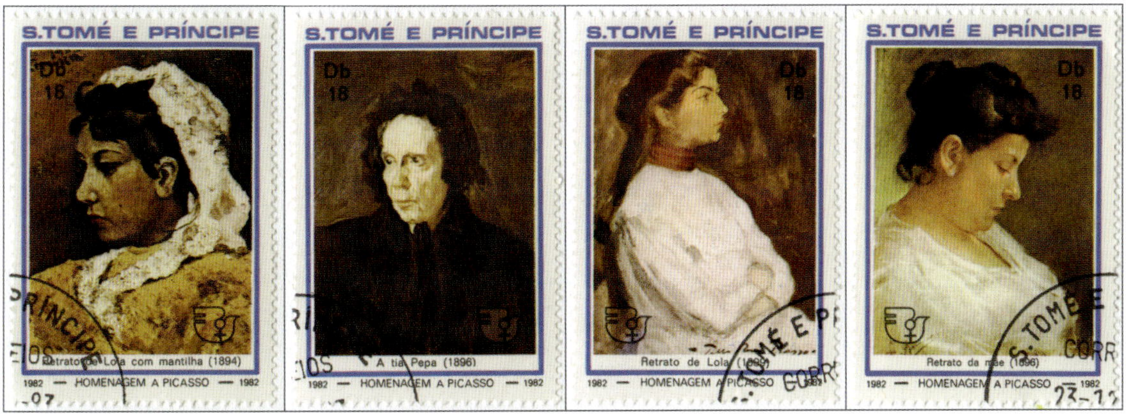

Portraits of Sister, Aunt, and Mother Pablo Picasso painted these portraits of his sister Lola, Aunt Pepa, and mother during his early years (1894–1899).

patron: Someone who gives an artist money to live on while the artist tries to sell their artwork. Spanish industrialist Pedro Manach was Picasso's first patron and financial supporter in Paris. Picasso painted a portrait of Manach.

philately: A formal name for the stamp hobby or stamp collecting

picture: A painting or pictorial representation

portrait: A painting or drawing of a person that tries to capture a true likeness

postmark: A mark struck upon envelopes, generally to indicate the name of the post office, date of mailing, etc.

primary colors: Red, blue, and yellow. All other colors can be made by mixing these colors together.

professional: An artist who is paid for work created and sold

Rose Period: A time (1905–1906) when Picasso's paintings were more-joyful, more-vibrant works, emphasizing the use of pinks ("rose" in French) and other warm hues to express a shift in mood and subject matter

self-portrait: A painting or drawing made by the artist of himself/herself

se-tenant: A French expression meaning "joined together." It has a specific meaning to stamp collectors because it refers to two or more stamps joined together of different denominations, colors, etc.

stamp: A small piece of adhesive paper that can be affixed to an envelope or package to send a letter or item through the mail

still life: A painting or drawing of objects such as flowers, vases, food, animals, fruit, books, etc. Objects placed in an arrangement as the subject of a painting.

studio: An artist's workplace or workroom

surrealists: Artists who painted strange images from their imagination. Picasso's surrealist paintings were characterized by dreamy depictions of figures with disorganized facial features and twisted bodies.

talk-balloon: A cloud shape next to a person where the words of the person are written to show the person is talking. In this book, several talk balloons are used to express quotes made by Picasso.

topical collecting: A popular field of collecting stamps. The list of topical collections is very long and covers hundreds of subjects. Simply speaking, if you were interested in stamps containing images of Picasso paintings, you may be interested in the following topical collections: Picasso paintings, famous paintings, famous painters, or Pablo Picasso.

unused: A stamp with or without original gum that has no cancellation or other evidence of postal duty

used: A stamp that has done postal duty, as evidenced by the cancellation

violent paintings: Picasso's paintings during the "Violent Years" (1936–1945) were deeply marked by personal and political catastrophes. The Spanish Civil War and World War II greatly affected Picasso, and the horror of war was highlighted in many of his paintings.

watercolor: A kind of paint that can be mixed with water

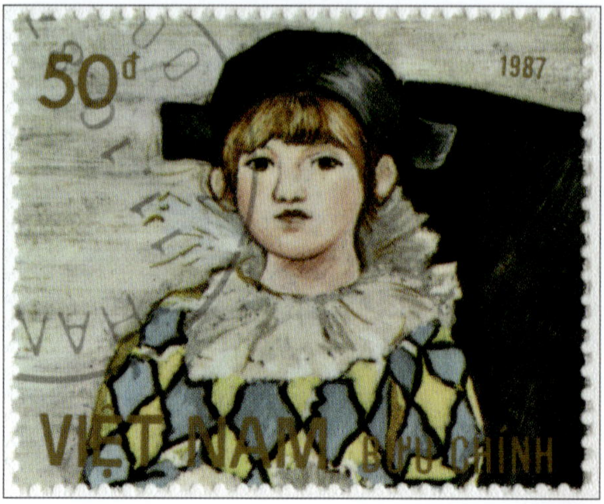

***Paul as Harlequin* (1925)**

This painting (*Paul as Harlequin*, 1925) shows Picasso's oldest son, Paulo (Paul), in pierrot costume. The stamp souvenir sheet was issued in 1987 by Vietnam (see p.87).

BIBLIOGRAPHY

Barr, Alfred H., Jr. *Picasso: Fifty Years of His Art*. New York: Arno, 1980.

Beardsley, John. *Pablo Picasso*. New York: Harry N. Adams, 1991.

Bernadac, Marie-Laure. *Picasso Museum Paris: The Masterpieces*. Munich: Prestel-Verlag, 1991.

Berger, John. *The Success and Failure of Picasso*. New York: Pantheon Books, 1989.

Bois, Yve-Alain. *Matisse and Picasso*. Paris: Flammarion, 1998.

Buchholz, Elke, and Beate Zimmermann. *Pablo Picasso*. Cologne: Könemann, 1999.

Freeman, Judi. *Picasso and the Weeping Woman*. New York: Rozzoli International, 1994.

Horodisch, Abraham. *Picasso as a Book Artist*. Cleveland, OH: World Publishing, 1962.

McDonald Jesse. *Pablo Picasso*. New York: Barnes and Noble, 1993.

Payne, Laura. *Essential Picasso*. London: Parragon, 1999.

Rubin, William, ed. *Pablo Picasso: A Retrospective*. New York: Museum of Modern Art, 1980.

Scarborough, Kate. *Pablo Picasso*. London: Franklin Watts, 2002.

Schiff, Gert. *Picasso at Work at Home*. Miami, FL: Center for the Fine Arts, 1985.

Serres, Alain. *And Picasso Painted Guernica*. Crows Nest, Australia: Allen & Unwin, 2010.

Walther, Ingo R. *Pablo Picasso, 1881–1973*. Cologne: Benedikt Taschen, 1986.

Warncke, Carsten-Peter. *Pablo Picasso, 1881–1973*. Cologne: Taschen, 2001.

Wertenbaker, Lael. *The World of Picasso, 1881–1973*. New York: Time-Life Books, 1974.

INDEX

A

Absinthe Drinker 20, 51
Acrobat on a Ball 22, 62
Art Institute of Chicago 53
Aunt Pepa 17

B

Beggars by the Edge of the Sea 55, 56
birth, Picasso's *16, 101, 107*
Blue Period, the *13, 18, 20, 21, 51, 83*
Boy with a Dog 22, 63, 64
Barque, Georges *24*
Bullfight: Death of the Toreador 28

C

Card Player 24, 35, 78
Cassagemas, Carles *17, 18*
Cat Devouring a Bird 30
Cavalier with Pipe 36
Celestina 18, 57
Child Holding a Dove 20, 42, 43
Children Drawing 32
Civil War *11, 13, 112*
Claude 14
Claude and Paloma at Play 32
Claude Drawing 32
Cleveland Museum of Art *18, 54*
Corina Pere Romeu 52
Crucifixion 86
cubism *13, 24, 25*

D

death, Picasso's *34, 100*
Dutch Girl 90

E

Els Quatre Gats 17, 41
End of the Act 19

F

Family of Traveling Entertainers 22, 66
First Communion 16
four cats (see *Els Quatre Gats*)
Francoise, Claude, and Paloma 32
Francoise with a Flower 101

G

Gilot, Francois *12-14, 101*
Girl in Front of a Mirror 28, 35, 90
Gouel, Eva *14*
Guernica 11, 13, 30, 94
Guitare J'aime Eva 24, 76

H

Harlequin 26, 35, 77, 79
Harlequin and His Companion 20, 44, 45
Harlequin Leaning on a Table 20, 46
Harlequin with Glass 22, 65

I

Interior with a Girl Drawing 35, 109

J

Jacqueline with Flowers 32, 104

K

Koklova, Olga 13, 14, 26, 83, 111
Korea *37, 102, 103*

L

La Belle Hollandaise 90
La Couffre 22, 35, 71
Las Meninas 36, 105
Landscape 7
Large Heads 36
late works *34-37*

Les Demoiselles d'Avignon 3, 13, 24, 35, 74, 75
Life 18, 54
Lola 14, 17
Lola with Mantilla 14, 17

M

Maar, Dora *11, 14, 83, 93, 100, 104*
Manach, Pedro *48*
Mandolin and Guitar 26
Massacre in Korea 32
Matisse, Henri *15*
maximum card 11, 19, 41, 72, 94, 97, 105, 106, 108, 111
Maya 14, 30, 96
Metropolitan Museum of Art *46*
Minotaur 28, 91
modern art 15
Mother 16
Mother and Child 22
Museum of Modern Art *35, 36, 86, 91, 98, 100, 109, 111*

N

National Gallery in London *42*
National Gallery of Art *48, 55*
neoclassicism *13, 26, 27*
Night Fishing at Antibes 98, 99

O

Olga in an Armchair 26
Olga (see Koklova, Olga)
Oliver, Fernande *18*

P

Paloma 14
Paloma at Three Years Old 32
Paloma in Blue 32
Paloma with an Orange 32
Paul as Clown 28
Paul as Harlequin 20, 87, 112
Paul as Pierrot with Flowers 28
Paul (Paulo) on a Donkey 26
Paulo (Paul) 14
Peace 32, 103
PHILEXFRANCE '89 *4-5, 63, 67*
Picasso Museum (Barcelona) *36, 41, 105, 106, 111*
Picasso Museum (Paris) *36, 40, 57, 97, 111*
Pierrot Seated 26, 80
Portrait of Artist's Father 16
Portrait of Artist's Mother 16
Portrait of Dora Maar 11, 93
Portrait of Gertrude Stein 22, 68-70
Portrait of Madame 5, 32
Portrait of Maya with Her Doll 96
Portrait of Pedro Manach 48
Portrait of Sabartes 17, 30
Portrait of Sylvette 32
postwar years *32, 33*
Pushkin Museum of Fine Arts *44, 67*

R

Rembrandt Figure and Eros 36
Roque, Jacqueline *13, 14, 104*
Rose Period *13, 22, 23, 66*

S

Sabartes, Jaime *36, 97, 111*
School of Fine Arts 16
Science and Charity 17, 41
Seated Old Man 36
Seated Woman 30, 36, 95
Self-Portrait 22, 24, 30, 47, 49, 50, 72, 73, 76, 104
souvenir sheet *49, 50, 66, 67, 86, 90*
Spanish Civil War *11, 13, 112*
Spanish Woman from Majorca 7
stamp sheet *3, 15*
Stein, Gertrude *22, 68-70*
Still Life on a Pedestal Table 28, 88
Studio with Plaster Head 28, 86
surrealism *24, 27-29*

T

Tete de Femme 36, 107
The Artist and His Model 36, 108
The Artist's Sister Lola 14, 17
The Barefoot Girl 16, 40
The Bathers 26
The Charmed House 36
The Doves 36
The Dream 28
The Kiss 36
The Ladies of Avignon (see Les Demoisells d'Avignon)
The Muse 28, 90
The Old Guitarist 18, 20, 53
The Old Jew 20
The Pigeons 106
The Rescue 28
The Three Dancers 28, 84, 85
The Toilette 22, 60, 61
Three Musicians 26, 35, 81, 82

V

Velazquez, Diego *105*
violent years *30, 31*

W

Walter, Marie-Therese *14, 109*
War 32, 102
Weeping Woman 30, 104
Woman Dressing Her Hair 30, 100
Women of Algiers 14, 36
Women Running on the Beach 26, 90
Woman with a Crow 58, 59
Woman with a Dog 32
Woman with a Flower 28, 89
Woman with a Hat 92
Woman with Pears 24, 35
World War II *30, 32, 112*

Y

Young Ladies of d'Avignon 90

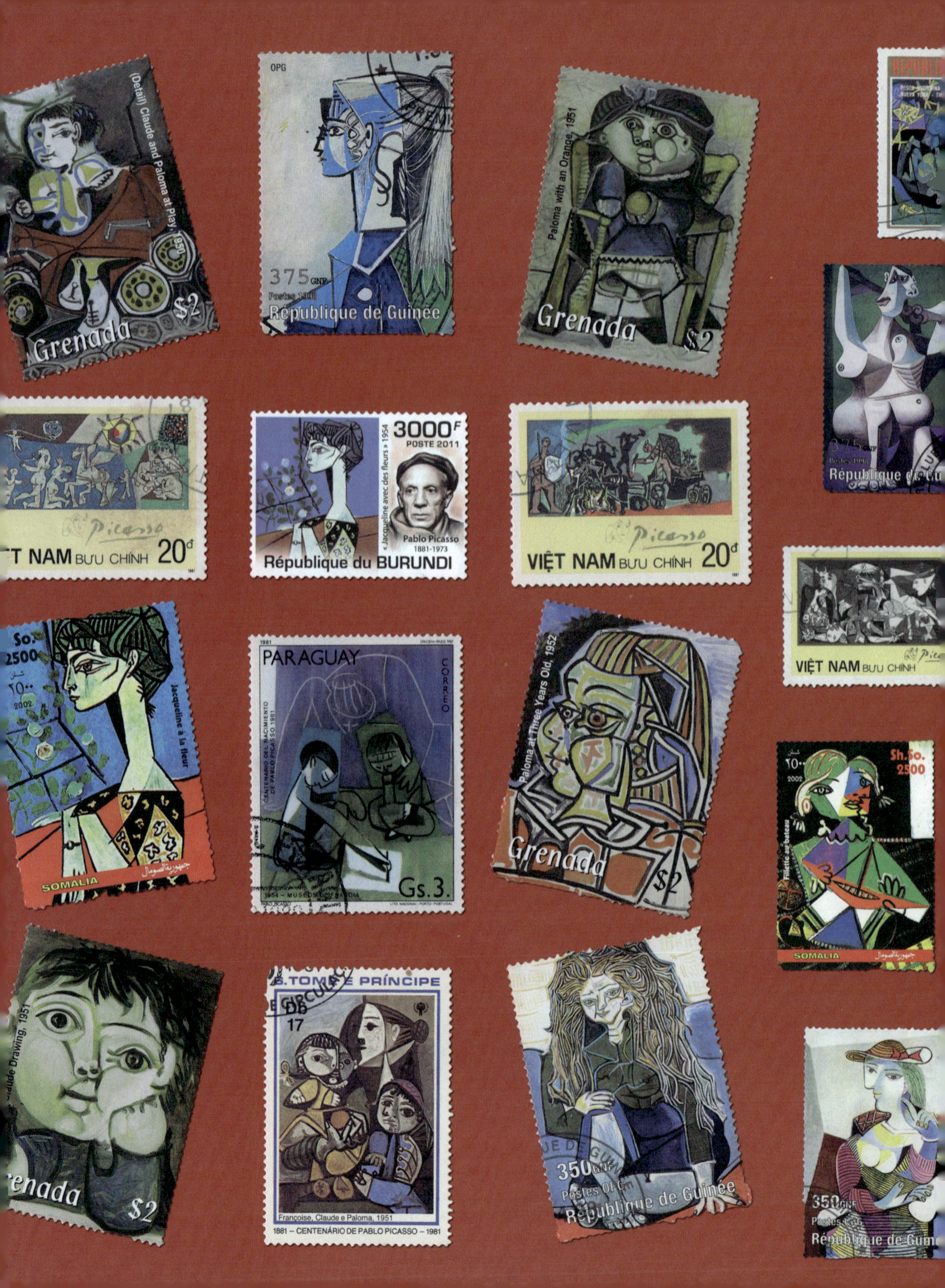

(Detail) Claude and Paloma at Play, 1950
Grenada
$2
OPG
375 GNF
République de Guinée
Paloma with an Orange, 1951
Grenada
$2
VIỆT NAM BƯU CHÍNH 20đ
Picasso
3000F
POSTE 2011
« Jacqueline avec des fleurs » 1954
Pablo Picasso
1881-1973
République du BURUNDI
VIỆT NAM BƯU CHÍNH 20đ
Picasso
So. 2500
2002
Jacqueline à la fleur
SOMALIA
جمهورية الصومال
1981
PARAGUAY
CORREO
CENTENARIO DEL NACIMIENTO DE PABLO PICASSO 1881
Gs.3.
Paloma at Three Years Old, 1952
Grenada
$2
VIỆT NAM BƯU CHÍNH
Sh.So. 2500
2002
Fillette au bateau
SOMALIA
جمهورية الصومال
Claude Drawing, 1951
Grenada
$2
S.TOMÉ E PRÍNCIPE
Db 17
Françoise, Claude e Paloma, 1951
1881 – CENTENÁRIO DE PABLO PICASSO – 1981
350 GNF
Postes OPG
République de Guinée
350 GNF